T0254114

Scripting Farming Simulator with Lua

Unlocking the Virtual Fields

Zander Brumbaugh
Manuel Leithner

Scripting Farming Simulator with Lua: Unlocking the Virtual Fields

Zander Brumbaugh
Seattle, WA, USA

Manuel Leithner
Buttenheim, Bayern, Germany

ISBN-13 (pbk): 979-8-8688-0059-7
https://doi.org/10.1007/979-8-8688-0060-3

ISBN-13 (electronic): 979-8-8688-0060-3

Copyright © 2024 by GIANTS Software GmbH

Managing Director, Apress Media LLC: Welmoed Spahr
Acquisitions Editor: Spandana Chatterjee
Development Editor: James Markham
Editorial Assistant: Jessica Vakili

Cover designed by eStudioCalamar

Cover image designed by GIANTS Software – Sandra Meier

Distributed to the book trade worldwide by Springer Science+Business Media New York, 1 New York Plaza, Suite 4600, New York, NY 10004-1562, USA. Phone 1-800-SPRINGER, fax (201) 348-4505, e-mail orders-ny@springer-sbm.com, or visit www.springeronline.com. Apress Media, LLC is a California LLC and the sole member (owner) is Springer Science + Business Media Finance Inc (SSBM Finance Inc). SSBM Finance Inc is a **Delaware** corporation.

For information on translations, please e-mail booktranslations@springernature.com; for reprint, paperback, or audio rights, please e-mail bookpermissions@springernature.com.

Apress titles may be purchased in bulk for academic, corporate, or promotional use. eBook versions and licenses are also available for most titles. For more information, reference our Print and eBook Bulk Sales web page at http://www.apress.com/bulk-sales.

Any source code or other supplementary material referenced by the author in this book is available to readers on GitHub. For more detailed information, please visit https://www.apress.com/gp/services/source-code.

Paper in this product is recyclable

Table of Contents

About the Authors..xiii

About the Technical Reviewer xv

Introduction xvii

Foreword xix

Chapter 1: Introduction, GDN, ModHub, Modding Tutorial Videos,
LuaDoc, FarmCon... 1

    Technical Requirements...1

    Exploring the GDN 1

        Modding Resources..3

        Video Tutorials 3

        Documentation 4

        Community Forum 5

        Downloads..8

        LuaDoc...9

        YouTube 10

    Looking at the ModHub..10

        Financial Opportunities of Mod Creation 11

    How to Attend FarmCon 12

    Participating in the Mod Contest...14

    Summary...15

Chapter 2: Getting Started with the GIANTS Editor 17

Technical Requirements 17

Installing the GIANTS Editor 18

The Viewport 19

    Movement and Camera Manipulation 20

    Viewport Options 21

The Scenegraph Panel 23

    Entities and the Parent-Child Hierarchy 24

Application Menus 25

    The File Menu 26

    The Edit Menu 27

    The Create Menu 29

    The View Menu 30

    The Scripts Menu 31

    The Window Menu 31

    The Help Menu 31

The Attributes Panel 32

The Toolbar 34

    File Section 35

    Play Section 35

    Mode Section 36

    Miscellaneous Section 39

    Terrain Section 39

Scripting 42

    The Console 43

Summary 44

Chapter 3: The Lua Programming Language 45

Technical Requirements...46

Learning About Data Types and Creating Variables.....................46

    Data Types 47

    Setting and Manipulating Variables...48

    Numbers...49

    Booleans...50

    Strings 51

    Tables 54

    Dictionaries 57

Conditional Statements..59

Declaring and Using Loops 64

    for Loops..64

    Iterator Function 66

    while Loops 68

    repeat Loops..69

Learning About Functions 70

    Functions in Programming 70

    Recursion 74

Classes..78

Demonstrating Programming Style and Efficiency 80

    General Programming Style Rules...80

Summary..82

Chapter 4: The GIANTS Studio...85

Technical Requirements...85

Installing the GIANTS Studio 86

Application Menus 86

    The File Menu 86

The Edit Menu...87

The View Menu..88

The Debug Menu 89

The Window Menu 89

The Help Menu 90

New Project...90

Starting the Game 94

Debugging Scripts...97

Using Breakpoints 98

Using the Locals Tab and the Callstack 99

Summary...101

Chapter 5: Making a Diner with a Rotating Sign 103

Technical Requirements...104

Preparing the Mod Folder Structure..104

Creating Mod Scripts 109

Creating XML Files..109

Creating Lua Files...117

Testing the Mod 123

Summary...124

Chapter 6: Rotating Mower Mod...127

Technical Requirements...128

Creating Mod Scripts 128

Creating XML Files..128

Creating Lua Files...144

Testing the Mod 172

Summary...172

Chapter 7: Speed Trap Trailer Mod **175**

Speed Trap Trailer Mod..175

Technical Requirements...176

Creating Mod Scripts 176

    Creating XML Files...176

    Creating Lua Files..193

Testing the Mod 204

Summary..205

Chapter 8: Mileage Counter HUD Mod...**207**

Technical Requirements...208

Creating Mod Scripts 208

    Creating XML Files...208

    Creating Lua Files..210

Testing the Mod 222

Summary..223

Chapter 9: Multibale Spawner Mod **225**

Technical Requirements...226

Creating Mod Scripts 226

    Creating XML Files...226

    Creating Lua Files..236

Testing the Mod 252

Summary..252

Chapter 10: Money Cheat Mod 255

Technical Requirements..256

Creating Mod Scripts 256

    Creating XML Files..256

    Creating Lua Files..262

Testing the Mod 270

Summary..270

Chapter 11: Publishing on the ModHub 273

Technical Requirements..273

What Is the ModHub?...273

Creating an Account..274

ModHub Creation Guidelines..276

Using the TestRunner 279

Uploading Your First Mod 280

Getting Feedback and Updating Your Mod 282

Rewards and Awards 283

Summary..284

Chapter 12: Documentation and Appendix 287

Debugging..287

    print 287

    printCallstack 288

Position, Orientation, and Size 288

    getWorldTranslation...288

    setWorldTranslation...289

    setTranslation 289

    getTranslation 289

    worldToLocal 290

localToWorld 290

localToLocal 291

setRotation 291

getRotation 292

getWorldRotation 292

setWorldRotation 293

localRotationToWorld 293

worldRotationToLocal 293

worldDirectionToLocal 294

localDirectionToLocal..294

localDirectionToWorld 295

setDirection 296

setScale..296

getScale..296

Entities 297

clone..297

createTransformGroup..297

setName 298

getName 298

setVisibility 298

getVisibility..299

setUserAttribute..299

getUserAttribute 299

getHasClassId..300

ClassIds Enum 300

Entity Relations 301

link..301

unlink..301

getParent..302

getChild 302

getChildAt..302

getNumOfChildren 303

getRootNode..303

Camera...303

getCamera..303

setCamera 304

I3D..304

loadI3DFile..304

loadSharedI3DFile 304

LoadI3dFailedReason Enum 305

streamI3DFile 305

cancelStreamI3DFile 306

streamSharedI3DFile 306

releaseSharedI3DFile 307

Physics...308

getRigidBodyType...308

RigidBodyType Enum 308

setRigidBodyType 308

getCenterOfMass 309

setCenterOfMass 309

getMass..309

setMass 310

raycastAll...310

raycastClosest 311

raycastCallback 312

overlapBox...312

overlapSphere 313

overlapCallback 314

Network 314

streamReadBool 314

streamReadFloat32 314

streamReadInt16 315

streamReadInt32 315

streamReadInt8 316

streamReadIntN 316

streamReadString 316

streamReadUInt16 317

streamReadUInt8 317

streamReadUIntN 317

streamWriteBool 318

streamWriteFloat32 318

streamWriteInt16 318

streamWriteInt32 319

streamWriteInt8 319

streamWriteIntN 319

streamWriteString 320

streamWriteUInt16 320

streamWriteUInt8 320

streamWriteUIntN 320

Index...**323**

About the Authors

Zander Brumbaugh is a programmer, game designer, technical author, and AI researcher based in Seattle, Washington. His work as an independent developer on the Roblox platform has been played more than 300 million times. He has created popular games like *My Salon*, *Power Simulator*, *Munching Masters*, and more. Zander is also a multiple-time best-selling textbook author, with works on programming and game development. He currently attends the the Paul G. Allen School of Computer Science and Engineering at the University of Washington where his research focuses on the improvement of language models for real-world settings.

Manuel Leithner is a senior gameplay programmer based in Buttenheim, Germany. While working on his bachelor's and master's degrees in business informatics/information systems, he started modding for Farming Simulator 2008, the first title of the series. A few years later, he worked as a freelancer for GIANTS Software on several DLCs and major game releases. In 2015, a branch office in Erlangen, Germany, was opened, and he became the head of the office as a branch manager. Since then, he has also become the lead gameplay programmer and responsible for gameplay across the whole franchise.

About the Technical Reviewer

 **Simon Jackson** is a long-time software engineer and architect with many years of Unity game development experience, as well as an author of several Unity game development titles. He loves to both create Unity projects as well as lend a helping hand to educate others, whether it's via a blog, vlog, user group, or major speaking event.

His primary focus is with the Reality Toolkit project, which is aimed at building a cross-platform Mixed Reality framework to enable both VR and AR developers to build efficient solutions in Unity and then build/distribute them to as many platforms as possible.

Introduction

About Farming Simulator

Since its initial release in 2008, Farming Simulator has been the premier farming simulation video game. As new generations of the game have been released, there have been increasingly new ways to play and build any farm you can imagine. Something that makes Farming Simulator truly unique is the ability to create your very own mods.

Mods are a way for you to make Farming Simulator your own, unique experience through modifying the game in a variety of ways. With mods, you can create something as simple as a new vehicle or a whole map, give yourself infinite money, or even change the game in its entirety. With many resources available and a large community of passionate creators, getting started with mod development is easier than ever.

The best part of this system is that many creators are already earning a living by making new mods. Whether you wish to be a mod creator only as a hobby or want to pursue it full-time, there are plenty of opportunities for you.

What You'll Learn

This book will take you on a deep dive into the many resources, tools, techniques, and opportunities available to you as you begin or continue your journey as a mod creator. By the end, you should feel confident in your ability to make programs in the Lua programming language, import 3D models, and ultimately create any mod you can envision.

Foreword

As the CEO of GIANTS Software, I am pleased to introduce this book on scripting with Farming Simulator Lua. The modding community has always been an essential part of Farming Simulator's success, and our developers have worked tirelessly to ensure that they have the tools they need to create incredible mods.

Since its inception in 2008, the Farming Simulator franchise has seen tremendous growth. Our community has been a significant factor in this success, and we continue to support and encourage modders to create innovative and exciting mods for our game. Scripting is a critical aspect of modding in Farming Simulator, and we recognize that it can be challenging for newcomers to grasp. With this book, we aim to demystify the scripting process and provide a comprehensive guide to creating Lua scripts that can enhance gameplay and introduce new features.

This book is the result of our collaboration with Zander Brumbaugh. The book provides a step-by-step approach to scripting, starting with the basics and progressing to more advanced topics, making it suitable for beginners and experienced modders alike. Our hope is that this book will inspire and encourage modders to push the limits of what is possible in Farming Simulator. I am constantly amazed by the creativity and ingenuity of our community, and we believe that this book will help take modding to the next level.

Finally, I would like to express my gratitude to the global Farming Simulator modding community for their continued support and contribution to the Farming Simulator franchise. With this in mind, we have made every effort to ensure that this book is accessible to modders of all backgrounds and skill levels. We have included examples and explanations that are easy to understand, regardless of your experience with scripting. In conclusion, I would like to thank the two authors of this book for their hard work and dedication. They have done an outstanding job of creating a comprehensive guide to scripting with Lua in Farming Simulator. I am confident that this book will become an invaluable resource for modders and will help drive the modding community forward.

Happy modding!

Christian Ammann

Founder and CEO, GIANTS Software

CHAPTER 1

Introduction, GDN, ModHub, Modding Tutorial Videos, LuaDoc, FarmCon...

In this chapter, we will explore the GIANTS Developer Network (GDN) and other important resources and materials available to mod creators (you!).

Technical Requirements

You will not need any software or additional materials for this chapter as it will mostly cover information. However, it may be beneficial to have an Internet connection and web browser available to you to search any topics covered in further detail or visit any websites mentioned.

Exploring the GDN

The **GIANTS Developer Network (GDN)** is the hub for all mod creation-related materials for Farming Simulator. Through the GDN, you can talk with other mod developers, view documentation for Farming Simulator

© GIANTS Software GmbH 2024
Z. Brumbaugh and M. Leithner, *Scripting Farming Simulator with Lua*,
https://doi.org/10.1007/979-8-8688-0060-3_1

and mod creation tools, watch tutorials, and make sure all the software you are using is up to date. Please note that **you need to create an account** to access the full feature set of the website. You can see a preview of the GDN website in Figure 1-1.

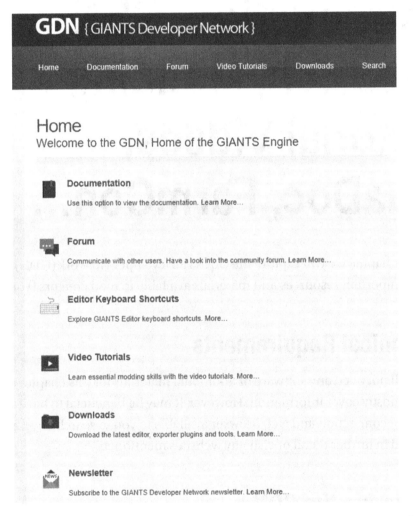

Figure 1-1. *The GDN contains all of the necessary resources to make great mods of your own*

In this section, we will explore all aspects of the GDN. If you want to navigate the website yourself while reading, you can use the following link:

https://gdn.giants-software.com

Modding Resources

The GDN includes different sections that can prove to be excellent resources at any level of mod creation experience. In this section, we will cover each section and discuss what information they cover.

Video Tutorials

The **Video Tutorials** section of the GDN contains groups of videos which give you a step-by-step guide on how to create a variety of in-game systems for your mods from scratch. Some of these topics include map creation, gameplay mods, sound design, effects, and more. These tutorials can be a helpful addition to this book for learning critical modding skills.

In addition to the free tutorials, there are other video contents from events such as FarmCon, which we will discuss in greater detail in the FarmCon section of this chapter. These videos are a good source of information about the best techniques and practices when creating mods of your own.

The newest 5.0 tutorials are paid tutorials that cover most recent release content. While access to these tutorials is paid, they are included with the collector's edition of Farming Simulator.

Documentation

The documentation section is one of the most important parts of the GDN, as it contains all official information for working with the GIANTS Editor, in-game interactions, mod creation, and the Lua programming language. Do note that the documentation section of the GDN is different from the documentation section on the main Farming Simulator website, which teaches you how to play the game rather than develop mods.

Under the **Fundamental Reading** section, there are links to the **Editor** and **Studio** documentation. The Editor documentation contains detailed information about using the **GIANTS Editor**, the main piece of software you will use when creating your mods. The editor allows you to combine both programming elements and physical, 3D elements to create more advanced mod types. You will learn how to navigate and use the GIANTS Editor in Chapter 2, "Getting Started with the GIANTS Editor." The Editor section of the GDN is something we will refer back to frequently.

The **GIANTS Studio** is a new tool for creating, editing, and debugging script mods. It works as an editor and a "remote" debugger in one. It interacts with the game as you create your mod and provides you with valuable information. Because of how the application is designed, it is a powerful environment that allows you to work on multiple mods at once. The studio is a separate application from the editor and will be important when you begin creating your own scripts in Lua.

The **Scripting** section of the GDN covers all of the vital information relating to the Lua programming language and how it relates to creating mods for Farming Simulator. We will cover this section in more detail in the *LuaDoc* section later in this chapter.

The **Content Creation** section covers fundamental information about importing 3D assets from various popular 3D modeling applications, including Maya and Blender. For clarity, **3D modeling** is the process of making all of the items you see and are able to interact with in the game; people who make 3D models are called **3D modelers**. To put it simply, 3D models include all of the "things" you see in the environment around you.

Community Forum

The forum is an excellent place to connect with other mod creators. Here, you can ask for help with specific issues you run into when developing your mods and get answers from other experienced users in a short amount of time. Additionally, you can have general developer discussion about best practices, software tips, and more. Like the Documentation section, do note that the forum of the GDN is different from the forum on the main website, which is for general discussion about Farming Simulator and the player community rather than mod creation. Figure 1-2 contains a preview of the forum.

Community Forum

View New Posts

```
[                                    ]  [ Search ]
```

Engine

Topics	Description	Threads	Posts	Last Post
Scripting	Scripting with LUA	747	3099	2 weeks ago
Editor	GIANTS Editor	1605	7702	2 weeks ago

Exporter

Topics	Description	Threads	Posts	Last Post
Maya Exporter	Autodesk Maya Exporter	93	370	6 months ago
3Ds MAX Exporter	Autodesk 3Ds MAX Exporter	48	180	2 months ago
Blender Exporter	Blender Exporter	130	638	Today (16:45)

Modding

Topics	Description	Threads	Posts	Last Post
Farming Simulator 22	Farming Simulator 22 Modding	387	1304	Today (19:43)
Farming Simulator 19	Farming Simulator 19 Modding	1100	4271	2 weeks ago
Farming Simulator 17	Farming Simulator 17 Modding	707	2580	3 weeks ago
Farming Simulator 15	Farming Simulator 15 Modding	447	1704	One month ago
Farming Simulator 2013	Farming Simulator 2013 Modding	173	695	17 months ago
Farming Simulator 2011	Farming Simulator 2011 Modding	192	663	20 months ago
Farming Simulator 2009	Farming Simulator 2009 Modding	174	764	2 months ago
Ski Region Simulator	Ski Region Simulator Modding	6	22	5 years ago
Demolition Company	Demolition Company Modding	17	52	21 months ago

Miscellaneous

Topics	Description	Threads	Posts	Last Post
Feedback	General suggestions	79	167	2 weeks ago
Feature Requests	Discussion about new features	87	262	12 days ago
Documentation	Discussion about documentation	23	83	6 months ago
Off Topic	Off Topic Discussions	43	150	2 weeks ago

Figure 1-2. *The GDN Forum is valuable for getting feedback and support from other creators*

Let us look now at each category of the forum and its purpose.

The **Engine** category of the forum is dedicated to discussion about the game engine of Farming Simulator. If you are a beginning developer, you will likely not need to interact with this section as it mostly covers advanced topics of how the programming language interacts with the game engine or how applications like the GIANTS Editor are implemented at the technical level.

The **Exporter** category of the forum is where mod creators can request help or talk about methods of using 3D modeling applications for creating or importing models for use with their mods. For example, if there is a tractor model you want to include in your mod but are having difficulty exporting it, you can post in this section and see if other creators have a solution to your problem.

The **Modding** category is an important part of the forum as it is where you should post any questions related to your work on mods. For instance, if you are not sure how to accomplish some sort of behavior or have an idea but are running into an issue, you can post your question here and have other members of the community assist you.

Additionally, there is a **Miscellaneous** category which includes four subcategories, those being **Feedback, Feature Requests, Documentation,** and **Off Topic**. The Feedback category is where you can make general comments about your experience with Farming Simulator or any applications you use for making your mods. The GIANTS Software team always values community feedback when making updates and deciding which direction to take the game.

The Feature Requests category is like the Feedback category but specifically where you can request new features or make suggestions for changes. While your suggestions are not guaranteed to be implemented, features and other additions that improve the gameplay or development experience will always be considered.

The Documentation category of the forum is where you can ask questions or make suggestions regarding the Documentation section of the GDN.

The Off Topic category is used for general development discussions or any topics that do not fall into any of the other categories.

Downloads

The **Downloads** section of the GDN is where you should always look to find the newest, updated versions of development applications made by GIANTS Software, including the GIANTS Editor and the GIANTS Studio. In addition to applications, there are also plug-ins and other add-ons for third-party software to make a more streamlined development experience. In this section, we will review which each category of the Downloads section offers.

The **Editor** category contains a list of releases for the GIANTS Editor. To ensure that you are able to take advantage of the newest features, make sure to download the most recent release version. We will walk you through the download process in Chapter 2, "Getting Started with the GIANTS Editor," which covers the GIANTS Editor.

The **Exporter** category includes plug-ins for various popular 3D modeling applications. These plug-ins create a more streamlined development experience by handling metadata and doing certain tasks as you export your 3D models for use in Farming Simulator mods. The applications currently supported include Blender and Maya.

The **Studio** category has a list of releases for the GIANTS Studio. As mentioned in the "Documentation" section, the Studio is a relatively new tool, so there are fewer versions released compared to the editor. Like the GIANTS Editor, you will want to make sure you have the latest version of the application installed to take advantage of the newest features and bug fixes. We will also cover the setup process for this application in Chapter 4, "The GIANTS Studio."

The **Other Tools** category of the Downloads section includes a limited amount of task-specific tools that may improve your experience creating mods. You are unlikely to interact with these tools until you are somewhat advanced as a creator but you are encouraged to explore nonetheless.

The **Modding** category includes applications, documents, images, and other media related to mod creation.

The **Miscellaneous** category includes any relevant downloads that do not fall into any other listed categories.

LuaDoc

In Chapter 3, "The Lua Programming Language," you will learn how to use the Lua programming language. **Programming** is what brings life to games and game systems. Any interactions you see, such as clicking a button and causing something to happen, are a result of programming. Those who program are called **programmers**. Lua is a fast, lightweight programming language that uses many universal programming constructs. So whether you are already an experienced programmer or have never done any programming before, you will learn everything from the basics to intermediate concepts in this book.

LuaDoc refers to the Lua documentation made by GIANTS Software. This documentation is included under the Documentation section of the GDN. For convenience, a link directly to the FS22 version of LuaDoc has been included here:

```
https://gdn.giants-software.com/documentation_scripting_
fs22.php
```

LuaDoc includes information not only about the Lua language but specifically how your programs are meant to interact with existing systems within Farming Simulator. Furthermore, much of the source code for the game systems within Farming Simulator are documented here and available to view through the GIANTS Studio.

YouTube

YouTube and other video streaming platforms also have many video tutorials available that you may find useful. Often, these videos may make a specific system or cover a specific issue that you will not find on the official site. However, as these videos are not official, they may not use the best practices and are not officially endorsed.

Looking at the ModHub

The ModHub is where you will publish your mods for all players to be able to use. The ModHub has different categories including maps, many different types of vehicles, and different buildings or farm technologies for players to include in their game.

The best-performing and highest-quality mods can appear in several algorithmic categories including *Latest* and *Top Downloaded*. These categories are then featured to players on the front page of the ModHub.

When users download your mod, they can leave a review on a five-star scale. Naturally, mods with a higher rating are more likely to be downloaded by other players and find their way into the sorts shown earlier. With dedication, your mods can also see wide usage and be shown at the top of these sorts. You can see a preview of the ModHub and the mentioned categories in Figure 1-3.

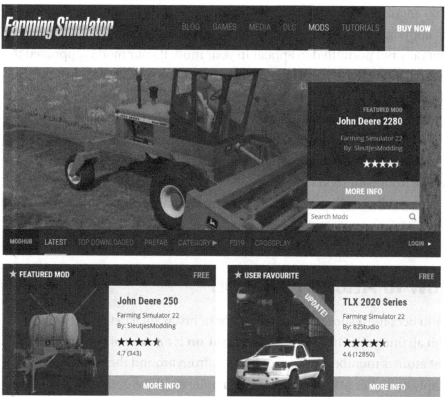

Figure 1-3. *The ModHub lets users discover new mods and enhance their Farming Sim experience*

Next, we will look at how many mod creators are already earning money by making their Farming Simulator mods available to the community.

Financial Opportunities of Mod Creation

As mentioned in the introduction, there are ways to earn money by creating mods and making them available for all Farming Simulator players to use. Once you create a quality mod, it must go through a manual approval process. This process ensures that the mod does what it claims to do and that it is free of any prohibited content. This content can vary, but copyrighted material, such as specific brands or companies, are generally not permitted to appear in your mod. If your mod is approved to be published on the ModHub, you may be eligible to receive payouts from GIANTS Software based on how many times your mod is downloaded. Remember, quality mods that receive the best reviews are more likely to appear in certain categories of the ModHub. When your mod is featured, more users will be able to see it and download, allowing you to earn more money from your mod.

In the next section, we will look at the annual Farming Simulator event, FarmCon.

How to Attend FarmCon

If you become a successful mod creator or just want a new way to engage with all things Farming Simulator, **FarmCon** is an annual convention that attracts members of the community from around the world. There is simply no better place to connect with other mod creators and community members.

FarmCon attendees are often the first to see new teasers, trailers, and announcements about the future of FarmCon. There are also many presenters with talks focusing on best techniques for players to build their farming empires and the best tips and tricks for mod creation. You can see a promotional image from FarmCon 22 in Mannheim, Germany, in Figure 1-4.

Figure 1-4. *FarmCon is an annual convention for all things Farming Simulator*

You may have some questions about what your FarmCon experience might look like or about the logistics of going. The following are some FarmCon FAQ that might be insightful:

- Do I need a ticket for FarmCon?

  A ticket is generally required for admission into the venue and in-person attendance.

- Do I have to visit FarmCon to get all the new info?

  We will not hide any new information about Farming Simulator at the event. You can follow announcements on the blog after the event.

- What language is FarmCon presented in?

  Most presentations at FarmCon in person will be held in German.

- I have further questions, how can I contact you?

  If you have any further questions about FarmCon, you can
  contact us via email at farmcon@giants-software.com.

If you want to stay informed about FarmCon, Farming Simulator, and
other exciting GIANTS Software projects, follow our social media accounts
listed here:

@farmingsimulator   @farmingsim   @FarmingSimulator

In the next section, we will look at official mod creation contests hosted
by GIANTS Software.

Participating in the Mod Contest

With each major release of Farming Simulator, there is a contest for mod
creators to participate in. Those who create the best mods or maps can win
some incredible prizes when the winners are announced at the FarmCon
the year following the release. For the winners, prizes have included
computer accessories, cameras, high-end computer graphics cards, and
trips to the factories of various farm equipment manufacturers.

If this excites you, you will have all the skills you need to participate
by the end of this book. The following are some of the general rules for
participating in the contest:

- Contestants – Teams or individuals may create
  submissions.

- Allowed in submission – New mod or map. No skins or
  prefabs.

- Origin – Only self-created mods (3D models, 2D textures, programming) will be accepted.

- Entry – A person or team may only enter once.

In the next section, we will briefly review what you have learned in this chapter and what to expect in the next.

Summary

In this chapter, you learned about the GIANTS Developer Network and what resources are available to you as you begin your journey as a mod creator. You also learned how to engage with other members of the community and the best ways to learn about events and see important updates relating to Farming Simulator.

With what you have learned about the mod-making process and environment from this chapter, you have been set on the path of being able to make anything you can envision in your mods. In the following chapter, you will familiarize yourself with the GIANTS Editor, the main software you will be using for creating your mods.

CHAPTER 2

Getting Started with the GIANTS Editor

The GIANTS Editor is the main application you will use to create mods. In the editor, you can run scripts, preview and manipulate models, and stage your creations before publishing them to the ModHub. In this chapter, we will explore the features and tools of the GIANTS Editor. Familiarizing yourself with the interfaces that mod creators work with is the first step in the path to making your own.

After reading this chapter, you will know the tools and features of the GIANTS Editor, be able to create and change the properties of objects in your mod, and manage application settings.

Technical Requirements

You will need to download the GIANTS Editor and optionally additional software for this chapter. As such, you will need an Internet connection and web browser available to you. The minimum requirements for the GIANTS Editor and other applications are as follows:

- Farming Simulator 22

- Windows 10 64-bit

- Intel Core i5-3330 or AMD FX-8320 or better

© GIANTS Software GmbH 2024
Z. Brumbaugh and M. Leithner, *Scripting Farming Simulator with Lua*,
https://doi.org/10.1007/979-8-8688-0060-3_2

- Nvidia GeForce GTX 660, AMD Radeon R7 265 graphics card or better (min. 2 GB VRAM, DX11/DX12 support)

- 8 GB RAM

- 35 GB free hard drive space

Installing the GIANTS Editor

To begin this chapter, we will return to the GDN website (`https://gdn.giants-software.com`) and head to the *Downloads* section. If you have not already made a GDN account, you will need to do so before you can download any of the free software on your computer. When you have navigated to the Downloads page, look for the most recent version of the GIANTS Editor available for your platform and game (e.g., Farming Simulator 22). By clicking the product name, you should be prompted to download the executable for the GIANTS Editor. You can see the relevant section of the Downloads page in Figure 2-1.

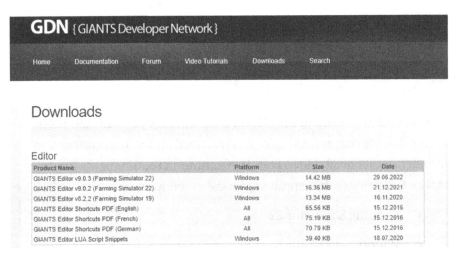

Figure 2-1. *All GIANTS Software applications can be downloaded through the GDN*

Once you have downloaded the executable, run it and proceed through the steps listed in the setup wizard. When the setup tasks have been completed, launch the GIANTS Editor application, and you should be greeted by a welcome menu. That is the first step complete!

In the next section, you will learn how to navigate the GIANTS Editor.

The Viewport

With the GIANTS Editor opened for the first time, a "Getting Started" window will pop up showing some useful information to get help about the editor. After closing it, you should see several panels on each side of a gray space. This space, called the viewport, is where you will see the models, map elements, and any other visual part of your mod. Your viewport will not be very interesting without any objects in your scene. Let's follow these steps to create your first object:

1. Go to the **Create** menu at the top left of the editor window.

2. Click the *Cube* button from the **Primitives** dropdown menu.

We will explore the Create menu and other application menus in greater detail in the "Application Menus" section of this chapter. For now, you should see the cube you have inserted into your scene. Your viewport should look something like what is depicted in Figure 2-2.

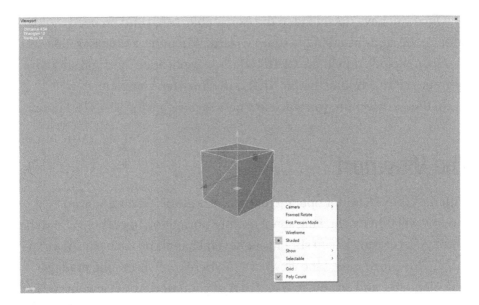

Figure 2-2. *The viewport is the main element you use to see and interact with your scene*

Let us now look at how to examine this cube and anything else you may add to your scene.

Movement and Camera Manipulation

Manipulation of your camera in the GIANTS Editor is quite simple. Your camera will move relative to the direction you are facing **while holding the right mouse button (RMB)**:

- The *W* key will move your camera forward.

- The *A* key will move your camera left.

- The *S* key will move your camera back.

- The *D* key will move your camera right.

- Holding the *Shift* key while moving your camera will cause movement to occur at a faster rate, which is convenient for moving across large areas in the scene.

If you feel that the camera is moving too fast or too slow, you can adjust the speed of the camera by pressing *KEY_NUM_MINUS* and *KEY_ NUM_PLUS*, respectively. For clarity, these are the plus (+) and minus (−) buttons on the number pad of a keyboard. The current navigation speed is displayed in the bottom-right corner of the window.

Let us now cover how you interact with objects in your scene. To select an object in your viewport, simply click the physical object with the left mouse button (**LMB**) or via the Scenegraph Panel, which we will cover in more detail in the "The Scenegraph Panel" section of this chapter. When you have an object selected, you can press *F* to bring your camera to the object. This is convenient when you have many objects in your scene and want to move your camera to one specifically.

Let us now look at some of the options available to change how we look at objects with the viewport and more.

Viewport Options

By right-clicking anywhere in the viewport, you will bring up a new menu with a list of options as seen back in Figure 2-2. Let us now look at what each of these options does.

Camera

The first option from this list is *Camera*, which allows you to set your perspective to any camera object within your scene. You may find this feature useful in instances where you want to test a camera object players will eventually use as part of your mod or simply to have multiple viewpoints available in different areas of your scene while in the Editor. Note that you cannot delete a camera object if your perspective is currently set to it.

Framed Rotate

The next option from the list is a toggle for **Framed Rotate** mode. When this option is enabled, you can move your camera around an arbitrary point in space; this is a very useful feature for examining an object in your scene. To do this, enable Framed Rotate, select an object and press the *F* key to bring your camera to it, zoom out, and press *ALT+LMB* to move your camera around its new pivot point.

First-Person Mode

This option enables a special mode that is useful for creating maps. It allows the user to walk through a map like a player using the mouse and the *A, S, D, W* keys for movement. Note that you should only enable this mode when editing a map as it requires a terrain object in the scene. Use the *ESC* key to disable the mode again.

Shading Modes

Listed after these options are two modes for viewing your scene; these two modes are called **wireframe** and **shaded**. When viewing your scene in shaded mode (the default mode), objects will be rendered (displayed) with shadows and appear as they would in the game. In wireframe mode, you will always be able to see the topology of objects in your scene and see objects through other objects. If you are unfamiliar with the process of 3D modeling, topology refers to the layout of the smaller 3D components that make up your model, often called polygons or tris (triangles).

Show and Selectable

Following these viewing mode options are options for what objects you can see and interact with in your scene. The first *Show* option includes a dropdown menu and list of object types that are shown only when enabled. Similarly, the *Selectable* option also produces a dropdown menu where you can choose which types of objects you are able to select with your mouse in the viewport. These settings are convenient when you are working in complex scenes and want to filter only for the types of objects you want to interact with.

Grid

The *Grid* option shows a grid with 1×1 squares when enabled. The grid can help to give you a frame of reference when creating your scene when terrain is not present as well as keeping objects aligned.

Polycount

Lastly, the *Polycount* option when enabled will show you additional information about objects you are selecting. This relates back to what you are able to see in the wireframe viewing mode. Because of how computer processing works, the lower the polycount of an object, the less computationally expensive it is to render.

In the following section, we will learn how objects in your scene are structured and how to navigate them all most efficiently.

The Scenegraph Panel

As previously mentioned, the Scenegraph Panel is an important menu that allows you to see all of the objects in your scene. This will become important when you begin programming as you will need to refer to objects in your scene, and this reference will be based on the organization of objects in your scene. You can see how your Scenegraph Panel might look when there are multiple objects in your scene in Figure 2-3.

Figure 2-3. *The Scenegraph shows all of the objects contained within your scene*

You may notice some objects in Figure 2-3 seem to be a list under another object. This descent is related to how objects are organized in the GIANTS Editor. Let us now explore what this hierarchy is called and how to navigate it.

Entities and the Parent-Child Hierarchy

In the GIANTS Editor (and many other applications like it), objects are stored in what is called a **parent-child hierarchy**. A parent-child hierarchy is one where an object is stored inside of something (its parent) and the object is the child to its parent. Each object in the engine is an **entity** with a unique ID used to access it. Please keep in mind that this ID is not persistent and can change on every game or editor startup. An entity can be a TransformGroup, a shape, a camera, etc. The entity type defines a feature set for the object. For example, a camera entity can be used as a viewport camera, a Shape entity has special functions like materials, and Transform entities can be used in the parent-child hierarchy and have a position in the world. Looking at Figure 2-4, you can see three objects: the Scenegraph, a Camera object named *perspectiveCamera*, and two Transform Group objects named *parentTransformGroup* and *childTransformGroup*. In the GIANTS Editor, the Scenegraph is always at the top of the parent-child hierarchy; that is, any objects in your scene are a descendant of the Scenegraph. In this example, *perspectiveCamera* and *parentTransformGroup* are direct descendants of the Scenegraph or its **children**. The Transform object named *childTransformGroup* is the child of *parentTransformGroup*; you can alternatively say that *childTransformGroup* is **parented** to *parentTransformGroup*:

Figure 2-4. *This example shows the parent-child hierarchy of the GIANTS Editor*

In the next section, we will look at the application menus of the editor

Application Menus

In this section, we will explore the various application menus in the GIANTS Editor and discuss which options you should know about as a beginning mod creator.

The File Menu

The **File menu** contains many options related to what you are currently working with inside of the GIANTS Editor. Let us look at each menu option and what they do.

The **New** button will reset the editor to an empty environment when pressed. Before the environment is cleared, you will be prompted to save any unsaved changes to the current file or to create a new file if you have not saved your work before.

The **Open** button will open your file explorer and allow you to open any .i3d files you have saved and continue editing them.

The **Save** and **Save As** buttons will save your current environment to an .i3d file. If you have not previously saved your work to a file, only the Save As button will be available and will prompt you to select a location on your computer and file name for the file to be stored with. If you have previously saved your work to a file, only the Save As button will prompt you to choose a new location and file name, whereas the Save option will simply overwrite your existing file.

Clicking the **Open Mod** button will allow you to open mods that have already been exported to mod file formats such as .zip or .xml instead of an .i3d file. Alternatively, selecting the **New Mod from Game** option will allow you to import game assets to your environment and use them to create a new mod, creating all of the relevant files in a directory of your choice. You can freely use any of the assets or components of them in your new creations.

The **Import** and **Import as Reference** options allow you to add 3D models and assets in .i3d or .fbx file formats to your scene. The difference between these options is that Import as Reference will create a link to the file you import. That is, any modifications you make to the original file you imported as a reference will be instantly shown in the file you imported to. This behavior does not occur when using the Import feature – with this, you would need to reimport the file if you wish to bring over any changes you have made.

If you wish to export the 3D elements of your mod, there are three options to choose from. The **Export all with Files**, **Export Selection**, and **Export Selection with Files** options all allow you to convert the objects in your environment into 3D model file formats, such as .i3d and .obj. The meaning of *with Files* is that it will include files like textures in addition to the base .i3d file. Without exporting with files, textures are referenced only with absolute or relative file paths and thus will not appear if shared with others. The functional difference between the *export all* and *export selection* is that *export selection* will only include objects that you are currently selecting in your scene as opposed to every object in your scene.

The **Preferences** button will open a menu that contains various settings related to the tools and interfaces of the GIANTS Editor. Not all of these settings will be relevant to you as a beginner, but feel free to explore each of them. If you have set preferences in a previous version of the GIANTS Editor, you can select the **Import Preferences** option, and the editor will automatically transfer over your preferences.

Lastly, hovering over the **Recent Files** button will produce a dropdown menu of any files you have recently worked with in the GIANTS Editor. Do note that opening recent files from this menu will change your scene without prompting you to save. Save any changes you have made to your scene before opening a recent file from this menu.

In the next section, we will discuss the **Edit menu** and the meaning of each option it contains.

The Edit Menu

The Edit menu contains a list of options related to actions you make in the editor in addition to the key bindings associated with them. Let us look at some of these options and what each of them does:

- *Undo* – Undo your last action

- *Redo* – Redo your last action

- *Clear History* – Clear the list of last actions

- *Cut* – Copy and remove an item from your scene

- *Copy* – Copy an item from your scene

- *Paste* – Add a copied item to your scene

- *Delete* – Delete a selected item from your scene

- *Duplicate* – Duplicate a selected item in your scene

- *Replace* – Replace objects of one type with another throughout the scene

Some other options this menu provides include Freeze Transformation, Move to Camera, and Interactive Placement. Freeze Transformations will allow you to set the frame of reference for a selected object to its parent for different properties. For example, if an object parented to your scene (top of the hierarchy) is moved from the origin (global center of your scene) and you apply this option to the Translate property, it will treat it as unmoved from the origin. Another example is if your object is rotated and you apply this option with the Rotate property selected, the rotation arcs will reset as if the object was not rotated. You will likely not need to use this option until you are a more advanced creator or find a situation where this is particularly helpful.

The Move to Camera option allows you to set the position and orientation of a selected object to that of your camera. This is convenient if you want to orient something based on your camera's perspective rather than trying to estimate with your tools.

Finally, the interactive placement button lets you freely place a selected object where your mouse is when the left mouse button is held down if your mouse is intersecting another object in your scene.

Do note the key bindings associated with each action we have covered as pressing these will be quicker than navigating to the menu.

You are also able to detach this application menu for quick access.

In the next section, we will look at the options in the **Create menu**.

The Create Menu

The Create menu displays options to insert objects into your scene. In the GIANTS Editor, there are six primary types of objects:

1. Transform Group

2. Light

3. Camera

4. Audio Source

5. Spline

6. Navigation Mesh

7. Note

8. Primitives (e.g., Cube, Plane, etc.)

Clicking a create option will create the object (see Figure 2-5), add it in the Scenegraph, select it, and show its values in the attribute window on the right-hand side of the GIANTS Editor. The Edit Menu section, we already created a cube primitive by using the Create menu. Try to explore the other actions of the *Edit* menu and see the effects of each.

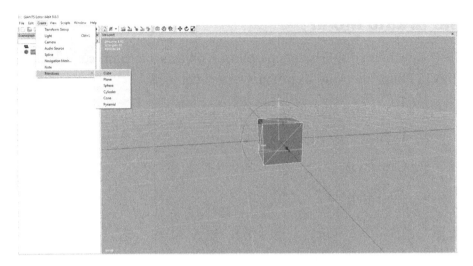

Figure 2-5. *You can insert primitive objects and more via the Create menu*

In the next section, we will look at the **View menu**.

The View Menu

The View menu is, as the name implies, important to how you view your scene – particularly in viewing 3D models. Most of the options contained in this menu were covered in the earlier "Viewport Options" section. We will discuss only the options that were not covered previously.

The first of these is the *Enable TAA* option; when enabled, temporal anti-aliasing will be used in rendering your scene, resulting in less jaggedness around objects and textures which creates a better appearance.

The *Profile* menu produces a dropdown menu when hovered over that shows presets for graphical quality in the viewport. If you are experiencing a low frame rate or other poor performance while editing, you should lower this setting.

Debug and **Texture Streaming** items show more advanced features of the editor that are normally not used by modders. They are included in the editor because the GIANTS Editor is also used by the GIANTS Software team internally to develop the game.

The following section will explore the contents of the **Scripts menu**.

The Scripts Menu

The Scripts menu contains a list of all available scripts. Through this menu, you can select the *Create new script* option to create new scripts. We will explore this more in the "Scripting" section of this chapter. For now, we will continue to the next section and discuss the **Window menu**.

The Window Menu

The Window menu allows you to toggle visibility or window mode for the various menus of the GIANTS Editor. Many of these windows are visible by default, including the Scenegraph, Viewport, Console, and Attributes windows. Feel free to look at any windows that are not visible by default, but we will cover almost all of these in future chapters as they become relevant. In the meantime, you can change where in the application most windows are displayed by clicking and dragging the top of most windows you currently have visible. This is a point of customization for you to make your environment as efficient for you to work in as possible.

We will now look at the options in the **Help menu**.

The Help Menu

The final application menu of the GIANTS Editor is the Help menu. This menu contains a list of options related to information about the editor itself and additional resources for its use. Almost all of these options will redirect you to the GDN, which we covered in the first chapter. This serves as a good reminder of the value of the resources that can be found on the GDN.

Now that we have covered all of the application menus of the GIANTS Editor, we will look at other windows and elements you should familiarize yourself with.

The Attributes Panel

When an object in your scene is selected, you will see **properties** about the object displayed in the **Attributes Panel**. Properties are values that change the behavior or appearance of an object in your scene. For objects of the Primitive type, some properties include Translate, Rotate, and Scale which refer to the position, orientation, and size of the object, respectively. The properties displayed in the Attributes Panel will change depending on the type of object you have selected as different objects have different functionalities. You can see what the Attributes Panel might look like when a Cube is selected in Figure 2-6.

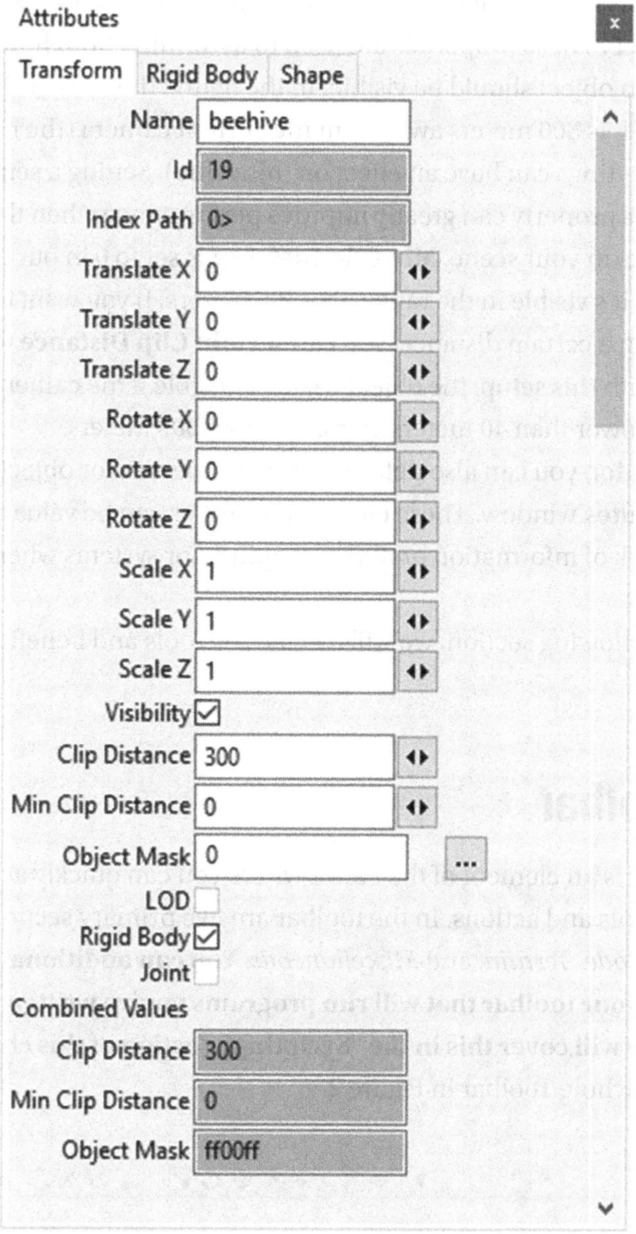

Attributes

Transform   Rigid Body   Shape

Name	beehive
Id	19
Index Path	0>
Translate X	0
Translate Y	0
Translate Z	0
Rotate X	0
Rotate Y	0
Rotate Z	0
Scale X	1
Scale Y	1
Scale Z	1
Visibility	☑
Clip Distance	300
Min Clip Distance	0
Object Mask	0
LOD	☐
Rigid Body	☑
Joint	☐

Combined Values

Clip Distance	300
Min Clip Distance	0
Object Mask	ff00ff

Figure 2-6. *The Attributes Panel shows the properties of a selected object, a cube in this case*

An important attribute shown in Figure 2-6 is **Clip Distance** and **Min Clip Distance**. These properties are used to determine from how far or near away an object should be visible. In the figure, the cube will not be visible once it is 300 meters away from the current camera (the hardware scalability settings can have an effect on this value). Setting a sensible value for this property can greatly improve performance when there are many objects in your scene. **Min Clip Distance** is set to 0 in our example. That means it's visible in the range of 0–300 meters. If you want to hide an object within a certain distance, you can set **Min Clip Distance** to 40, for example. With this setup, the object will be invisible if the camera to object distance is lower than 40 meters or greater than 300 meters.

As a creator, you can also define custom properties for objects via the **User Attributes** window. These custom properties can be valuable for keeping track of information or making settings for systems when creating your mods.

In the following section, we will discuss the tools and benefits of the **Toolbar**.

The Toolbar

The Toolbar is an element of the editor where you can quickly access a variety of tools and actions. In the toolbar are five primary sections called *File, Play, Mode, Terrain,* and *Miscellaneous.* **You can additionally create buttons in your toolbar that will run programs you've written when pressed; we will cover this in the "Scripting" section of this chapter.** You can see the whole Toolbar in Figure 2-7.

Figure 2-7. *The Toolbar contains buttons for different actions and tools*

File Section

The File section includes nine buttons as shown in Figure 2-8. The following actions are available:

1. Create a new i3D file

2. Open an existing i3D file

3. Open the current file in a text editor

4. Reload the current file

5. Save the current file

6. Save the current scene in a new file

7. Import an i3D file to the current scene

8. Undo the last action

9. Redo the last action

Figure 2-8. *File toolbar*

Play Section

The Play toolbar allows you to test your mod, in different ways. The first test option, indicated by the play button icon (Figure 2-9), will begin physics simulation, play sounds, and additional rendering like showing particle emission and animations. The option indicated by the eye icon lets you test your mod in first-person mode. In this mode, you will be able to walk around the map of your mod and interact with objects from a first-person perspective and feel the effects of gravity like walking around in Farming Simulator.

Figure 2-9. *Play toolbar*

Mode Section

Let us now look at some of the different options shown in the Mode section of the Toolbar for manipulating objects within your scene (Figure 2-10).

Figure 2-10. *Mode toolbar*

Local/World Mode

This button toggles the object mode between world space and local space manipulation. In the scenegraph hierarchy, the transform attributes of an object are stored relative to the parent object, so-called local space attributes. By default, the manipulation of the object within the viewport is based on local space transformation. You can change this by activating the world space mode. Now the movement is independent of the parent object.

Snapping

With the snapping button, you can toggle the snapping mode. Using the down pointing arrow, you can set the snap deltas. For example, if you set the snap value to "1.000" and try to move an object, it will move in 1 m steps.

Let's now have a look at the different manipulation modes. Note that when none of these modes are selected (default), all three tools are available when an object is selected. If you gain mastery over these different modes, this setting may be preferable to quickly manipulate an object without any switching.

Translation Mode

When in **Translation** mode (shortcut: *W* key), selected objects will show three arrows and three planes through which to move the selected object. When using the arrows, the object will simply follow in the direction you drag your mouse along the axis indicated by the arrow you grab.

When using the planes to move objects, the object will freely follow the movement of your mouse except on the axis of the plane you selected. Try translating a primitive object using the arrows; notice how the Translate attributes change and how each axis (X, Y, or Z) is affected by exactly one of the arrows. You can see a reference for these axes and their color-coded handles in Figure 2-11.

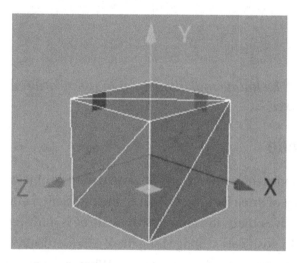

Figure 2-11. *The Translate tool allows you to move objects along the X, Y, and Z axes*

Rotation Mode

The Rotation mode (shortcut: *E* key) shows three arcs with which to rotate a selected object. Like the Translate mode, each color-coded arc corresponds to an axis of rotation. Try rotating a primitive object and seeing how the Rotate attributes are changed. Do note which arc corresponds to which axis may not be intuitive as the arcs rotate around the previously illustrated axes. Figure 2-12 visualizes this difference.

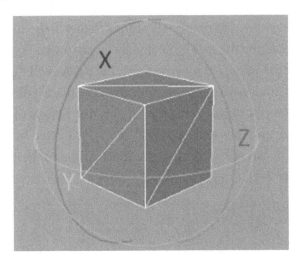

Figure 2-12. *The Rotate tool allows you to rotate around the Translation axes*

Scaling Mode

The Scaling mode (shortcut: *R* key) allows you to scale objects in your scene with a set of three handles similar to the translation arrows. When scaling a primitive object, the amount you scale by is mirrored across the axis. That is, positively scaling along the Y axis (vertically) 1 unit in this mode increases the total size by 2 units. Whenever you want to make something bigger or smaller in your scene, you should use this mode.

Miscellaneous Section

The Miscellaneous section brings up three different actions (Figure 2-13):

1. Prefab Explorer to download existing objects (e.g., buildings)

2. Reload all textures of the current scene

3. Reload textures of the selected object

Figure 2-13. *Miscellaneous toolbar*

Terrain Section

If you want to create maps of your own, you will need something to stand on; this is where terrain comes in. The toolbar (Figure 2-14) has the following elements to modify the terrain:

1. Terrain sculpting

2. Terrain painting

3. Mesh/object painting

4. InfoLayer painting

5. Procedural painting

6. Foliage painting

Figure 2-14. *Terrain toolbar*

But first of all, you need a terrain node in your scenegraph. To add one, follow these steps:

1. Go to the File menu.

2. Select the New Mod From Game option.

3. Import one of the maps from the *Item* dropdown menu.

This will import all of the files and assets from the game into a new working directory of your choice. With a map now imported, we can begin to modify its terrain with the different terrain modification modes of the GIANTS Editor. Before exploring the tools and modes for editing, we will need to open the **Terrain Editing** window from the *Window* application menu to see and control how we modify our terrain. With this window opened, we will start by using the **Terrain sculpt mode** as an example.

Let us first select terrain sculpt mode, which is indicated in the Toolbar by the icon with the up and down arrows as seen in Figure 2-15.

Figure 2-15. *Terrain sculpt mode can be toggled via the Toolbar*

Once you have the tool selected, you will not be able to move your camera as usual until you deselect the tool, which can be done by clicking the icon again. To move your camera when in this mode, you can use *Alt+RMB* to move forward and backward in the direction the camera is facing. Additionally, you can use *Alt+LMB* to rotate the camera and *Alt+LMB+RMB* to move the camera along the relative X and Y directions. Do note these movement modes are also available when not using the terrain editing modes.

Returning to the sculpt mode, you can use *LMB* to grow terrain upward, *RMB* to shrink terrain downward, and middle mouse button (MMB) to smooth terrain by default. Additionally, by pulling your mouse wheel back, you can increase the size of the area that will be affected by the tool. Oppositely, you can push the mouse wheel forward to decrease the size of the affected terrain area. These settings, among others, can be changed in the *Brush* section of the Terrain Editing window. Note also that from this window you can change the shape of your brush from a circle to a square. You can see what sculpting grass-textured terrain in your scene with a circular brush might look like in Figure 2-16.

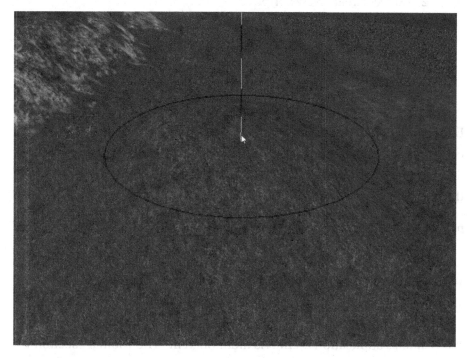

Figure 2-16 *You can use terrain sculpt mode to modify terrain in your scene*

While there are more terrain editing features and modes, these will be the most relevant to you as a beginner making your mod. As with other topics we have covered, you are encouraged to explore anything we did not cover. The next section will give you a first look at programming and some of the elements of the GIANTS Editor relevant to it.

Scripting

In this last section, you will get your first taste of programming by creating your first **script**, which is what we call a file that holds code. To add a new script, follow these steps:

1. Navigate to the *Scripts* application menu.

2. Select Create New Script.

3. You will be prompted to enter a name for your script.

4. Enter a name of your choice – perhaps *test*.

The Script Editor should appear within a new window in the GIANTS Editor and include some comments by default. Comments are lines of code that don't do anything and simply hold text; in Lua, comments are lines that begin with two dashes (--). After these lines, add a new line with the following content:

print("Hello world!")

Hello world! is a traditional first line of code for many programmers. With this line written in your script, click *Save* and then *Execute*. You should see the output of your program in the Output window of the GIANTS Editor. Note that you can access the Script Editor at any time via the *Windows* application menu. As mentioned in "The Toolbar" section of this chapter, you can assign a script you create to a button in one of five custom script toolbars. Having a shortcut to a script in the toolbar is a handy way to speed up the modding process. For example, as a map creator, you could create a script that perfectly aligns fences. With the shortcut button in the toolbar, you would simply need one click to align the fences.

To add a script to the toolbar, open it in the Script Editor; at the top of the window, select one of the script button slots from the dropdown menu next to the *Toolbar* label for your script to be assigned to, as seen in Figure 2-17. You can upload an icon so that you can easily identify each of your scripts. Once you've done this, simply click the button with your chosen icon in the Toolbar, and you should see the output of the script in the console.

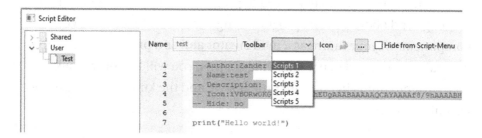

Figure 2-17. *You can bind scripts to Toolbar buttons to be conveniently run when pressed*

There you go, your first program is complete! You will learn the fundamentals of Lua and how to make more complex systems in Chapter 3, "The Lua Programming Language." For now, let's look at what other editor elements are relevant to writing and running Lua code.

The Console

The Console is a window of the GIANTS Editor that can be used to write and execute Lua code. After writing your code in the textbox of the Console, press *Shift+Enter* to have that code execute instantly. This is useful when running simple commands or doing math with what's offered by the Lua libraries but also to affect things in your scene, such as changing fog or other properties. In the next chapter, you will gain experience with the Console as you execute simple programs to gain familiarity with the Lua programming language.

Summary

In this chapter, you learned how to use the GIANTS Editor and what tools and features it offers. You should now feel comfortable creating and changing the properties of new objects, managing application settings, creating and executing a script, and manipulating elements of your environment like terrain with built-in tools.

The next chapter will teach you to program in the Lua programming language and about general programming constructs that will be key components of your future as a mod creator and as a programmer more generally. By the end of the following chapter, you will be able to make your own programs in Lua with proper style and the knowledge to produce optimized code.

CHAPTER 3

The Lua Programming Language

The Lua language is a fast, procedural programming language used by the GIANTS Engine and many other applications. Lua was originally created in 1993 due to software trade barriers in Brazil, which prevented many from buying specialized software from outside the country. Because of this, the language was designed to be highly customizable with a simple API in the C programming language so that programmers could easily make changes to fit their needs.

The goal of this chapter is to give you the knowledge you need to make your first programs in Lua so that you're ready to become a fully proficient programmer. No prior programming experience is assumed, so we will start by covering the concept of variables and other universal programming constructs. Then, within a few chapters, you will be able to create full programs to interact with your Farming Simulator mods. If you find some material difficult, don't be worried! You're taking a crash course in a skill that you will build upon for the rest of your life, and this is just the beginning. If you feel the need to move between different sections or review some earlier ones, you are encouraged to do so!

© GIANTS Software GmbH 2024
Z. Brumbaugh and M. Leithner, *Scripting Farming Simulator with Lua*,
https://doi.org/10.1007/979-8-8688-0060-3_3

Technical Requirements

In this chapter, you will be working entirely in the GIANTS Editor and must meet the requirements mentioned in the "Technical Requirements" section of Chapter 2, "Getting Started with the GIANTS Editor." While releases are infrequent, make sure you are always using the most recent version of the GIANTS Editor. This will ensure that you are able to take advantage of any new features. You can find all the code used in this chapter in the book's code repository on the GDN at the following link:

https://gdn.giants-software.com/lp/scriptingBook.php

Learning About Data Types and Creating Variables

In programming, a **variable is a way for your code to hold a piece of information**; different types of information are called data types. Variables are convenient because when you create one, you can give it an **identifier** (a name) so that it may be easily referenced and used later. In many programming languages, these variables are **typed**; this means that the type of the variable, be it a number or a word, must be decided when it is created. In Lua, variables are untyped which means you may assign any type of data to a variable without stating what that type is.

It is important that you know what the most common data types are before you begin programming.

Data Types

In Lua, the **number** data type can hold both whole and fractional portions of numeric values. Examples of a number can include 1, 0.33, −1.2, etc. This is the only numeric type used in Lua, but it may be helpful to remember that an integer is simply a whole number, positive, negative, or zero. The number data type is actually named a **double-precision floating-point number**, though it is more commonly called a **double**, which is a type of float. Some values cannot be perfectly represented by this system because of how computers work; such inaccuracies are referred to as **floating-point errors**. An example of how one of these errors might look is when the value 0.2 is instead shown as 0.20000000000000018. It's important to be aware of these errors when processing data, and you may run into them in a game development environment.

Booleans are a simple data type with a binary true or false value; when stored in a variable, they are more frequently called **bools**. It is important to note that in Lua, 1 and 0 only have numeric values and do not have any uses in Boolean logic, as seen in other languages. That is to say, 1 and 0 only represent numbers, not true or false or any other value.

Strings, as a data type, are best explained as any kind of text. Strings can represent words, sentences, letters, and more. In most languages, strings are an array or sequence of individual characters; in Lua, however, characters are not a data type.

In Lua, **tables** are a data structure that can be used in many different ways. We will discuss two uses of tables in this section: **arrays** and **dictionaries**. Unlike arrays in other programming languages, tables when used as an array can act more like lists, as they are not limited to an initialized size, nor do they require one; as a result, additional table positions do not need to be preemptively reserved. Elements contained in these tables are indexed from 1 to n, with n being how many elements are in your table. It should be noted that in most other languages, the starting index value of a table is 0, whereas it is 1 in Lua; these are called zero-based and one-based indexing styles, respectively. Additionally, tables are not typed by default; it could be said that this has many advantages, as in other languages you would be restricted to only adding values of the same type into a single array. However, you should still keep your tables organized and not loosely throw any type of data into them like a virtual colander.

The greatest benefit of using a table as a **dictionary** is the ability to index anything with a convenient key instead of numbered indices. For example, if you had a farm in your experience and you wanted all the apples in your experience to have one functionality and all bananas to have another, you could use the name of the fruit as a dictionary key that has an associated function; you could even use the physical fruit itself as the key since keys are not limited just to strings. As before, dictionaries have an infinite capacity, and elements within them can be of any type.

Setting and Manipulating Variables

Initializing and changing variables in Lua is a process that utilizes a variety of different operators to achieve a desired result. A convenient way to check the value of your variable is by using the print() function. You learned this function in Chapter 2, "Getting Started with the GIANTS Editor," where you used it to output *Hello world!* in the Console. The print() function is a vaLuable tool when following along in your program and for observing what your code produces when it would otherwise not be visible. In this section, we will begin writing new lines of code that hold and manipulate data. To get started, open the GIANTS Editor and create a new script. Once you write a program, you will need to click *Save* and then *Execute*. Output from your program will be seen in the console as shown in the "Scripting" section of Chapter 2, "Getting Started with the GIANTS Editor."

Numbers

Number variables are easy to set and change. We initialize variables using the "*local*" keyword followed by its name and then its value which determines its type. If you do not use the "*local*" keyword, then the variable is declared globally for the entire script which can lead to problems later on. After writing local, you put the name of your variable. A variable name cannot start with nonalphabetical characters and cannot contain any characters that are not alphanumeric except for underscores. For example, if you wanted to have a variable that simply held the value of 99, your code would look like this:

```
local myNumber = 99
```

There are many different operators we can use to change the variable, and libraries of special functions, but for this example, we simply want the value to increment by *1* to reach a total value of 100. To accomplish this, we can think of setting the variable to itself plus *1* by using the addition operator (+):

```
myNumber = myNumber + 1
```

When we are referencing a variable, we simply use its name, so stating "*myNumber* = ", we are saying we want to update the existing variable we declared earlier. The local keyword is only used when we first initialize the variable. Depending on the scenario, it may be more practical to simply set the variable to 100 directly. In this case, you would simply set the variable to the value, similar to what you did when initializing it (without the local statement, of course).

Lua supports the arithmetic operators that are standard across most languages, those being for addition (+), subtraction (-), multiplication (*), division (/), and modulo (%).

While you are likely familiar with most of these operations, the concept of modulo may be new to you. A modulo operation simply returns the remainder when a is divided by b. For example:

$$7 \% 4 = 3$$

$$8 \% 4 = 0$$

For more advanced operations, Lua provides a library with the same functionality as the standard math library in the C language. This library provides trigonometric functions, value conversions, and specific values with convenience and accuracy. To utilize this library, we can use the math keyword.

Here is an example of getting an accurate approximation of pi by using the math library:

```
myNumber = math.pi
```

Moving forward, we will discuss the **Boolean** data type.

Booleans

Setting a **Boolean** is simple as there are only two initialization options: using the true or false keyword. An initialization statement for a Boolean value may look something like this:

```
local myBool = true
```

To change the value of this variable, you simply need to set the bool as true or false. For example, we will set *myBool* equal to false with the following line of code:

```
myBool = false
```

There is a trick for setting a bool to its opposite value in one line, as opposed to using a conditional. We can do this by making use of the not operator, which will be covered more once we get to conditional statements. The not operator serves to simply return the opposite of the input following it. For example, if we wanted to change the preceding *myBool* variable from false back to true, we could simply use the following line of code:

```
myBool = not myBool
print(myBool)
```

```
Output: true
```

Continuing, we will cover another primitive data type, **strings**.

Strings

To declare a **string**, you should use the same variable initialization style and write your text inside double quotes. We use double quotes to describe strings, for example, "*My String.*" If the string itself contains double quotes, then we can use a single quote instead:

```
local myString = "Hello"
```

If you are using double quoted strings, Lua uses the backslash (\) as an escape character. This means that any character that would normally be special is treated as text within a string. For example, if someone in some game dialog is speaking from the third person, you could create double quote marks, like this:

```
myString = "He said \"I don't like apples!\""
```

Conversely, this backslash operator makes some normal text special. Two characters that are made special by the backslash character are the letters n and t.

\t: A tab will be added in that place.

\n: A new line is inserted at that point.

The following code shows the usage of both special chars:

```
myString = "Separated\tby\ttabs"
print(myString)
```

```
Output: "Separated by tabs"
```

```
myString = "Separated\nby\nlines"
print(myString)
```

```
Output:
"Separated
by
lines"
```

If you have multiple lines in your string, you do not necessarily need to utilize the \n operator. Lua, unlike some other languages, supports the use of multiline strings. Aside from being able to simply press your Enter key to create new lines, you can more conveniently format paragraph-sized strings in your programs. To initialize a paragraph string, you must capture your text within double brackets, as shown here:

```
myString = [[This string
can span
multiple lines.]]
```

One of the most common ways string variables can be changed is by **concatenating** them. By following any string with .. and providing another string, the latter string will be attached at that position:

```
myString = "Hello"
myString = myString.. " World!"
print(myString)
```

```
Output: "Hello World!"
```

The ability to concatenate is particularly useful when you're presenting different information to a player via a UI element. For example, if you wanted to announce that some event has come to an end, you can append the name of that event to a string:

```
local eventName = "rain"
myString = "Weather event over! The ".. eventName.. "
has ended."
print(myString)
```

Output: "Weather event over! The rain has ended."

Similar to how numeric data has a library for mathematical operations, there exists a library of string functions for more complex manipulations, as well as data management. This library can be accessed by writing the string keyword. Some functions include the ability to change the case of all letters within a string, the ability to split strings at certain points, and even to find all strings within a string that match a certain pattern, which is useful for systems such as in-game search bars. For example, all the letters in the following string will be converted into uppercase using one of the string library's functions:

```
myString = "iT iS wARm tOdaY."
print(string.upper(myString))
```

Output: "IT IS WARM TODAY."

Using strings in numeric arithmetic should be avoided when possible, but there may be situations where this happens. Whenever a string is used where a number is required, Lua will attempt to automatically convert that string into a number. For example, if you try to add the string "50" to the number *100*, it will function correctly, as shown here:

```
print("50" + 100)
```

Output: 150

However, if the string you are attempting to perform an operation on contains nonnumeric characters, the string-to-number conversion will fail. To prevent this, you can check if a string is fully numeric by using the *tonumber()* function. If the string that's been passed to the function cannot be converted into a number, the value that's returned will be **nil**; nil is a value that represents something nonexistent. If we attempt to add the string "Hello" to the number *100*, an error will occur:

```
myString = "Hello"
print(tonumber(myString))
```

```
Output: nil
```

```
local myNumber = 100 + myString
```

```
Output:  "local myNumber = 100 + myString:3: attempt to perform
arithmetic (add) on number and string"
```

Next, you will learn about **tables**, which have a wide variety of applications.

Tables

Tables are straightforward but less intuitive to set and manipulate than the other data types we have covered so far, as you must make use of a library for some operations. If you are already familiar with other programming languages, you might compare tables with an array or a list.

To create a new, empty table, you must set your variable to a set of braces ({}), as shown here:

```
local myTable = {}
```

When initializing a new table, you do not need to have it start out empty; you can include elements within your table when it is first created. It is important to note that elements in tables require a separating character; in this case, that character is a comma (,). For example, if a player was tasked with retrieving items from a grocery list, you could initialize a table of predetermined foodstuffs this way:

```
local myTable = {"Tofu", "Milk", "Bacon"}
```

Once you've created your table, you will need to be able to index what items exist within your list. Without loops, which will be covered later in this chapter, you can only index items individually. Remember that tables use one-based numeric indexing, so indexing items is just done with a number within brackets ([]). All items from the grocery list could be either assigned to a variable or acquired directly, as seen in the following print line of code:

```
local myTable = {"Tofu", "Milk", "Bacon"}
local firstItem = myTable[1]
print(firstItem, myTable[2], myTable[3])
```

Output: "Tofu Milk Bacon"

To add or remove elements from a table, you can use the table library, which can be accessed by using the table keyword. This library allows you to alter the structure of tables by changing how they are sorted, what their contents are, and where existing table entries are located. In order to add new elements to a table, you should use the *table.insert()* function. The function requires a minimum of two arguments, with the first being the table being targeted and the second being the value that you wish to add to the table. If three arguments are provided, the first argument is the targeted table, the second is the desired table position, and the third is the value to be added. When using the function with three arguments, it is important to remember that all the elements following or at the desired position are shifted to the right. Furthermore, there are no restrictions to the provided index, meaning the index can be negative or be an element that hasn't been reached yet by the length of the table, though you should avoid this as it internally converts the array-like table to a dictionary. Here is an example of adding an element to the beginning of a table and an element without a position specified, which will, by default, go to the end of the table:

```
local items = {"Elephant", "Towel", "Turtle"}
table.insert(items, 1, "Rock")
table.insert(items, "Cat")
-> items = {"Rock", "Elephant", "Towel", "Turtle", "Cat"}
```

To remove an item from the list, you need to know the exact index of the item within the table. For example, if the list is only supposed to contain living things, we would want to remove the Rock and Towel items. We can do this by using the *table.remove()* function. It is important to note that removing an element from a table will shift all the elements that follow it to the left. So, if the rock was removed from the table first, the indices of all the other items in the table would be one less than they were before. This can be seen in the following code:

```
items = {"Rock", "Elephant", "Towel", "Turtle", "Cat"}
table.remove(items, 1)
```

```
-> items = {"Elephant", "Towel", "Turtle", "Cat"}
```

```
table.remove(items, 2)
```

```
-> items = {"Elephant", "Turtle", "Cat"}
```

To confirm that the correct number of elements is within your table at any given time, you can preface a table or table variable with the # operator to return the number of elements within it. Additionally, you can use the table.getn() function to return the same result, though this is longer to write. You can prove these techniques return the same result by making the following comparison:

```
print(#items == table.getn(items))
```

```
Output: true
```

We'll cover how to make more comparisons when we learn about conditional statements. In the following section, you will learn about **dictionaries**.

56

Dictionaries

As we mentioned previously, **dictionaries** are tables that use custom, key-based indexing as opposed to sorted numeric indexes. Conceptually, you can think of entering values into a dictionary as declaring a variable, except the local keyword is not applicable here. While elements in a dictionary can be laid out like a table, it is more common for each entry to have its own line; the separating character for elements is a comma. If you had a restaurant's menu within your experience, you could arrange the items within a dictionary, with the key being the name of the meal's course and the value being the name of the dish:

```
local menu = {
    appetizer = "House salad",
    entree = "Ham sandwich",
    dessert = "Ice cream",
}
```

Indexing these declared elements is quite intuitive as you must simply follow the path to the desired value. In this case, let's say you wanted to capture what dish was being served as the entrée on the menu with a new variable:

```
local meal = menu.entree
print(meal)
```

```
Output: "Ham sandwich"
```

Setting elements is equally as straightforward; by following the path, you can set or alter the element based on its data type like any other variable:

```
menu.entree = "Turkey sandwich"
```

One of the advantages of using these keys in Lua is that they are not restricted to only string indexes. By using brackets ([]), you can use any data type as an index of your value. This is particularly useful if you want one data type to have a direct association with another at a given value. For example, if you wanted to set a list of threshold prices that correlated with a describing string, you could use a number as an index. Bear in mind that in order to index non-string keys, you must also use brackets:

```lua
local prices = {
        [0] = "Free",
        [5] = "Cheap",
        [20] = "Average",
        [50] = "Expensive",
}
print(prices[0])
```

```
Output:   "Free"
```

Something to note is that tables can have another table as a value; whenever something exists within another entity of the same type, we call this **nesting**. You can create structures by nesting tables within each other and fetching them with the same key-based style. When we discuss classes and specializations, you'll see that nesting tables is a somewhat common practice for organizational and functional purposes. For instance, if you wanted to maintain sets of information where you can retrieve data with a key, you can format your dictionary like so:

```lua
local configInfo = {
        ["Peach Tree"] = {
                spawnRate = 16,
                health = 50,
        },
        Chicken = {
                eggsPerMinute = 3,
```

```
        health = 15,
    },
}
```

Now that you know how to set and alter these data types once they have been assigned to variables, you will learn how to check the values of them to determine what type of behavior should occur as a result.

Conditional Statements

Conditional statements or **conditional expressions** are used in code when you want different behaviors to occur only when some requirement is met. These are important for determining different information about data and what your program should do to handle that data accordingly.

The if statement is the core component of conditional expressions. These statements consist of three elements: the if keyword, the case that must be met for the contained code to be executed, and the then keyword, which serves as an identifier for the end of your case. To give you a direct example of this, the following code shows a conditional where the condition is simply true, meaning the contained instructions will always be executed:

```
if true then
        print("Executed")
end
```

Output: Executed

Here, you can see that the conditional closes with the end keyword. In Lua, anything that acts as a single block of code (defines a scope) will have end designate the conclusion of that block.

Returning to the condition portion of if statements, determining whether a condition has been met is based on Boolean logic, a system of evaLuating any type of data. We end up with a true or false value as the result. To do this, evaLuations are made using a system containing various **logical operators** and **relational operators**. Like many languages, Lua uses two equal signs (==) to check equality between values; this is a relational operator. As an example, let's say you want to print the string "Play motor sound" only if another string representing the state of an object is equal to "motorOn":

```
if ignitionState == "motorOn" then
     print("Play motor sound")
end
```

For this operator, there exists an opposite: the not equal to expression (~=). Like the use of its counterpart, this relational operator is used to make comparisons of an explicit value.

To check finite or infinite ranges of numbers, you can use the relational operators of greater than (>) and less than (<). These operators have variations that include the value they are being compared to in the form of greater than or equal to (>=) and less than or equal to (<=). A practical application of these operators could be only playing a sound when the engine of a vehicle is revved:

```
if motorRPM >= 750 then
     print("Play loud motor sound")
end
```

The not operator serves to negate whatever value is provided to it. As we saw previously when we switched the state of a bool variable, the not operator returned the opposite of what was given to it. In terms of conditional statements, this can be used in similar situations as the inequality operator (~=):

```lua
if movementDirection ~= -1 then
     print("Moving forward or standing")
end
```

The logical and operator is used to compare two values and requires that the values provided to it are both true. In the following example, we want to ensure that both variables hold Fruit as their value. When this condition is not met because one is defined as Vegetable, we will not see any output since a true value is not present on both sides of the operator:

```lua
local item1 = "Fruit"
local item2 = "Vegetable"
if item1 == "Fruit" and item2 == "Fruit" then
     print("Both fruit.") --No output as requirements not met.
end
```

Output:

The logical or operator only requires that at least one of the values it receives is true. We can see in this instance that the item is defined as Vegetable. The condition says that the item must be defined as either Fruit or Vegetable, meaning we will see output since one of the values on either side of the operator is true:

```lua
local item = "Vegetable"
if item == "Fruit" or item == "Vegetable" then
     print("Is produce.") --Prints as one requirement is met.
end
```

Output: "Is produce."

As we mentioned previously, you can check multiple cases using one conditional expression, though this does not require the use of multiple if statements. The else keyword grants additional functionality to these expressions by executing an alternate case if the first condition was not

61

passed. Let's look at an example where lifting a heavy object requires 100 strength, but an object that is not heavy requires only 50 strength. Notice that our heavy variable, being a bool, will only be true or false, and, consequently, we do not need to use the equality operator (==):

```lua
local heavy = true
local strengthRequired = 0
if heavy then
      strengthRequired = 100
else
      strengthRequired = 50
end
print(strengthRequired)
```

```
Output:   100
```

While this has great uses, it does not allow us to explicitly check additional cases – it merely gives us an idea of what to do if the previous condition was not satisfied. The elseif keyword is used when you want to check additional cases that may occur under different conditions. You can have as many elseif statements as desired, allowing you to create a chain of various conditions and cases. When using elseif statements, you can still utilize an else expression, but it must be at the end of the overall conditional statement. Let's look at an example where a machine has been supplied random produce and we must count fruits, vegetables, as well as any other item that managed to find its way into the supply:

```lua
local numFruits = 0
local numVeggies = 0
local notProduce = 0
local item = "Fruit"
if item == "Fruit" then
      numFruits = numFruits + 1
elseif item == "Vegetable" then
```

```
        numVeggies = numVeggies + 1
else
        notProduce = notProduce + 1
end
```

Lastly, there exist implicit conditional statements, which are expressions where, through the use of logical operators, you can set a condition and alternate cases without ever explicitly writing an if statement. In most languages, this behavior is called a **ternary expression**.

In the following code, the goal is to assign a string to the *isEven* variable based on whether some value assigned to a variable called number is, in fact, even. While this could be accomplished with an if-else statement, it is shorter to use this new expression here instead:

```
local isEven = number % 2 == 0 and "Even" or "Odd"
```

As you can see, if number is even, that side of the and operator will be true when assigning "Even" to the variable by using short-circuit logic, meaning conditional evaLuation stops after one condition is met or violated. If number is not even, it will go to an alternate case, which is "Odd". You may have observed that the or operator acts similarly to the else keyword in this instance because of the nature of this implicit expression.

Like in mathematics, certain operators take **precedence** over others; this means that they are evaLuated first. In Lua, mathematical operators have the same precedence as they do in the real world, and relational operators typically take precedence over logical operators. Because of this, the use of parentheses in your conditions can help make your code more readable and help ensure it executes as you intend it to. You can see the full order of operator precedence from the linked page from the Lua documentation website:

https://www.Lua.org/pil/3.5.html

Conditional statements are a core component in programming and, as you have seen, have a multitude of applications for even the most basic programs. In the next section, we will cover loops. **Loops** often go hand in hand with conditional statements, since they can feed whole sets of data into a conditional expression or repeat manipulation as needed to accomplish a desired behavior.

Declaring and Using Loops

Loops are vaLuable components when it comes to programming, especially when working with sets of data. It would, of course, be quite unrealistic to expect a programmer to index and assign all 1000 elements of a hypothetical table to variables in order to perform some sort of operation. To accomplish behaviors like this, loops are key. They function by jumping back to the beginning of their code block if a condition is still met, executing until they reach their terminating case.

for Loops

for loops are a type of loop that are primarily used for iterating over datasets. In Lua, those datasets are typically related to tables or numbers. In Lua, there are two types of for loops: **numeric for** loops and **generic for** loops. The primary difference between these is what determines how they are executed. For numeric for loops, a variable is assigned to a defined start value, end value, and optionally an increment value; if the increment is not included, Lua sets the increment to 1. The numeric for loop will then execute the contained code a specified number of times, treating the endpoints of the number range inclusively. Additionally, the assigned variable serves to tell you what the current value of the loop is. Much like the use of if and then in conditionals, for loops use for and do as their declaration keywords.

The following example prints numbers going from 0 to 10, incrementing by 1 with each loop completion. Note that the increment in this case did not need to be specified but has been shown to aid with your understanding:

```lua
for i = 0, 10, 1 do
    print(i)
end
```

Let's create a more practical example using a numeric for loop where we find the sum of all integers ranging from 1 to n. Additionally, we can test that the for loop works correctly by plugging in the same value for n into the theorem for this operation seen in Figure 3-1.

$$\sum_{I=1}^{N} = 1+2+3+...+N = \frac{N(N+1)}{2}$$

Figure 3-1. *Theorem for the sum of the first n natural numbers*

In this demonstration, you will notice the use of *tostring()*, which functions much like the aforementioned *tonumber()*. This is used because while *print()* will automatically convert other data types into strings, you cannot append other data types, except for numbers to strings. In this example, we will find the sum, print it, and then print whether the sum that was found by the for loop matches the value expected by the theorem:

```lua
local n = 17
local theoremValue = (n * (n + 1)) / 2
local sum = 0
```

```
for i = 1, n, 1 do
      sum = sum + i
end
print(sum)
print("Function working = ".. tostring(sum == theoremValue))

Output:
153
"Function working = true"
```

Returning to the for loop types, we have generic for loops. While the name seems to imply that they are not useful or special, you will likely utilize them more than numeric for loops – or most other types of loops for that matter. Generic for loops allow you to traverse all indices and values returned by an **iterator function**.

Iterator Function

In programming languages, an iterator function is designed to allow programmers to process every element of a data structure while making those returned values isolated from the data structure itself except when the element is passed by reference, rather than by value. We'll cover what this means in the "Recursion" section of this chapter. For now, keep in mind that things like tables and instances are passed in directly where values like numbers or strings are copied. Modifying the former types in the loop will modify them directly. This isolation of copied types, which can be seen when defining a variable in a code block, relates to the concept of **scope**. This means that something that's declared in a block cannot be referenced outside of that block. In the following example, we have a dictionary called items that contains three strings. By providing this data structure to the pairs() iterator function, you can nicely display every index and value being provided by the iterator:

```lua
local items = {
      Animal = "Elephant",
      Food = "Egg",
      Plant = "Flower",
}
for index, value in pairs(items) do
      print(index, value)
end
```

As mentioned previously, the index and value provided by the iterator are not components of the actual data structure that is passed to pairs(). This means you are free to manipulate these as desired without the risk of affecting the elements currently being processed. In the following code, the goal is to double any odd numbers to make them even. While we could assign the number that results from using modulo to a new variable, it is alright in this case to simply use the value variable directly. Notice that in order to actually change the element of the table that value corresponds to, you must use the index provided by the iterator with the table itself. In this example, we use the **ipairs()** iterator function. ipairs() should be used with tables being used as arrays as it ensures elements are processed in order, whereas pairs() does not. While you could continue to use pairs(), elements may be processed in a nonsequential order, for example, the second element (60) before the first element (37):

```lua
local values = {37, 60, 59, 20, 4, 10, 100, 75, 83}
for index, value in ipairs(values) do
      value = value % 2
      if value == 1 then --Odd number
            values[index] = values[index] * 2
      end
end
print(values)
```

Output: {74, 60, 118, 20, 4, 10, 100, 150, 166}

You will now learn about a different type of loop that will always run, so long as a condition is met.

while Loops

while loops are loops that run continuously, as long as some specified condition is met. Though they can be used for similar purposes as for loops, it is best to think of them as a repeating conditional statement. In the following example, the while loop increments a value by 1 only if that value is less than 10:

```
local num = 0
while num < 10 do
      num = num + 1
end
print(num)
```

```
Output:   10
```

As long as the condition is not **false** (false or nil in Lua), the loop will execute, and if the condition itself is a function, that function will execute and the loop will also run if the function returns a value. This is also true of the condition of conditional statements. You should remember to use good style when doing this, which we will discuss more in the "Demonstrating Programming Style and Efficiency" section.

Another variation of the while loop is the while true loop. This type of loop will always execute as the condition is always true. This variation of a while loop can be useful or simply a preference over the previously shown way of creating one; however, it can cause a script to crash as the loop stacks on top of itself infinitely. To avoid this, we can use a break statement which terminates the loop. The break statement is usually wrapped in some conditional statement as it would otherwise immediately terminate the loop after running once. You can see this loop is equivalent to the previous loop example but makes use of the new syntax:

```
local num = 0
while true do
        num = num + 1
        if num >= 10 then
                break
        end
end
print(num)
```

```
Output: 10
```

In the next section, you will learn about a similar type of loop that can be used in slightly different applications.

repeat Loops

repeat loops execute their contents until a condition is met. While this may seem much like a while loop, the difference is that while loops run only if a condition is met, checking the condition before running. Unlike other loop types, repeat loops always run at least once, checking the terminating condition only after execution, much like a do-while loop in other languages. The keywords for repeat loops are repeat and until, where the code to be executed follows the repeat keyword, closed by until, and ends with the condition to leave the loop. The following loop shows a number variable being decremented until its value is equal to 0:

```
local num = 12
repeat
        num = num - 1
```

```
until num == 0
print(num)
```

```
Output:  0
```

With loops now at your disposal, you can process large sets of data and make systems that require consistent, repetitive behavior. Next, you will learn about a new way of feeding data to loops, as well as condensing them if they are frequently used.

Learning About Functions

In programming, a function is a code block that is able to be called repeatedly, typically designed to accomplish a single task. Functions are important for abbreviating common jobs being done and help reduce the amount of redundancy within your programs. In this section, you will learn different ways to format functions, as well as when you should be using them.

Functions in Programming

We primarily use functions to define code that can be easily referenced and executed repeatedly. For the sake of terminology, many programming languages distinguish functions from **procedures** or **subroutines**; the difference here is that a function executes code to compute some data that is returned, whereas a procedure simply accomplishes a task without returning a value to where it was called. The following function has been designed to create a new table and fill it with fruits, vegetables, or a nonproduce item based on a randomly generated value. See that the function is locally defined, much like a variable, followed by the function keyword and the name of the function, and ends with a set of parentheses (()); this part of a function is called the **header**. To select a random item, we need to generate a random index using the random function of the math library. This function will generate a random integer between the min and max value that's provided to it inclusively. This output of the function can then be used with one of the examples seen in the "Conditional Statements" section. Notice how we declare a new variable item but do not assign it a value. This is proper syntax and the variable will hold a value of nil by default. If you feel comfortable, try making a produce counter using the conditional statement from the previous section, a loop, and this function:

```lua
local function fillStoreSupply()
    local storeSupply = {}
    for i = 1, 10 do
        local ranVal = math.random(1,3)
        local item
        if ranVal == 1 then
            item = "Fruit"
        elseif ranVal == 2 then
            item = "Vegetable"
        else
            item = "Shoe"
        end
        table.insert(storeSupply, item)
    end
    return storeSupply
end
local supplyTable = fillStoreSupply()
```

One of the main aspects of using functions is providing information to them when you call them for a task. To do this, values need to be added to the call statement of the function and defined in the line where the function is declared. When a value is being provided to a call, it is referred to as an **argument**. However, when referring to this data inside a function,

it is referred to as a **parameter**. The following function creates a factorial
from the provided number, n. A factorial is the result of multiplying all
whole numbers less than a number, by that number. See how a number
is provided as the argument in the function call. When the function runs,
that value is automatically assigned to n, which can then be manipulated
as needed:

```
local function factorial(n)
    assert(n == math.floor(n), "n must be a whole number.")
    local factorial = 1 --Empty product should be 1
    while n > 1 do
        factorial = factorial * n
        n = n - 1
    end
    return factorial
end
print(factorial(12))
```

```
Output:   479001600
```

You may have noticed the use of the *assert()* function. Much like the
use of *throw()* in the Java programming language, you can use this to
throw an error and terminate a process if some condition is not met. The
second argument is a string that is sent to the output and will look like
any other naturally occurring error message. Do note that while this is
useful for testing, you should not include assert statements in your final
production code.

In the case that you do not know how many arguments are going
to be passed to a function, you can create a **variadic function**. Variadic
functions are like regular functions, though they possess the ability to take
any number of arguments in a tuple state. The following variadic function
returns the sum of all numbers provided to it. Notice the use of the three
dots (...); these dots represent whatever arguments are passed to the

function and are most often put directly into a table for processing. In the following code block, you can see a random amount of number arguments being passed to the sum function. The parameters are added and returned as a single value:

```lua
local function sum(...)
    local args = {...}
    local sum = 0
    for _, number in pairs(args) do
        sum = sum + number
    end
    return sum
end
local num = sum(7, 9, 12, 3, 2, 6, 13)
print(num)
```

Output: 52

As you may have found out on your own, all the loops we have covered have the ability to yield; that is to say that when they run, they pause the current thread, meaning that the loop must finish before any code following it can be executed. Make certain when writing your loops that they reach a terminating case; otherwise, the program will crash.

You may also notice that we use the special character "_" in the for loop definition. It is common practice to use the "_" character for unused elements. In the sample, the pairs iterator function returns two values in each loop. But in the loop block, we only use the second one ("number"). The first return value is unused so we could mark or replace it with "_" and clearly define we don't use it in the following code path.

The next section will cover recursion, a useful technique for solving some types of problems.

Recursion

One of the invaLuable features of functions is their ability to call themselves. When properly structured, this can create what you might think of as a loop in a process called **recursion**. The difference between something like a while loop and a recursive process is that a loop jumps back to its beginning, whereas recursion actually **stacks** upon itself. In programming, a **stack** can be a data structure or, as in the case of recursion, simply the state of something in your program. Like a stack of plates or pancakes, the one that was most recently added will be the first one to be removed.

To demonstrate this stacking, let's return to the factorial function we created earlier in the "Functions in Programming" section. Though a while loop was able to accomplish the goal, you could also achieve the same result by using recursion. In the following function, notice that the call and header of the function remain unchanged; the recursive elements exist in the return statements. For the if statement, the first case simply returns 1 if n is less than 1, because we cannot create a factorial from any values less than this; in the case of n being 0, its factorial would also be 1 by convention. The next case is the most important: if n is greater than 1, then it is multiplied by the value that's returned by the factorial function, where n is one less than the current value of n. As you may begin to see, this causes the function to stack until n has been decreased down to 1. This is the **base case**, where no function call is made, and we work back down the stack:

```
local function factorial(n)
    assert(n == math.floor(n), "n must be a whole number.")
    if n <= 1 then
        return 1
    else
        return n * factorial(n - 1)
```

```
        end
end
print(factorial(6))
```

Output: *720*

To give a better visualization of how this process is being executed, let's look at a mapped-out example of the previous call to the factorial function, using 6 for n. Observe that each call, n, is set to be multiplied by the returned value of the function and continues to be stacked until a case without a function call is reached. Then, each function stops and is taken off the stack, returning the value to the return statement that called it. Once this process finishes, our original function returns the final value to wherever it was called from:

```
factorial(6)
6 * factorial(5)
6 * (5 * factorial(4))
6 * (5 * (4 * factorial(3)))
6 * (5 * (4 * (3 * (factorial(2)))))
6 * (5 * (4 * (3 * (2 * factorial(1)))))
6 * (5 * (4 * (3 * (2 * 1))))
6 * (5 * (4 * (3 * 2)))
6 * (5 * (4 * 6))
6 * (5 * 24)
6 * 120
720
```

Now that you have a firmer grasp of the concept of recursion, let's look at another practical example. When working with tables, setting a variable to an already existing table will not follow normal behavior and simply copy that value to the new variable; instead, tables use **references**. References work to save resources, essentially causing new variables to act only as pointers to a previously declared table; the pointer can actually be seen by printing the table. With this behavior, assigning a table to a variable and changing anything within that table would change it everywhere it is referenced. You can test this with the following code. Here, you can see that when a variable's value is set to a table that has already been created, the variables contain the same reference:

```
local function checkEquality(table1, table2)
     print("Variable 1: ".. tostring(table1))
     print("Variable 2: ".. tostring(table2))
     print("First and second variable same table = "..
     tostring(table1 ==  table2))
end
local group = {"Manuel", "Christian", "Zander"}
local groupRef = group
checkEquality(group, groupRef)

Output:
Variable 1: table: 0x0000020215384838
Variable 2: table: 0x0000020215384838
First and second variable same table = true
```

If a table were cloned every time it was assigned to a variable, that would make indexing libraries or any other large table structure extraordinarily expensive. There are scenarios, however, where you may need to clone a table or dictionary. While for loops may be viable in some cases, the presence of nested tables, as seen at the end of the "Dictionaries" section, could potentially require that you use any number of for loops to accomplish your task. To get around this, we can once again use recursion. The following example creates a copy of our items table by creating a new table and adding each element to it by index and value. In the case that the value to be cloned is a table, the function recurses with the nested table as the argument. Once it's done this, the completely new

table is returned to where it was called from, and the checkEquality()
function from the previous example is used to verify that the tables
are unique:

```lua
local items = {
      Egg = {fragile = true},
      Water = {wet = true},
}
local function recursiveCopy(targetTable)
      local tableCopy = {}
      for index, value in pairs(targetTable) do
            if type(value) == "table" then
                  value = recursiveCopy(value)
            end
            tableCopy[index] = value
      end
      return tableCopy
end
local itemsClone = recursiveCopy(items)
local areEqual = checkEquality(items, itemsClone)
print(areEqual)
```

Output: false

Like loops, calls to recursive functions can yield, but typically, they
finish in a short enough amount of time to where nothing in your thread is
affected. If, for some reason, your recursive function runs long enough to
cause a noticeable pause for the rest of your program, consider reviewing
the efficiency of your function.

We will next look at how to create **classes** and what purpose they serve.

Classes

Classes are a convenient way in programming to organize code into templates with fields, methods, and events easily defined. For your mods, you will need to create classes to define the functionality and attributes of new items you create. The following code shows a sample class without any functionality:

```
SampleClass = {}

function SampleClass.new()
      local self = {}
        setmetatable(self, {__index=SampleClass})
        return self
end
```

That's all. Quite simply right. We only need a table and a constructor function. But as stated earlier, this class has no functionality at all.

So in a more practical example, you may want to create a vehicle for your mod. You will need to define behavior for when it is turned on, turned off, and how fast it is able to go. Let us say you want to make a new tractor – you can see how to create a class for the vehicle called Tractor in the following example:

```
Tractor = {}

function Tractor.new(name, maxSpeed, maxPower)
      local self = {}
      setmetatable(self, {__index=Tractor})
      self.name = name
      self.maxSpeed = maxSpeed
      self.maxPower = maxPower
      return self
end
```

```lua
function Tractor:turnOn()
    print(string.format("Turned on tractor '%s'",
    self:getName()))
end

function Tractor:turnOff()
    print(string.format("Turned off tractor '%s'",
    self:getName()))
end

function Tractor:getMaxPower()
    return self.maxPower
end

function Tractor:getMaxSpeed()
    return self.maxSpeed
end

function Tractor:getName()
    return self.name
end
```

With the class now created, we can create new Tractor **objects**. In
programming, an object is a single instance of a class. Using objects as
opposed to functions and procedural logic to create programs is called
object-oriented programming (OOP). Languages that use objects and
OOP as the primary means of doing tasks are called object-oriented
languages. While Lua is not an object-oriented language, creating classes
and objects can still be convenient in certain environments as their
creation, properties, and methods are uniform and neatly put together.
To create a new object from the class, we simply call the new constructor
of the class and assign what it returns to a variable. We can then call the
methods of our class and use the returned values as needed as seen in the
example:

```
local tractor1 = Tractor.new("Fendt Vario 700", 50, 280)
local tractor2 = Tractor.new("New Holland T8", 50, 381)
tractor1:turnOn() -> Turned on tractor 'Fendt Vario 700'
tractor2:turnOn() -> Turned on tractor 'New Holland T8'
print(tractor1:getMaxPower())
print(tractor2:getMaxPower())
```

```
Output:
280
381
```

We will now look at how to write programs with proper style and what to be aware of to ensure they remain efficient.

Demonstrating Programming Style and Efficiency

Writing code with good style not only improves the quality of your work, but it also prepares you to pursue programming in more professional environments or when working with other people. We will cover these universal programming style rules in this section.

General Programming Style Rules

Readability is an important aspect of maintaining good style. Not only do others who may read your code need to understand what is happening, but being able to easily follow your own code will greatly increase your workflow. Having a clean coding style will also enable you to be more conscious of other style factors you should be implementing. The two ways you can make your code the most readable are to use proper indentation and observe appropriate line length. For line length, most college programming courses will likely suggest that you limit your lines of code to 80–100 characters.

In the Script Editor of the GIANTS Editor, there are line numbers but not an indicator for which column you are on for a line. Generally, your line length should not exceed your viewport size, which means that you should not require the use of a horizontal scrollbar to see the entirety of your line. Out of all the readability rules, you should arguably observe indentation style the most carefully. Make sure what you write follows the code examples in this chapter until you feel confident with your ability to follow this rule. Alternatively, you can use the GIANTS Studio which provides a more dedicated programming environment with more quality-of-life features. We will cover the IDE in Chapter 4, "The GIANTS Studio."

Thinking again about working with multiple programmers, comments are an invaLuable part of letting others, as well as your future self, know what your code is doing. While readability is also needed to make others aware of what a script's purpose is, comments can be used to more explicitly tell fellow programmers where a code block is being used, what it requires, or what behavior to expect from it.

Looking back at implicit conditionals, there are situations where it may make more sense to use logic within a variable declaration than to use an explicit conditional statement. This decision is ultimately up to you, but only use it when it's practical. If you need to create more than two or three cases, you should likely just use a conditional. Additionally, remember to consider previously mentioned style points, such as line length.

As mentioned briefly previously, you should ensure that you are not grouping random data together in tables or dictionaries. For organizational purposes, you should be using tables for a significant purpose, and the elements of data within them should be at least loosely associated with each other. If necessary, there is no harm in creating additional tables to accommodate different sets of data being used in your code.

A **naming convention** refers to how you format the names of your variables, functions, constants, and more when programming. There are many conventions – the first two you'll likely encounter being Pascal case and camel case. Camel case is where the first letter of the variable is lowercase with the first letter of any other words in the variable being capitalized, for example, camelCase. Pascal case is where the first letter of all words in the variable name are capitalized, such as PascalCase. The convention you use can depend on what you're defining, but for the purpose of this book, it is sufficient to say you should stylistically use camel case when programming in Lua.

Lastly, you should **optimize** your code when possible. Optimizing a program generally means writing it so that it accomplishes its goal while taking up the least amount of computational or memory resources. For example, if you are using a value in multiple places, consider using one variable instead of defining another. If you are using repeated lines of code in your program, consider using a single function – while this will have little impact on your program, it will help greatly with readability.

Summary

In this chapter, you learned about programming constructs that exist in a wide variety of languages, such as variables, data types, loops, and some data structures, as well as those that are exclusive to Lua. With this knowledge, you can begin making your own mental connections by experimenting with the examples from this chapter and making your own programs.

In the next chapter, you will learn about the GIANTS Studio to help you find errors and fix your programs. Following that, you will utilize the new information you have learned about to start making your first mod-oriented systems, which will lead to you making full mod creations in the following chapters.

CHAPTER 4

The GIANTS Studio

Another essential application in the Farming Simulator modding environment is the GIANTS Studio. It is an **integrated development environment** (IDE) made specifically to assist with programming mods for Farming Simulator. An IDE is an application that provides additional resources to programmers for software development. The GIANTS Studio consists of a script editor and many debugging tools, which we will cover in this chapter.

Technical Requirements

You will need to download the GIANTS Studio and optionally additional software for this chapter. As such, you will need an Internet connection and web browser available to you. The minimum requirements for the GIANTS Studio and other applications are as follows:

- Farming Simulator 22
- Windows 10 64-bit
- Intel Core i5-3330 or AMD FX-8320 or better
- Nvidia Geforce GTX 660, AMD Radeon R7 265 graphics card or better (min. 2 GB VRAM, DX11/DX12 support)
- 8 GB RAM
- 35 GB free hard drive space
- Sound card

© GIANTS Software GmbH 2024
Z. Brumbaugh and M. Leithner, *Scripting Farming Simulator with Lua*,
https://doi.org/10.1007/979-8-8688-0060-3_4

Installing the GIANTS Studio

Like installing the GIANTS Editor, you will need to navigate to the *Downloads* section of the GDN (https://gdn.giants-software.com). You should have a GDN account at this point, but do remember you will need one before you can download any software available from the GDN. When you have navigated to the Downloads page, install the GIANTS Studio available for your platform (it should again be at the top of the list). You can see the relevant section of the Downloads page in Figure 4-1.

Studio / IDE / Debugger			
Product Name	Platform	Size	Date
GIANTS Studio v9.0.1 (Farming Simulator 22)	Windows	6.02 MB	01.10.2023

Figure 4-1. *All GIANTS Software applications can be downloaded through the GDN*

Once the executable has been downloaded, run it and proceed through the steps listed in the setup wizard. When the setup tasks have been completed, launch the GIANTS Studio application, and you should be greeted by the same welcome menu as the GIANTS Editor.

The next section will teach you how to navigate the GIANTS Studio.

Application Menus

In this section, we will explore the various application menus in the GIANTS Studio and discuss which options you should know about as a beginning mod creator.

The File Menu

The contents of the File menu of the GIANTS Studio are almost the same as that of the GIANTS Editor. However, there are two new options, **New Project** and **Open Project**. The New Project option will prompt you to create a new mod project. Your new project will be saved as a .gsp file, and you will be prompted to configure certain project settings. We will walk you through this process in the "Debugging Scripts" section of this chapter. The Open Project option will simply open one of your .gsp files, allowing you to pick up from where you left off.

In the next section, we will look at the **Edit menu**.

The Edit Menu

The **Edit** menu provides several new functionalities, the first being the **Find** tool. While there are many options you can use with this tool, the most commonly used are the standard **Find** action (*Ctrl+F*), **Find in files** (*Ctrl+Shift+F*), and **Go to Line** (*Ctrl+G*) tools. The **Find** action is straightforward and simply looks for strings in the current script that match your input. **Find in files** searches all the current scripts within your project for strings that match your input; the results will be returned to you in the **Find Results** tab. Finally, **Go to Line** will bring up a new modal window with a box that asks for you to input a line number. Once inputted, your line selection will move to the specified number, and the box will close.

The **Replace** action will bring up a menu in the IDE in the same window as the Find tool and will prompt you to provide two strings. The first string is what you want to find in your script, while the second is what you want that string to be replaced by. This feature can be applied to more than one script at a time, but make sure you know what you are replacing to avoid creating new bugs.

In this menu are also some quick actions for commenting or uncommenting your Lua code. You can comment or uncomment highlighted code by pressing *Ctrl+K* or *Ctrl+Shift+K*, respectively.

In the next section, we will look at the options in the **View menu**.

The View Menu

The **View** menu contains a list of the menus within the GIANTS Studio. By selecting an option from this menu, it will display the associated tab. Let us now look at each of these menus and what information they show.

The **Globals** and **Locals** tabs will show you the names and values of globally and locally defined variables in your script. These are valuable because when combined with other tools, you can see if a variable is taking on the value you expect it to at different points in your program's execution.

The **Watch** tab will allow you to specify variables you want to keep track of. These variables will be tracked even as your program switches between scopes, giving it a different use case than the **Globals** or **Locals** tabs.

The **Script Console** functions much like the Console menu of the GIANTS Editor, allowing you to write and execute Lua code. The main difference is that the Script Console of the GIANTS Studio only executes code when in a debugging session and directs output toward the Output menu, which is covered later in this section.

The **Callstack** tab allows you to see what series of calls have been made at a point in your program. For example, if you halt execution while in a function that was called by another function, then the call to both functions would be visible in the callstack. This is particularly useful in tracing the source of an error for more complex programs.

To actually halt the execution of your program, you will need to use **Breakpoints**. The **Breakpoints** tab will allow you to see and manage the breakpoints in your program. We will discuss this menu and the concept of breakpoints more in the "Using Breakpoints" section of this chapter.

Through the **Memory** and **Allocations** tabs, you can see how much memory is being used by each part of your program. If you encounter a **memory leak**, that is, a fault in your program that causes computer memory to be used but never freed up, this tool can be used to fix that problem.

The **Output** tab is where the output from Farming Simulator, your mod files, and Script Console executions are directed.

The **Error List** tab will show you the current syntax errors in your program. If there is an error in your code at runtime, this will be shown via the Output tab.

When using the Find in Files tool discussed in the "The Edit Menu" section, results will be directed to the **Find Results** tab.

Like in the GIANTS Editor, the GIANTS Studio has a Toolbar containing buttons for quickly doing actions. You can again customize which sets of actions are visible via the **Toolbars** option.

The **Navigate Forward** and **Navigate Backward** options will move your cursor to places it has been previously within a script or across files you have opened in the script editor portion of the IDE. Note that the key bindings associated with action are *Alt+Left* and *Alt+Right*, respectively.

Lastly, **Reset Window Layout** will reset the layout of all windows and menus in the GIANTS Studio to their default positions.

The following section will explore the contents of the **Debug menu**.

The Debug Menu

The Debug menu contains a list of actions for using various tools offered by the GIANTS Studio. You will learn how to use all of these actions in the "Creating and Debugging Scripts" section of this chapter. For now, we will continue to the next section and discuss the **Window menu**.

The Window Menu

The **Window menu** in the Studio contains only three options: **Reopen Tab**, **Close Tab**, and **Close All Tabs**. The Reopen Tab option will reopen the most recently closed editing tab. The Close Tab button will only close the tab you are currently focused on, while Close All Tabs will close all editing tabs you have opened.

We will now look at the options in the **Help menu**.

The Help Menu

The Help menu of the IDE is identical to that of the editor. You can see the overview of these options in the "The Help Menu" section of Chapter 2, "Getting Started with the GIANTS Editor."

Now that we have covered all of the application menus of the GIANTS Studio, we will look at other windows and elements you should familiarize yourself with.

New Project

Before you create any script files, we will create a new mod project. To do this, we will navigate to the File menu and select the *New Project* option. After choosing a name for your project, a menu like that in Figure 4-2 will be displayed. If Farming Simulator 22 is installed on your computer, the GIANTS Studio will take care of setting the correct paths. Make sure that the option "Auto create mod folder" is activated.

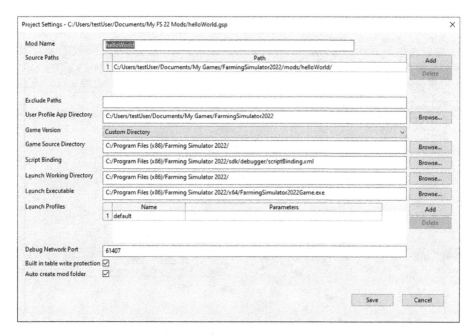

Figure 4-2. *You can configure project settings with the Project Settings option from the file menu*

Once you've created your project, the Project Browser on the left side of the application should already display a sample mod layout (Figure 4-3).

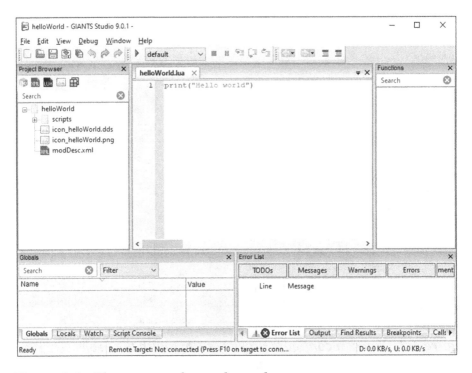

Figure 4-3. *The generated sample mod*

The *helloWorld.lua* file is already opened in the main script editor window. But first we should also have a look at the *modDesc.xml* file which is the entry point of each mod.

To do so, double-click the *modDesc.xml* file, and it will open it in the main script editor window of the IDE. You should see the following code in the *modDesc.xml*:

```
<?xml version="1.0" encoding="utf-8" standalone="no" ?>
<modDesc descVersion="72">
    <Author>GIANTS Software</author>
    <version>1.0.0.0</version>
    <multiplayer supported="true" />
    <title>
        <en>Sample Mod - Hello World</en>
```

```
    </title>
    <description>
        <en>A sample mod</en>
    </description>
    <iconFilename>icon_helloWorld.png</iconFilename>
    <extraSourceFiles>
        <sourceFile filename="scripts/helloWorld.lua"/>
    </extraSourceFiles>
</modDesc>
```

Let us break down what each part of the .xml tells the game about your mod and why they are needed. In the first line, we specify the XML declaration which describes some information about the .xml file. It is read by XML editors to get more information about the .xml format. This is not relevant to the functionality of your mod but is needed for .xml files. Next, we have the **descVersion** field which specifies the minimum feature set of the game needed to run the mod. The **descVersion** field should always be set to the current available game patch version; that value can be found in the newest ModHub Guidelines (see the "ModHub Creation Guidelines" section of Chapter 11, "Publishing on the ModHub").

The next field is the **author** section which records who the mod author is, which is you! It's important to include this field so that you are credited for your mod when it is published to the ModHub. The **version** field defines the current version of the mod; this is required so that you can specify different versions when you update the mod and publish again to the ModHub. The **multiplayer supported** field specifies whether your mod supports multiplayer gameplay. If enabled, the mod will be selectable when creating a multiplayer game and hidden otherwise.

Next, we specify the title of your mod using the **title** field. The text in this field will be used when your mod is displayed in the mod menu and you support multiple languages by wrapping the text with the locale. In the preceding example, we say this is English with an <en></en>.

Similarly, the **description** field will be used to display a description of your mod under the title in the mod menu and can also be localized with different wrappers. You can also define an icon for when your mod is displayed by defining the **iconFilename** field. The field should contain the path to the image file relative to the mod folder.

Lastly, we specify what scripts should be loaded by using the **extraSourceFiles** field. Here, you should list each .lua file in a **sourceFile** wrapper, setting the file name to the path of your script relative to the mod folder. As you can see, we want to include a script called *helloWorld. lua*. Studio already created this file during the setup process of the sample mod.

Starting the Game

GIANT Studio successfully set up a sample mod for us. Before doing the next steps, let's first test if the mod successfully loads in the game.

To launch the game, navigate to the Toolbar and click the **Start** button which is indicated by the icon in Figure 4-4. Alternatively, you can use the Start without Debugging option from the Debug application menu for a faster startup time. Farming Simulator should launch automatically and present you with the main menu. If you launched the game without debugging, you must press *F10* to connect the GIANTS Studio to the game; you should see the IDE connected in the Output tab.

Figure 4-4. *You can start the game by clicking the depicted icon in the Toolbar*

Once on the game's main menu, go to *Options* ➤ *Display Settings* and select the *Windowed Mode.* When you debug your program in the next section, the application will halt processes, preventing you from switching applications if the application is in fullscreen mode. Next, return to the main menu and select *Career*, pick an empty save slot, and then select any difficulty and any map. Once you have selected a map, click *Continue* and you will be able to select the mod(s) you would like to run in your game as seen in Figure 4-5. If this menu does not appear, make sure you have placed your Mod Directory folder in the correct location under the mods folder of the Farming Simulator game directory. Additionally, you can look in the *log.txt* file or Output tab and check if your mod is listed in an *Available mod: (Hash: a random md5 hash) (Version: 1.0.0.0) myMod* format.

Figure 4-5. *You can choose which of your mods should be active when debugging via this menu*

With your mod selected, click *Start*. Any output from your program should be directed to the Output window. As we haven't changed anything to the helloWorld.lua yet, you should find a single line "Hello world" in the Output window.

Debugging Scripts

The most powerful feature of GIANTS Studio is the debug option. It's natural that mistakes happen during development. But often it's really hard to find the issue just by looking at the code lines. Debugging is a great option to do a step-by-step execution of your script code and analyze the variable values and the execution path.

In the previous chapter, we already introduced the factorial function. Let's reuse it to explore the debugging tools offered by the GIANTS Studio.

Replace the content of the helloWorld.lua file with the following **incorrect** implementation of the factorial function:

```lua
print("Hello World")
local function factorial(n)
    assert(n == math.floor(n), "n must be a whole number.")

    if n <= 1 then
        return 1
    else
        return n * factorial(n - 2)
    end
end
print("Factorial value: ".. factorial(6))
```

In the next sections, we will begin using the tools of the GIANTS Studio to debug our broken script.

Using Breakpoints

Breakpoints are one of the debugging tools provided by the GIANTS Studio. Breakpoints will pause your program once the line of code they are associated with is reached. To add a breakpoint, you can simply click the space to the right of a line number when inside of a script. You should note that by right-clicking a breakpoint, you have the options to delete it or simply disable it for the time being. You should add a breakpoint on line 5 as shown in Figure 4-6, so we can see the state of our program when we reach the base case of our recursive function.

```
helloWorld.lua  X    modDesc.xml  X

 1
 2    print("Hallo world")
 3
 4    local function factorial(n)
 5        assert(n == math.floor(n), "n must be a whole number.")
 6
 7        if n <= 1 then
 8            return 1
          else
10            return n * factorial(n - 2)
11        end
12    end
13
14    print("Factorial value: ".. factorial(6))
15
```

Figure 4-6. *You can halt the execution of your program with breakpoints*

The setup is now done, and you can **start the game again**. Click the "Start" button in the toolbar which is indicated by the icon in Figure 4-4. Follow the same steps like in the previous section "Starting the Game."

Once a breakpoint has been reached, you can continue through the code line by line by using the **Step Into**, **Step Over**, and **Step Out** options under the Debug application menu. **Step Into** will continue through your code line by line, entering any functions or blocks of code that exist elsewhere that are referenced. The **Step Over** action will skip over any code blocks if the next line would otherwise bring you into one. Finally, the **Step Out** action will take you out of a code block immediately if you have reached one, bringing you to the next line following the container.

We will now learn to use breakpoints with some other menus of the GIANTS Studio to fix our program.

Using the Locals Tab and the Callstack

Under the View application menu, you can find the **Locals** and **Callstack** tabs. Both serve to provide additional information about what your code is executing when debugging. By viewing the Callstack menu, you can see which processes are currently on the stack; that is, you can see if you are currently in a function, view the order in which functions are called, and see which lines those calls are made from. You may find this feature particularly useful if you are working with a recursive function, as you can see the order of calls. To aid you as you follow your code, you can also view the Watch window to see the exact values of the variables and types of expressions within your script. Look at the advantages of using both tools to follow a recursive function, similar to the one shown in Figure 4-7.

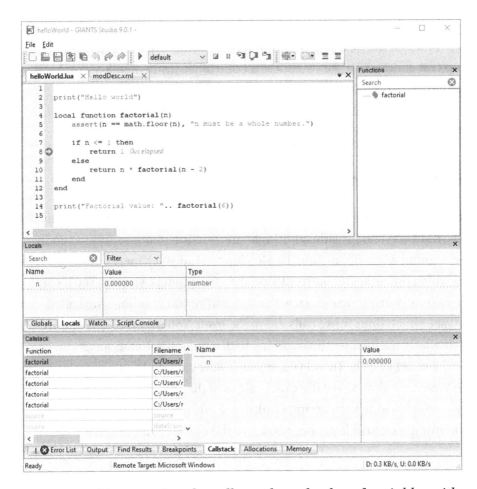

Figure 4-7. *You can view the calls made and value of variables with the Callstack and Watch menus*

We can see that the factorial function was only called four times. We know that the function should be called as many times as our input – that is, factorial(6) should call the factorial function six times. What might be causing the function to reach the terminating or base case early? Upon closer inspection, we can see that the input to the next function call is being decreased by 2 instead of 1. With this correction, you should see the factorial function is called a number of times equal to the input.

Summary

In this chapter, you learned how to use the GIANTS Remote Studio to debug your scripts and follow their execution step by step. You should now feel comfortable creating new mods, testing them via the IDE, and using the IDE to edit and debug your scripts with the tools it provides.

In the next chapter, you will create your first mod by introducing a placeable and configurable roadside diner.

CHAPTER 5

Making a Diner with a Rotating Sign

With the knowledge and programming skills you have gained in the previous chapters, you are ready to create your first complete mod. In this chapter, we will create a mod that allows players to place a diner with a rotating sign (see Figure 5-1). This will require that you organize 3D assets in your mod, creating a placement system, and write the necessary code to make the sign of the diner spin. Let's begin!

Figure 5-1. *The diner with its rotating sign makes for an attractive decoration in your town*

© GIANTS Software GmbH 2024
Z. Brumbaugh and M. Leithner, *Scripting Farming Simulator with Lua*,
https://doi.org/10.1007/979-8-8688-0060-3_5

Technical Requirements

In this chapter, you will be working entirely in the GIANTS Editor and Studio and must meet the requirements mentioned in the "Technical Requirements" section of Chapter 2, "Getting Started with the GIANTS Editor." While releases are infrequent, make sure you are always using the most recent version of the GIANTS Editor. This will ensure that you are able to take advantage of any new features. You can find all the code and assets used in this chapter in the book's code repository on the GDN at the following link:

https://gdn.giants-software.com/lp/scriptingBook.php

Preparing the Mod Folder Structure

Creating a new mod in GIANTS Studio always starts with the creation of a new project. If you don't know how to properly set up a new project, check the "New Project" section of Chapter 4, "The GIANTS Studio," again to get familiar with this process. This is essential for all following chapters.

So let's create a new project called "**restaurant**." GIANTS Studio will create a project setup that will look similar to Figure 5-2. As you can see, it is just a simple helloWorld project with a modDesc.xml, helloWorld.lua, and an icon.

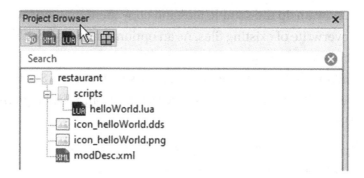

Figure 5-2. *The restaurant project*

In this sample mod, we want to create a diner with a rotating sign. Therefore, we need the source files for the restaurant. Once you have downloaded the sample files from the GDN, you should right-click the project root to open the mod folder in the explorer (Figure 5-3).

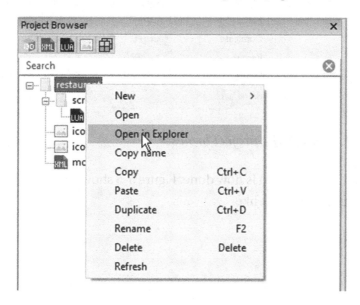

Figure 5-3. *Go to the mod directory*

You can now unzip the sample files and copy them into the mod folder. Accept the overwrite of existing files. As an optional step, you could delete all files in the mod folder first.

To get an updated view in the project browser of GIANTS Studio, you need to refresh it. Right-click again on the root node and click *Refresh* (Figure 5-4).

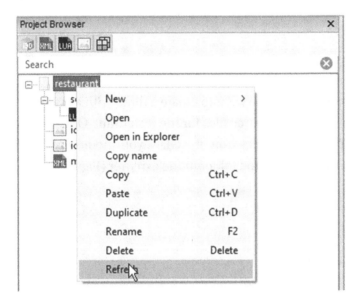

Figure 5-4. *Refresh the project browser*

The setup of this mod is now done. Figure 5-5 shows how the Project Browser should now look like.

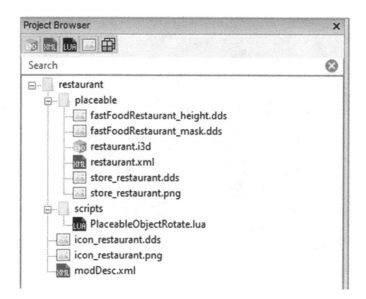

Figure 5-5. *The mod structure*

Let's now have a look at the actual visual representation of the diner. In the folder *placeable,* you should see the diner model contained within an .i3d file (*restaurant.i3d*). You are encouraged to look and explore the model in the GIANTS Editor. Recall you can open a model in the GIANTS Editor via the *Open* option of the File application menu or by pressing *Ctrl+O*. But you can also open it directly from GIANTS Studio. Just right-click the .i3d file and check *Open with Default.* The GIANTS Editor should start with the restaurant.i3d loaded. Assuming you are in the default viewing mode, the diner should look as it does in Figure 5-6.

Figure 5-6. *The diner model is the centerpiece of this mod*

The restaurant mod is now already working. So you could start and test it in game. But let's have a look at the files first. **Please note that all following chapters should be set up using the same steps:**

1. Create a project.

2. Download the sample files for the GDN.

3. Copy the files into the mod folder.

4. Refresh the Project Browser.

In the XML file and Lua file creation sections of the chapters, you will always be asked to create a file or add the content to files. You can ignore these lines if you use the sample files as a start because they already contain all these lines of code.

Creating Mod Scripts

In this section, we will create and explore the scripts needed for the mod. We will start by looking at the .xml files and then cover the .lua files. We will create and edit these files in GIANTS Studio. If you need a refresher on how to make and edit files, refer back to Chapter 4, "The GIANTS Studio."

Creating XML Files

Before we create scripts for the in-game systems of your mod, we will again need to set configurations for our mod via a file called modDesc.xml. Make sure that this file is in your mod directory and add the following content:

```xml
<?xml version="1.0" encoding="utf-8" standalone="no" ?>
<modDesc descVersion="72">
    <Author>GIANTS Software</author>
    <version>1.0.0.0</version>
    <multiplayer supported="true" />
    <title>
        <en>Sample Mod - Restaurant</en>
    </title>
    <description>
        <en>A sample mod</en>
    </description>
    <iconFilename>icon_restaurant.png</iconFilename>
    <placeableSpecializations>
        <specialization name="objectRotate" className="Plac
        eableObjectRotate"
                    filename="scripts/
                    PlaceableObjectRotate.lua" />
    </placeableSpecializations>
    <placeableTypes>
```

```
        <type name="restaurant" parent="simplePlaceable"
                filename="$dataS/scripts/placeables/
                Placeable.lua">
            <specialization name="objectRotate" />
        </type>
    </placeableTypes>
    <storeItems>
        <storeItem xmlFilename="placeable/restaurant.xml"/>
    </storeItems>
</modDesc>
```

While most of the fields in the file have already been discussed in the
"Debugging Scripts" section of Chapter 4, "The GIANTS Studio," there are
several new ones to discuss.

The first new field we define in the preceding code is a
placeableSpecializations field which includes several subfields. Placeables
use an internal specialization system that behaves like a plug-in system –
that is, each specialization is used for a specific placeable feature. For
example, the *placement* specialization adds functionality to support
dynamic placement via the construction screen, and the *leveling*
specialization adds support to level the area around the placeable.

We define a *specialization* field that includes the *filename* field which
defines the script our mod will use to handle the placeable object. The Lua
file we reference and will use is named *PlaceableObjectRotate.lua*, which
we will create later in this section.

Next, we define the *placeableTypes* field. Placeable types are used
to define a specific feature set for a placeable item. For example, the
restaurant model should use the functionality given by the internal
Placeable.lua file and the additional features of the *simplePlaceable* type
and *objectRotate* specialization.

Lastly, we need to make the restaurant a purchasable item from the in-game store. We do this by defining the *storeItems* field and referencing an .xml file for our restaurant, which should be titled *restaurant.xml*. Your *restaurant.xml* file should be in the *placeable* subdirectory mentioned in the previous section. That concludes the content for modDesc.xml; we will now explore the contents of **restaurant.xml** and the meaning of each section:

```
<?xml version="1.0" encoding="utf-8" standalone="no" ?>
<placeable type="restaurant" xmlns:xsi="http://www.w3.org/2001/
XMLSchema-instance" xsi:noNamespaceSchemaLocation="https://
validation.gdn.giants-software.com/fs22/placeable.xsd">
    <storeData>
        <name>Restaurant</name>
        <functions>
            <function>A deco object</function>
        </functions>
        <image>icon_restaurant.png</image>
        <price>55000</price>
        <lifetime>1000</lifetime>
        <rotation>0</rotation>
        <brand>NONE</brand>
        <species>placeable</species>
        <category>decoration</category>
        <brush>
            <type>placeable</type>
            <category>decoration</category>
            <tab>uncategorized</tab>
        </brush>
        <vertexBufferMemoryUsage>0</
vertexBufferMemoryUsage>
        <indexBufferMemoryUsage>0</indexBufferMemoryUsage>
```

```
        <textureMemoryUsage>0</textureMemoryUsage>
        <instanceVertexBufferMemoryUsage>0</
        instanceVertexBufferMemoryUsage>
        <instanceIndexBufferMemoryUsage>0</
        instanceIndexBufferMemoryUsage>
    </storeData>
```

The file starts with the XML declaration defining the information about the XML content. The root element is of the *placeable* type. The *type* attribute links the restaurant to the placeable type we defined in the *placeableType* section of the modDesc.xml.

The purpose of an XML schema is to define the allowed building blocks of an XML document. This includes the elements and attributes that can appear in a document, types of data for elements, the number and order of child elements, as well as default and fixed values for elements. The GDN also provides schema for vehicles, which will be covered in Chapter 6, "Rotating Mower Mod." You can always find the newest available XML schema from the GDN:

```
https://validation.gdn.giants-software.com/fs22/overview.html
```

The schema for placeables can be found at the following link:

```
https://validation.gdn.giants-software.com/fs22/placeable.xsd
```

Next, the file defines *configurations* for the restaurant model and its in-game behavior. Next, we define a *storeData* field which holds the *price, brand,* and *description* of the item which will be displayed in the shop.

Like the .xml file for the mod itself, we will also define basic information such as a *name* and *image* in the *name* and *image* fields. The *function* field holds a description about the item and its function. The price of the item, as seen in the Construction Mode, is set by the *price* field of this section. The *lifetime* field defines the lifetime of the object until it is fully aged; *maintenance* costs are calculated based on this value. The *rotation* field defines an initial rotation for our object, which we will set to 0 by default.

The *brand* field is used if the item is associated with a real-world brand; we will set it to NONE in our case as the restaurant is fictional. The *category* field determines what type of in-game object the asset is treated as – our restaurant serves no functional purpose, so we categorize it as a decoration. The *brush* field is important as it defines the tab and category that the structure will be displayed in when in the Construction Mode. The remaining fields are used internally by the GIANTS Engine and will be set by the ModHub team; you do not need to change these values yourself. Next, we will look at more of the contents of the restaurant.xml file:

```
<base>
        <filename>placeable/restaurant.i3d</filename>
</base>
<placement useRandomYRotation="false"
useManualYRotation="true" >
<testAreas>
        <testArea startNode="testArea1Start"
        endNode="testArea1End" />
        <testArea startNode="testArea2Start"
        endNode="testArea2End" />
</testAreas>
</placement>
<clearAreas>
        <clearArea startNode="clearArea1Start"
        widthNode="clearArea1Width"
```

```
                            heightNode="clearArea1Height"/>
    <clearArea startNode="clearArea2Start"
    widthNode="clearArea2Width"
                            heightNode="clearArea2Height"/>
</clearAreas>
<leveling requireLeveling="true" maxSmoothDistance="10"
maxSlope="75"
            maxEdgeAngle="30" >
    <levelAreas>
        <levelArea startNode="levelArea1Start"
        widthNode="levelArea1Width"
                        heightNode="levelArea1Height"
                        groundType="asphalt"/>
        <levelArea startNode="levelArea2Start"
        widthNode="levelArea2Width"
                        heightNode="levelArea2Height"
                        groundType="asphalt"/>
    </levelAreas>
</leveling>
```

This section of the file is necessary for the placeable specialization to function. Since this is mostly internal, we will cover each field quickly. The **filename** field holds the name of the .i3d file of our diner relative to the mod folder.

The *testAreas* field defines test areas that are used to identify possible placement conflicts. We use two points to create a test box, and in game we use an overlapBox check to get objects within the box to check conflicts. That is, if other objects are within the test areas, the object cannot be placed there.

```
<tipOcclusionUpdateAreas>
    <tipOcclusionUpdateArea
        startNode="tipOcclusionUpdateArea1Start"
        endNode="tipOcclusionUpdateArea1End" />
</tipOcclusionUpdateAreas>
<ai>
    <updateAreas>
        <updateArea
            startNode="tipOcclusionUpdateArea1Start"
            endNode="tipOcclusionUpdateArea1End" />
    </updateAreas>
</ai>
<objectRotate>
    <object node="roofLogo" rotAxis="2"
    rotDurationSeconds="10" />
</objectRotate>
```

The *clearAreas* field defines an area under the model where foliage and fields will be cleared once the model has been placed.

The *levelAreas* field also defines an area under the model where terrain will be leveled to more neatly support the diner.

The *tipOcclusionUpdateAreas* is used by the engine to determine whether certain environmental interactions like snow falling should still occur in locations around the restaurant or whether they have been blocked.

Similarly, the *updateAreas* field under the ai field instructs the AI system to sample the update area to get new information about collisions it has to avoid in the future.

Lastly, the *objectRotate* field defines which part of our model should rotate and information about the behavior of its rotation. Note that this is where we set the axis the object should rotate around as well as the time in seconds it takes for the object to make one revolution. Axis values of 1, 2, and 3 correspond to X, Y, and Z axes, respectively. Let us now look at the remaining content for the restaurant.xml file:

```
<i3dMappings>
      <i3dMapping id="roofLogo" node="0>0|0|0" />
      <i3dMapping id="blinker02Decal" node="0>0|0|0|1|0" />
      <i3dMapping id="blinker01Decal" node="0>0|0|0|1|1" />
      <i3dMapping id="dinnerDecal" node="0>0|0|0|1|2" />
...
      </i3dMappings>
</placeable>
```

This section of the file defines i3d mappings for the model. i3d mappings are automatically created by the Blender or Maya exporter. Using the i3dMapping field id instead of the node path in the upper part of the .xml file avoids errors as you do not have to adjust the node paths manually after changing the hierarchy within the .i3d file. Let us use the following line as an example:

```
<object node="roofLogo" rotAxis="2" rotDurationSeconds="10" />
```

In this line, we use *roofLogo* instead of the i3d path 0>0|0|0. The script will later automatically resolve the *roofLogo* ID to 0>0|0|0 and resolve this i3d path to a valid entity ID. So, if we would change the hierarchy of the i3d in Maya and reexport the file, we will not have to change anything in the object element as the Maya exporter will automatically recreate the i3dMapping sections with the new i3d paths. If you examine the restaurant.i3d file in the GIANTS Editor, you will see other reference points have already been physically created and our program references them by name.

Creating Lua Files

With our .xml files created, we will need to create a script to handle the placement of your diner model in the game environment; we will name this script *PlaceableObjectRotate.lua.* **If you already have this file from the GDN, you are still encouraged to follow along as we break down each part of the program.** Let's first look at what needs to be defined to declare the specialization:

```lua
local modName = g_currentModName

-- @category Specializations
PlaceableObjectRotate = {}
PlaceableObjectRotate.SPEC_TABLE_NAME = "spec_"..
modName..".objectRotate"

function PlaceableObjectRotate.prerequisitesPresent(specia
lizations)
    return true
end

-- @param table placeableType the placeable type
-- @includeCode
function PlaceableObjectRotate.registerEventListeners(plac
eableType)
    SpecializationUtil.registerEventListener(placeableType,
    "onLoad", PlaceableObjectRotate)
    SpecializationUtil.registerEventListener(placeableType,
    "onUpdate", PlaceableObjectRotate)
end
```

In this code, we assign the name of the mod to a variable called *modName*. Note that this value is determined by the name of your mod directory and is only available while the .lua file is loaded. As such, we want to store a copy in a local variable of the script to be able to access it later.

Next, we set *SPEC_TABLE_NAME* for our module, which will later serve as an index for functions related to our mod.

Next, we define the *prerequisitesPresent* function, which, for our purposes, will always return true. We include this function to ensure all specializations our mod depends on have been loaded before we attempt to use them. Errors will be produced if we try to access variables or functions from a specialization that has not yet been loaded. For example, if we want to use any part of the PlaceableLights specialization, we would add *SpecializationUtil.hasSpecialization(PlaceableLights, specializations)* in this function.

The *registerEventListeners* function will handle the creation of **events**. Events are signals that can be **triggered** or **fired** and have some associated function be called with relevant arguments from the event. For this mod, or more specifically the internal *placeable* specialization we declared we would be using in modDesc.xml, we want to create an event called *onLoad* and *onUpdate,* which we will define the functions for later in this section.

```
-- @includeCode
function PlaceableObjectRotate.registerXMLPaths(schema,
basePath)
    schema:setXMLSpecializationType("ObjectRotate")
    schema:register(XMLValueType.NODE_INDEX,
            basePath .. ".objectRotate.object(?)#node",
            "Node index or i3d mapping name of the object
            that should rotate")
    schema:register(XMLValueType.FLOAT,
```

```
        basePath .. ".objectRotate.object(?)#rotDurat
        ionSeconds",
        "Duration in seconds for one rotation", 1)
    schema:register(XMLValueType.INT,
            basePath .. ".objectRotate.
            object(?)#rotAxis",
            "Rotation axis (1-3)", 1)
    schema:setXMLSpecializationType()
end
```

Next, we define the *registerXMLPaths* function which allows .xml files associated with the mod to be read from. This is important as without this function, we would not be able to read information from .xml files we use to configure mod behavior. We now have the base of our specialization created. Let us look at the implementation for the placeable object, which is handled via the event functions we set listeners for earlier in the section:

```
function PlaceableObjectRotate:onLoad(savegame)
    local spec = self[PlaceableObjectRotate.SPEC_TABLE_NAME]
    spec.objects = {}

    self.xmlFile:iterate("placeable.objectRotate.object",
    function(_, key)
        local node = self.xmlFile:getValue(key ..
        "#node", nil, self.components, self.i3dMappings)

        if node ~= nil then
            local rotDurationSeconds =
            self.xmlFile:getValue(key ..
            "#rotDurationSeconds", 1)
            local rotAxis = self.xmlFile:getValue(key ..
            "#rotAxis", 1)
```

```
        if rotAxis < 1 or rotAxis > 3 then
            rotAxis = 1
            Logging.xmlWarning(self.xmlFile,
                "Invalid rotation axis for
                objectRotate '%s'! Using default
                axis '%d'!",
                key, rotAxis)
        end
        local object = {}
        object.node = node
        -- convert the duration to angle delta per
        -- millisecond
        object.anglePerMs = (2*math.pi) /
            rotDurationSeconds / 1000
        object.rotAxis = rotAxis

        table.insert(spec.objects, object)
    else
        Logging.xmlWarning(self.xmlFile,
            "Invalid node given for objectRotate
            '%s'!", key)
    end
    end)
end
```

In the preceding code, we first need to define the *onLoad()* function
which dictates the behavior for when the placeable item loads. Normally,
this is when the diner is placed in the world. This function defines some
additional values for the mod while preparing relevant objects to be
used in game. The spec variable we define indexes a table we refer to as a
namespace. Each specialization has its own namespace under which its
fields and functions are stored. With this defined, the function then uses
information from the restaurant.xml file we created previously to ensure

the model is correctly configured and to define behaviors for when it is present in the game.

To access .xml files via a script, we use special syntax to access its elements. Let's assume we have the following XML content:

```
<root>
     <element1 value="1" />
     <elements>
          <subElement>test</subElement>
          </subElement>test2</subElement>
     </elements>
<root>
```

If we want to access the value attribute of *element1*, we can simply read it with the following Lua code:

```
xmlFile:getString("root.element1#value")
```

The period (.) operator accesses the sub-elements of the current element, and the pound (#) operator accesses the attribute of the current element. If you want to select the second sub-element, you would write the following Lua code:

```
xmlFile:getString("root.elements.subElement(1)")
```

Unlike Lua, access to XML elements is zero based, so 1 is the second element. You may also find the Logging utility class useful. It contains functions such as the following which can print useful errors, warnings, or other information to the log file:

```
warning(text , ...)
xmlWarning(xmlFile, text, ...)
error(text, ...)
xmlError(xmlFile, text, ...)
```

```
info(text, ...)
xmlInfo(text, ...)
```

All of these functions internally use the *string.format()* function, so the text that is passed can contain placeholders that will be filled using the parameters provided in the function's arguments.

Returning to *PlaceableObjectRotate.lua*, you can see we set the *anglePerMs* field of the object by converting from the time it should take the sign to make one full rotation into a value used to change the rotation of our sign each time we update it. The *getValue()* script function can be used to access elements from the .xml file because we defined the XML elements and their types in the *registerXMLPaths()* function. The script now can evaluate the given element or attribute and convert its value to the correct type. Let's look at the following line of code:

```
local node = self.xmlFile:getValue(key .. "#node", nil,
                                    self.components,
                                    self.i3dMappings)
```

The script reads the node value (in our sample, *roofLogo)* and uses the passed *self.i3dMappings* to get the i3d path of it. Then, an internal function uses the i3d path and the *self.components* table to go through the i3d hierarchy to find the correct entity and then returns the ID of this entity. For each xml entry, we create a table with all of the settings for the object and put it into the *self.objects* table. This allows us to easily support multiple rotating objects in our mods.

```
-- @param float dt delta time since last update
-- @includeCode
function PlaceableObjectRotate:onUpdate(dt)
    local spec = self[PlaceableObjectRotate.SPEC_TABLE_NAME]

    for _, object in ipairs(spec.objects) do
        local rx, ry, rz = getRotation(object.node)
```

```
        local deltaAngle = object.anglePerMs * dt
        rx = rx + (object.rotAxis == 1 and deltaAngle or 0)
        ry = ry + (object.rotAxis == 2 and deltaAngle or 0)
        rz = rz + (object.rotAxis == 3 and deltaAngle or 0)
        rx = rx % (2*math.pi)
        ry = ry % (2*math.pi)
        rz = rz % (2*math.pi)
        setRotation(object.node, rx, ry, rz)
    end
    self:raiseActive()
end
```

For the sign to be updated, we need the *onUpdate()* function, which
is called repeatedly once the restaurant has been placed and will update
the rotation of the sign. That is, each time the function is called, the sign
will rotate a small amount around the Y axis, meaning the function must
be called quickly and consistently. To do this, the *onUpdate()* function
is bound to each **frame**. That means each time a frame of the game is
rendered by the player's computer, the function is called with how much
time has passed since the last frame was rendered as a parameter called *dt*,
which is short for *delta time*. For a game running at 60 **frames per second**
(FPS), the value of dt would be 1/60 or about 16.667 milliseconds. The last
statement in this function, *self:raiseActive()*, will ensure that the function is
called in the next frame.

Testing the Mod

Now that you have organized and written the assets and scripts required
for your mod, you are ready to test it. From the GIANTS Studio, you can
run the game without debugging from the Debug application menu.
After you begin a new game on the map of your choice, you should be

able to see the diner in the Construction Mode. Once placed, the sign on top of the diner should begin to spin, catching the attention of potential customers driving by.

Summary

In this chapter, you learned how to create your first playable mod. With this mod, players will now be able to place down a diner in their game and watch as the sign rotates. You should now feel comfortable implementing specializations yourself as well as making placement systems for any type of building model.

In the next chapter, you will learn to make a more complicated mod that involves both 3D models and programming.

CHAPTER 6

Rotating Mower Mod

In this chapter, you will build upon your experience with programming, working with models and .i3d files and making simpler mods to make a more complex mod. This mod focuses on creating a mower with rotating blades (see Figure 6-1). Unlike the previous mod example where we made a static structure with a rotating sign, we will be making a moving vehicle with rotating elements that also affects foliage and other elements of the game environment.

Figure 6-1. *The rotating mower is an excellent tool for clearing your fields*

© GIANTS Software GmbH 2024
Z. Brumbaugh and M. Leithner, *Scripting Farming Simulator with Lua*,
https://doi.org/10.1007/979-8-8688-0060-3_6

Technical Requirements

Like the previous chapter, you will be working entirely in the GIANTS Editor and Studio and must meet the requirements mentioned in the "Technical Requirements" section of Chapter 2, "Getting Started with the GIANTS Editor." Make sure you are always using the most recent version of the GIANTS Editor. This will ensure that you are able to take advantage of any new features. You can find all the code and assets used in this chapter in the book's code repository on the GDN at the following link:

https://gdn.giants-software.com/lp/scriptingBook.php

Creating Mod Scripts

This section will explore all of the scripts necessary for this mod. We will start by looking at the .xml files and then cover the .lua files. Please see the "Preparing the Mod Folder Structure" section of Chapter 5, "Making a Diner with a Rotating Sign," on how to set up a mod project and use the sample files provided on GDN.

Creating XML Files

Like in the previous chapters, we will need to create a *modDesc.xml* file. You should be familiar with the basic fields for setting a name, description, and icon for the mod. Let us now look at the contents of modDesc.xml:

```xml
<?xml version="1.0" encoding="utf-8" standalone="no" ?>
<modDesc descVersion="72">
    <Author>GIANTS Software</author>
    <version>1.0.0.0</version>
    <multiplayer supported="true" />
    <title>
        <en>Sample Mod - Rotate Mower</en>
    </title>
    <description>
        <en>A sample mod</en>
    </description>
    <iconFilename>icon_rotateMower.png</iconFilename>
    <materialHolders>
        <materialHolder filename="effects/particles.i3d" />
    </materialHolders>
    <extraSourceFiles>
        <sourceFile filename="scripts/events/
        RotorSpeedFactorEvent.lua"/>
        <sourceFile filename="scripts/
        FSDensityMapUtilExtension.lua"/>
    </extraSourceFiles>
    <specializations>
        <specialization name="rotateMower"
            className="RotateMower"
            filename="scripts/RotateMower.lua" />
    </specializations>
```

In this first section of the file, we define basic information about our mod. The first new field we include is *materialHolders* which includes one *materialHolder* field. Note that you can add more *materialHolder* fields as needed when designing your own mods. This field is used to load a specific material or effect like particles that are then added to a global material or effect database and can be accessed via a script. Here, we reference our *particles.i3d* file which contains particle effects which will be used with our mower to create an exhaust effect. The path to our file is once again relative to the mod directory. Next, we reference some Lua files to be used in our mod using the extraSourceFiles field. The two scripts we are including are *RotorSpeedFactorEvent.lua* and *FSDensityMapUtilExtension.lua*. Lastly, we create a new rotateMower specialization that uses our *RotateMower.lua file*. We will explore all of these Lua scripts in the following "Creating Lua Files" section. Let us now cover the remaining content of modDesc.xml:

```
<vehicleTypes>
        <type name="rotateMower" parent="baseAttachable"
              filename="$dataS/scripts/vehicles/Vehicle.lua">
                <specialization name="turnOnVehicle" />
                <specialization name="groundReference" />
                <specialization name="workArea" />
                <specialization name="workParticles" />
                <specialization name="rotateMower" />
        </type>
</vehicleTypes>
<storeItems>
        <storeItem xmlFilename="vehicle/rotateMower.xml"/>
</storeItems>
<actions>
        <action name="CHANGE_ROTOR_SPEED" axisType="FULL" />
</actions>
<inputBinding>
        <actionBinding action="CHANGE_ROTOR_SPEED">
                <binding device="KB_MOUSE_DEFAULT" input="KEY_n"
                        axisComponent="-" />
                <binding device="KB_MOUSE_DEFAULT" input="KEY_m"
                        axisComponent="+" />
```

```
     </actionBinding>
   </inputBinding>
   <l10n filenamePrefix="l10n/l10n" />
 </modDesc>
```

In the second half of the file, we define some additional fields you have not seen previously.

The *vehicleTypes* field is used to define a specific feature set for a vehicle. The base class for our new rotateMower specialization is *Vehicle. lua,* and the additional features, such as the ability to attach the vehicle, are all of the baseAttachable type and its specializations.

We also provide functionality to turn the vehicle on or off via the *turnOnVehicle* specialization. To manipulate the foliage and other elements of the ground, we need support for work areas which use the *workArea* specialization. We want our mod to only work if it has ground contact, so we need to add the *groundReference* specialization. Support for particles will be added by using the *workParticles* specialization. Finally, we link our own *rotateMower* specialization.

Like before, we make our mod purchasable in game by using the *storeItems* field. In this field, we reference the *rotateMower* configuration file called *rotateMower.xml* which will define all of the information about the physical mower, much like the restaurant.xml file from Chapter 5, "Making a Diner with Rotating Element." We will cover the contents of this file later in this section.

Another new field in this file is *actions*, which holds a list of *action* fields that can be triggered by the player. For our mod, we will define one input for the player which allows them to control the speed of the mower's rotor. This *action* is defined as a *FULL* axis. The game supports half and full axes. *FULL* means that the action can return values between −1 and 1, while a *HALF* axis only returns values between 0 and 1. Typical use cases for a *HALF* axis include simple toggle actions like turning on or off something. In this case, you only want to get the button press. Use cases

131

for a *FULL* axis include steering or, in our case, the speed control. We want to decrease and increase the speed using this one action. Both axis types support digital (e.g., keyboard) and analog bindings (e.g., joystick).

Next, the *inputBinding* field allows us to define inputs to control our previously defined actions. In our mod, we will bind the *N* key to decrease the rotor speed and the *M* key to increase the rotor speed. The *device="KB_ MOUSE_DEFAULT"* field binds this action to available keyboards. *KB_ MOUSE_DEFAULT* is a wildcard placeholder for all keyboards or mouses. There is also *DEFAULT_GAMEPAD* that links to all gamepads. There is also the option to link to a specific device with its device UUID, but this is not recommended in practice.

Lastly, we include the *l10n* field which allows us to provide translations for our mod so that players who speak different languages can still know the controls associated with the mower.

With modDesc.xml now defined, let us now cover the contents of rotateMower.xml and explore how the new fields interact with our mod:

```
<?xml version="1.0" encoding="utf-8" standalone="no" ?>
<vehicle type="rotateMower" xmlns:xsi="http://www.w3.org/2001/
XMLSchema-instance" xsi:noNamespaceSchemaLocation="https://
validation.gdn.giants-software.com/fs22/vehicle.xsd">
        <annotation>
                Copyright (C) GIANTS Software GmbH, All Rights
                Reserved.
        </annotation>
        <storeData>
                <name>Rotate Mower</name>
                <specs>
                        <neededPower>40</neededPower>
                        <workingWidth>2.4</workingWidth>
                </specs>
                <functions>
```

```
    <function>$l10n_function_mower</function>
</functions>
<image>vehicle/store_rotateMower.png</image>
<price>12000</price>
<lifetime>600</lifetime>
<rotation>0</rotation>
<brand>LIZARD</brand>
<category>mowers</category>
<shopTranslationOffset>0 0 0</
shopTranslationOffset>
<shopRotationOffset>0 0 0</shopRotationOffset>
<vertexBufferMemoryUsage>0</
vertexBufferMemoryUsage>
<indexBufferMemoryUsage>0</indexBufferMemoryUsage>
<textureMemoryUsage>0</textureMemoryUsage>
<instanceVertexBufferMemoryUsage>0</
instanceVertexBufferMemoryUsage>
<instanceIndexBufferMemoryUsage>0
</instanceIndexBufferMemoryUsage>
    </storeData>
```

Most of this section follows from the "Creating XML Files" section of Chapter 5, "Making a Diner with Rotating Element." Note that the vehicle schema can be found on the GDN at the following link. The vehicle.xsd provides all available elements that are allowed in a vehicle.xml file:

```
https://validation.gdn.giants-software.com/fs22/vehicle.xsd
```

You should already be familiar with fields like *name, function, price,* and several other fields present. We define a new field called *specs* which holds a *neededPower* and *workingWidth* field. The *specs* field is used to display information about an item in the shop. The two fields we've defined with it will be used to determine how much energy the mower consumes and the width of the area it cuts. You may have noticed that we set the brand field to *LIZARD* – LIZARD is a fictitious brand that many vehicles in Farming Simulator choose to use. Let us now look at more of the contents of rotateMower.xml:

```
<base>
      <typeDesc>$l10n_typeDesc_mower</typeDesc>
      <filename>vehicle/rotateMower.i3d</filename>
      <size width="3.2" length="1.5" lengthOffset="0.1" />
      <speedLimit value="20" />
      <components>
            <component centerOfMass="0 0.2 0"
                  solverIterationCount="10" mass="440" />
      </components>
      <schemaOverlay attacherJointPosition="0 0"
            name="IMPLEMENT" />
      <mapHotspot type="TOOL" />
</base>
<powerConsumer ptoRpm="470" neededMinPtoPower="10"
      neededMaxPtoPower="15"/>
<groundReferenceNodes>
      <groundReferenceNode node="groundRefNode"
            threshold="0.2" />
</groundReferenceNodes>
<workAreas>
      <workArea type="rotateMower" functionName="processRotate
      MowerArea"
                  disableBackwards="false" >
            <area startNode="workAreaStart"
                  widthNode="workAreaWidth"
                  heightNode="workAreaHeight" />
            <groundReferenceNode index="1" />
```

```
    <onlyActiveWhenLowered value="true"/>
  </workArea>
</workAreas >
```

In this portion of the file, we create a *base* field which holds basic information about the mower. Note how we reference the rotateMower. i3d as the file for the mower model, a *speed limit* for the mower to move at, and some information for how the model should be handled, including its *mass, center of mass*, and the overall *size* of the vehicle which is used to make sure the mower spawns correctly.

Next, we define a *powerConsumer* field so that the mower consumes engine power from its tractor. The *groundReferenceNodes* field defines reference points to see if the mower is currently touching the ground. The *workAreas* field holds *workArea* fields which define the area that is affected by the mower when it is active. Note that we use one of the ground reference nodes previously defined and specify mowing should only happen when the mower is lowered. Next, we will look at more of the file's contents:

```
<attachable>
    <inputAttacherJoints>
        <inputAttacherJoint node="attacherJoint"
                jointType="implement"
                topReferenceNode="topReferenceNode"
                upperRotationOffset="10"
                lowerRotLimitScale="0 0 0"
                lowerTransLimitScale="0 1 0">
            <distanceToGround lower="0.35" upper="1.0" />
        </inputAttacherJoint>
    </inputAttacherJoints>
    <support animationName="moveSupport" />
</attachable>
```

In this section, we define an attachment point where the mower utility will connect to the tractor. To do this, we include an *attachable* field which holds an *inputAttacherJoints* field, a list of *inputAttacherJoint* fields. The *inputAttacherJoint* field includes *configurations* for how the mower should attach to the tractor. The *node* attribute defines the position of the physics joint that connects the mower and the tractor – we also use the i3d-mapping for all i3d reference to avoid the more complex and user-unfriendly i3d paths like 0>0|0|0.

The *topReferenceNode* defines the position for the top bar of the three-point hitch. The *jointType* defines a preset for the physics joint – in our case, we use *implement*. By default, the script lowers and lifts the tools parallel to the ground. We want our mower to be a bit tilted when raised, so we add *upperRotationOffset="10"*. This causes the script to tilt our tool by 10 degrees when lifted. The *lowerRotLimitScale* and *lowerTransLimitScale* fields scale the joint limits.

Joint limits define the possible free (controlled by gravity and external impacts) movement of a joint for translation and rotation. The *distanceToGround* element defines the offsets of the tool when lifted or lowered. Lastly, the support element in our case defines an animation that is played when the mower is detached and played in reverse while the mower is attached.

```
<powerTakeOffs>
    <input inputAttacherJointIndices="1"
        inputNode="ptoInputNode"
        aboveAttacher="true" />
</powerTakeOffs>
<lights>
    <defaultLights>
        <defaultLight shaderNode="drum01Knife"
            lightTypes="0" intensity="300"/>
```

```
        <defaultLight shaderNode="drum02Knife"
            lightTypes="0" intensity="300"/>
        <defaultLight shaderNode="drum03Knife"
            lightTypes="0" intensity="300"/>
        <defaultLight shaderNode="drum04Knife"
            lightTypes="0" intensity="300"/>
    </defaultLights>
</lights>
```

The inclusion of the *powerTakeOffs* field determines whether a PTO
can be attached to the tractor. For clarity, a PTO is a power shaft that
transfers the tractor's engine power to the tool. Next, we define the blades
of the mower to be shader nodes if the lights on it are turned on by using a
lights field. For each blade, we define a new *defaultLight* in a *defaultLights*
field and reference the physical shader elements by name. The *lightType*
0 defines that the lights should be activated with the default light. There
are other light types such as 1, 2, or 3 – all of them are for special light
scenarios like *frontLight*, *workLight*, etc. They also depend on the tractor
the tool is attached to.

```
<ai>
        <needsLowering value="true" />
        <areaMarkers leftNode="aiMarkerLeft"
            rightNode="aiMarkerRight"
            backNode="aiMarkerBack" />
        <collisionTrigger node="aiCollisionNode" width="2.9"
            height="1.2"/>
        <agentAttachment width="2.3" height="1.2" length="1.2"
            lengthOffset="0.15"/>
</ai>
<turnOnVehicle turnOffIfNotAllowed="true"
            turnOffText="$l10n_action_turnOffMower"
```

```
            turnOnText="$l10n_action_turnOnMower" />
<foliageBending>
      <bendingNode minX="-1.4" maxX="1.4" minZ="-0.373"
          maxZ="0.7" yOffset="0.2"/>
</foliageBending>
<wearable wearDuration="480" workMultiplier="5"
      fieldMultiplier="2"/>
<washable dirtDuration="90" washDuration="1" workMultiplier="4"
      fieldMultiplier="2"/>
```

We also define an *ai* field, which dictates how AI vehicles and other agents should interact with our mower. For our mod, we define a *collisionTrigger* which is used by the AI tractor that uses our mower to detect other vehicles and objects in the world and also forces other AI vehicles to stop if they are near the mower. The AI *area markers* define the cut area of the mower used by the AI system to calculate the routes on the field it has to drive along. The *agentAttachment* element is used by the street AI system to calculate the correct route if you send a tractor with attached mower to a field or back to the farm. Next, the *turnOnVehicle* field allows us to display custom text when the mower is turned on or off. Note how we reference the translation .xml files from earlier in this field. We will need to define how foliage behaves when our mower interacts with it. We accomplish this by using the *foliageBending* field and including a *bendingNode* with configurations for how the foliage model should deform. As we use the mower, it will become dirty and see the effects of wear and tear. To reflect this, we create *wearable* fields which set the appearance of these environmental effects. With these general elements now included, we will define our custom element for the *rotateMower* in the file:

```
<rotateMower>
    <animationNodes>
        <animationNode node="drum01"
            rotSpeed="1000"  rotAxis="2"
            turnOnFadeTime="2.5"
            turnOffFadeTime="2"
            speedFunc="getRotorSpeedFactor"/>
        <animationNode node="drum02"
            rotSpeed="-1000" rotAxis="2"
            turnOnFadeTime="2.5" turnOffFadeTime="2"
            speedFunc="getRotorSpeedFactor"/>
        <animationNode node="drum03"
            rotSpeed="1000"  rotAxis="2"
            turnOnFadeTime="2.5"
            turnOffFadeTime="2"
            speedFunc="getRotorSpeedFactor"/>
        <animationNode node="drum04"
            rotSpeed="-1000" rotAxis="2"
            turnOnFadeTime="2.5"
            turnOffFadeTime="2"
            speedFunc="getRotorSpeedFactor"/>
    </animationNodes>
    <effects>
        <effectNode effectClass="ParticleEffect"
            effectNode="smokeEmitter"
            particleType="SMOKE"
            worldSpace="true" />
    </effects>
```

In our *rotateMower* element, we first define *animationNode* fields in an *animationNodes* container. Note that like other nodes and points of reference, these are already physically part of the mower model, and we refer to them by name. Two of the configurations we include in these elements are *turnOnFadeTime* and *turnOffFadeTime* which are used to let the blades speed up and slow down when the mower is turned on and off. The *rotSpeed* defines the rotation speed of the drum, and the *rotAxis* with value 2 defines that the object will rotate around its local Y axis. Next, we add a smoky particle effect for the dirt and exhaust from the mower by including an effects element with an *effectNode* field. The game supports different effect classes. We want to spawn a particle effect, so we need to set the value of *effectClass* to *ParticleEffect*. Also, notice that the *particleType* field is set to *SMOKE*, which directly connects to particle. i3d which holds our materials. In this material holder, we define a real particle system with user attributes and set *particleType* to *SMOKE*. Thus, the system can access the material holder and clone the defined particle system to be used in our *rotateMower*. Let's continue through the components of the *rotateMower* field:

```
<sounds>
    <start file="sounds/rotor_start.wav" innerRadius="5.0"
            outerRadius="65.0"
            fadeOut="0.1" linkNode="rotateMower_main_
            component1">
        <volume indoor="0.45" outdoor="1.1">
            <modifier type="ROTOR_RPM" value="0.00"
            modifiedValue="0.70" />
            <modifier type="ROTOR_RPM" value="1.00"
            modifiedValue="1.00" />
        </volume>
        <pitch indoor="1.00" outdoor="1">
```

```
            <modifier type="ROTOR_RPM" value="0.00"
            modifiedValue="0.50" />
            <modifier type="ROTOR_RPM" value="1.00"
            modifiedValue="1.0" />
        </pitch>
        <lowpassGain indoor="0.50" outdoor="1.00" />
    </start>
    <work file="sounds/rotor_work_loop.wav" innerRadius="5.0"
            outerRadius="65.0"
            fadeOut="0.1" linkNode="rotateMower_main_
            component1" >
...
    </work>
    <stop file="sounds/rotor_stop.wav" innerRadius="5.0"
            outerRadius="650.0"
            fadeOut="0.1">
...
    </stop>
</sounds>
</rotateMower>
```

We use this section of the rotateMower element to define the sounds it should use and how different mower actions affect these sounds. We start by creating a *sounds* element which includes *start, work,* and *stop* fields. Each of these fields references one sound which is used when the mower starts, is working, and when it stops. Importantly, as rotor revolutions per minute (RPM) increases, we want to increase the volume and pitch of the sound, which we achieve by using *pitch* and *volume* fields. Note that we can add *filters* to these sounds and change their behavior depending on whether the player's perspective is inside the cabin of a tractor or outdoors. This concludes the elements of the rotateMower field. Let us continue through the remaining contents of rotateMower.xml:

```
    <i3dMappings>
        <i3dMapping id="rotateMower_main_component1"
            node="0>" />
        <i3dMapping id="rotateMower_vis" node="0>0" />
        <i3dMapping id="attacherJoint" node="0>0|0|0" />
        <i3dMapping id="topReferenceNode" node="0>0|0|1" />
        <i3dMapping id="ptoInputNode" node="0>0|0|2" />
...
    </i3dMappings>
</vehicle>
```

We conclude our file with an *i3dMappings* field like we defined for our diner model in Chapter 5, "Making a Diner with Rotating Element."

With *modDesc.xml* and *rotateMower.xml* complete, we only need to create some supporting files before we jump into creating our Lua scripts. Earlier, we referenced two .xml files (*l10n_de.xml* and *l10n_en.xml*) in the l10n section of *modDesc.xml* that let us display custom text to players in different languages. We will start with *l10n_en.xml* which displays the controls for the mower to the player in English:

```
<?xml version="1.0" encoding="UTF-8" standalone="yes" ?>
<l10n>
    <elements>
        <e k="input_CHANGE_ROTOR_SPEED_1"
            v="Decrease Rotor Speed"/>
        <e k="input_CHANGE_ROTOR_SPEED_2"
            v="Increase Rotor Speed"/>
        <e k="input_CHANGE_ROTOR_SPEED"
            v="Change Rotor Speed (%d%%)"/>
        <e k="action_turnOffMower" v="Turn off mower"/>
        <e k="action_turnOnMower" v="Turn on mower"/>
    </elements>
</l10n>
```

In this file, we reference the custom actions we created in *modDesc. xml* by *name* and associate *text* with each input. We can do the same in German so that German-speaking players can more easily engage with the mod. Let us look at the contents of *l10n_de.xml*:

```
<?xml version="1.0" encoding="UTF-8" standalone="yes" ?>
<l10n>
     <elements>
          <e k="input_CHANGE_ROTOR_SPEED_1"
               v="Rotorgeschwindigkeit senken"/>
          <e k="input_CHANGE_ROTOR_SPEED_2"
               v="Rotorgeschwindigkeit erhöhen"/>
          <e k="input_CHANGE_ROTOR_SPEED"
               v="Rotorgeschwindigkeit anpassen (%d%%)"/>
          <e k="action_turnOffMower"
               v="Mähwerk ausschalten"/>
          <e k="action_turnOnMower" v="Mähwerk anschalten"/>
     </elements>
</l10n>
```

You can add support for additional languages by creating a new file with the translations and appropriate suffix. For example, to add support for French, create a new file called *l10n_fr.xml*. With these files created, we have finished making all of the .xml files for our mod! This is a good point to review everything you have created so far and double-check your understanding before we jump into creating our Lua files and bringing our mower to life.

Creating Lua Files

We're now ready to create our Lua files – we will start with
RotorSpeedFactorEvent.lua. The purpose of this script is to replicate
a user's input to other players over the network if they are playing in
multiplayer mode. Let us now examine the contents of the script:

```
RotorSpeedFactorEvent = {}
local RotorSpeedFactorEvent_mt =
Class(RotorSpeedFactorEvent, Event)
InitEventClass(RotorSpeedFactorEvent, "RotorSpeedFactorEvent")

function RotorSpeedFactorEvent.emptyNew()
      local self = Event.new(RotorSpeedFactorEvent_mt)
      return self
end

function RotorSpeedFactorEvent.new(vehicle, speedFactor)
      local self = RotorSpeedFactorEvent.emptyNew()
      self.vehicle = vehicle
      self.speedFactor = speedFactor
      return self
end
```

We start by creating a new table and using the *Event* base class to
create our new *RotorSpeedFactorEvent*, a subclass of *Event*. Next, we
define two constructor functions: *RotorSpeedFactorEvent.emptyNew()* and
RotorSpeedFactorEvent.new(). The first constructor takes no arguments
and creates an empty event for later use. The second constructor is passed
vehicle and *speedFactor* arguments which reference the vehicle the event is
for and the current speed of the rotor, respectively. With our constructors
defined, we can begin to implement the main functionality of this event:

```
function RotorSpeedFactorEvent:writeStream(streamId,
connection)
```

```
        NetworkUtil.writeNodeObject(streamId, self.vehicle)
        RotateMower.streamWriteSpeedFactor(streamId, self.
        speedFactor)
End

function RotorSpeedFactorEvent:readStream(streamId, connection)
        self.vehicle = NetworkUtil.readNodeObject(streamId)
        self.speedFactor = RotateMower.streamReadSpeedFactor
        (streamId)
        self:run(connection)
end
```

The *writeStream()* function writes the event data to the network stream. That is, it communicates the information about the event to all players. This function is largely for internal use but note that we send a signal to the network to update the *speedFactor* of the mower's rotors in this function.

We cannot directly send the object reference of a vehicle over the network as it could be different on different PCs connected to the game. Instead, the network creates a mapping of the local vehicle reference and a unique ID (integer). The *writeNodeObject()* function of *NetworkUtil* simply gets the network id of the passed vehicle object and writes that integer to the network stream.

Once we have written event information to the stream, we need to be able to read it – we do this through the *readStream()* function. A strict requirement is that the call order is the same for read and write; otherwise, the network protocol stack will be broken. You can see how the network stream looks like in Figure 6-2.

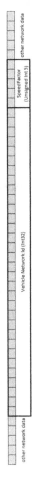

Figure 6-2. *This figure visualizes the network stream*

This function is again mostly for internal purposes, but like the *writeStream()* function, we must use the *readNodeObject()* function of *NetworkUtil* to remap the network ID back to a local vehicle object reference before we update the *speedFactor* field of the class and call the *run()* function to update the vehicle itself. The signal to perform this action was sent out at an earlier point in time by the *writeStream()* function.

```
function RotorSpeedFactorEvent:run(connection)
    if not connection:getIsServer() then
        g_server:broadcastEvent(self, false, connection,
        self.vehicle)
    end
    if self.vehicle ~= nil then
        self.vehicle:setRotorSpeedFactor(self.
        speedFactor, true)
    end
end
```

The *run()* function is where we execute the main physical changes as a result of the event. In our case, we need to update the vehicle to reflect the values set for *speedFactor* in our class. If a player (client) requested the change in motor speed via our custom action, we need to tell the server to replicate this action and *broadcast* the information to all other players in the game. Note that the network does not allow the client to directly tell the server or other users which behavior should be occurring for security purposes.

```
function RotorSpeedFactorEvent.sendEvent(vehicle, speedFactor,
noEventSend)
    if noEventSend == nil or noEventSend == false then
        if g_server ~= nil then
            g_server:broadcastEvent(RotorSpeedFactorEvent.
            new(vehicle, speedFactor),
```

```
                            nil, nil, vehicle)
            else
                g_client:getServerConnection():sendEvent(
                        RotorSpeedFactorEvent.
                        new(vehicle, speedFactor))
            end
        end
end
```

Lastly, we define the static helper function *sendEvent()* which is used by both clients and the server to perform replication. For example, the client can tell the server to replicate their action by sending this event. Additionally, the server can use this function to perform the client's request and replicate the change to other players from the server.

With *RotorSpeedFactorEvent.lua* completed, we will need to define an extension to an existing utility so that the mower can affect foliage it's used on. The GIANTS Engine uses what's called a *density map* to define where foliage is present. The purpose of this utility is to let our mod modify this density map based on the physical properties of the mower. Now we will cover the contents of *FSDensityMapUtilExtension.lua*:

```
function FSDensityMapUtil.updateRotateMowerArea(startWorl
dX, startWorldZ, widthWorldX, widthWorldZ, heightWorldX,
heightWorldZ)
        local functionData = FSDensityMapUtil.functionCache.
        updateRotateMowerArea
        if functionData == nil then
                local terrainRootNode = g_currentMission.
                terrainRootNode
                functionData = {}
                functionData.lastArea = 0
                functionData.lastTotalArea = 0
```

```
local multiModifier = DensityMapMultiModifier.new()
local modifier, filter
for _, desc in pairs(g_fruitTypeManager:getFruitT
ypes()) do
    if desc.terrainDataPlaneId ~= nil then
        if modifier == nil then
            modifier = DensityMapModifier.
            new(desc.terrainDataPlaneId,
                desc.startStateChannel,
                desc.numStateChannels,
                terrainRootNode)
        else
            modifier:resetDensityMapAndChanne
            ls(desc.terrainDataPlaneId,
                desc.startStateChannel,
                desc.numStateChannels)
        end
        if filter == nil then
            filter = DensityMapFilter.
            new(desc.terrainDataPlaneId,
                desc.startStateChannel,
                desc.numStateChannels,
                terrainRootNode)
        else
            filter:resetDensityMapAndChannels
            (desc.terrainDataPlaneId,
                desc.startStateChannel,
                desc.numStateChannels)
        end
```

```
                    filter:setValueCompareParams(DensityVal
                    ueCompareType.BETWEEN, 2,
                        desc.cutState)
                    multiModifier:addExecuteSet(desc.
                    cutState or 0, modifier, filter)
            end
        end
```

The program begins by defining a new function, *updateRotateMowerArea()*. This function will modify the foliage density map within a box as defined by the function's six arguments. We want to make multiple modifications to the foliage density map so we will need to create a *DensityMapMultiModifier*. For each type of foliage we want to affect, there is a different density map.

To modify these density maps, a new *DensityMapModifier* object must be created with the appropriate *DensityMap ID* and its value range (*startStateChannel* and *numStateChannels*). The *terrainRootNode* passed during the modifier's construction is used to calculate the affected range of pixels. For example, different density maps could have different sizes – the system must know the relationship between these sizes, so we use the *terrainRootNode* to calculate these. To save on performance, we only want to create the modifier once and cache (store) it.

We do not want all types of foliage to be affected by the mower, so we must create a new *DensityMapFilter* object for each type of mowable item. Like the density map modifier, we will also want to cache our filter. With the modifier and filters created, we call the *addExecuteSet* function of the *DensityMapMultiModifier* object we previously defined which will use our modifier and filter objects to update the foliage to a cut state. This is the main component of our extension on this utility. Let us now explore the rest of the script:

```
local weedSystem = g_currentMission.weedSystem
if weedSystem ~= nil then
    local weedTerrainDataPlaneId, weedStartChannel,
    weedNumChannels = weedSystem:getDensityMapData()
    modifier:resetDensityMapAndChannels(weedTerrain
    DataPlaneId, weedStartChannel, weedNumChannels)
    filter:resetDensityMapAndChannels(weedTerrainDataPlaneId,
    weedStartChannel, weedNumChannels)
    filter:setValueCompareParams(DensityValueCompareType.
    GREATER, 2)
    multiModifier:addExecuteSet(0, modifier, filter)
end
```

Weeds are kept in their own density map separate from the types of foliage we handled previously for our mower to affect. Like before, we will use our modifier and filter objects and update them to focus on the weed foliage layer. Then, using the density map multimodifier, we will update weeds under the mower to a cut state.

```
if g_currentMission.foliageSystem ~= nil then
    local decoFoliages = g_currentMission.foliageSystem:getDe
    coFoliages()
    local grassDesc = g_fruitTypeManager:getFruitTypeByIndex(
    FruitType.GRASS)
    for index, decoFoliage in pairs(decoFoliages) do
        if decoFoliage.terrainDataPlaneId ~= nil then
            -- reset the data plane and channels
            modifier:resetDensityMapAndChannels
            (grassDesc.terrainDataPlaneId,
                grassDesc.startStateChannel,
                grassDesc.numStateChannels)
            filter:resetDensityMapAndChannels
            (decoFoliage.terrainDataPlaneId,
```

```
                    decoFoliage.startStateChannel,
                    decoFoliage.numStateChannels)
                -- limit to visible deco foliage only
                filter:setValueCompareParams
                (DensityValueCompareType.GREATER, 0)
                -- execute the modifier for data pixels that
                -- match the filter
                multiModifier:addExecuteSet
                (grassDesc.cutState, modifier, filter)
            end
        end
end

functionData.multiModifier = multiModifier
FSDensityMapUtil.functionCache.updateRotateMowerArea =
functionData
end
```

Bushes are kept in their own foliage layer separate from the weeds or crops, and we will need to perform a similar process for them to also be cut. For all types of these *Deco Foliages*, we will once again use our modifier and filter objects to target their respective layers and update them to a cut state via our density map multimodifier.

```
DensityMapHeightUtil.clearArea(startWorldX, startWorldZ,
widthWorldX, widthWorldZ, heightWorldX, heightWorldZ)
local multiModifier = functionData.multiModifier
multiModifier:updateParallelogramWorldCoords(startWorldX,
startWorldZ, widthWorldX, widthWorldZ, heightWorldX,
heightWorldZ, DensityCoordType.POINT_POINT_POINT)
multiModifier:execute(false)
end
```

Next, we clear the area by calling the *clearArea()* function of *DensityMapHeightUtil*. This function removes everything that was forced to the ground in the area, such as straw or wheat. If a player mowed over some wheat or stones on the ground, the *clearArea()* function will remove those items. The *updateParallelogramWorldCoords()* function will update the coordinates of the area that should be affected by the execution of the *multiModifier*. Lastly, we execute the *multiModifier* which will run all of the operations we define in the main if statement of the function.

With the additions made to the density map utility, we are left with only *RotateMower.lua*, the main control script for our mower. Let us now look at the script's contents:

```
local modName = g_currentModName
RotateMower = {}
RotateMower.SPEC_TABLE_NAME = "spec_"..modName..".rotateMower"
RotateMower.MIN_SPEED_FACTOR = 0.1
RotateMower.MAX_SPEED_FACTOR = 2
RotateMower.STEP_SIZE = 0.1
RotateMower.NUM_BITS = 5

function RotateMower.streamWriteSpeedFactor(streamId,
rotorSpeedFactor)
    streamWriteUIntN(streamId,
    math.floor((rotorSpeedFactor * 10) + 0.5),
            RotateMower.NUM_BITS)
end

function RotateMower.streamReadSpeedFactor(streamId)
    -- read the speed factor from the network stream as
    -- an integer
    local speedFactor = streamReadUIntN(streamId,
    RotateMower.NUM_BITS)
```

```
    -- convert it back to float
    local rotorSpeedFactor = speedFactor / 10

    return rotorSpeedFactor
end
g_particleSystemManager:addParticleType("smoke")
```

This first part of our script creates the table for our specialization and adds five values to it. The first value we added defines our namespace like we have done in all previous specializations. The next two values define the min and max speed factors for the range of mower rotor speeds. The *STEP_SIZE* value defines the rate of change in the mower's rotor speed when the player makes an input. Lastly, *NUM_BITS* is used internally to represent a range of speed values; in this case, we will not need more than 5 bits if we treat our number as an unsigned integer. The first function we implement is *streamWriteSpeedFactor()* which is used in the network portion (writeStream()) of our scripts to write the *speedFactor* in a simplified way. Normally, the speedFactor is stored as a float. That means we would need 32 bits to send this data over the network. Using this function, we simply convert speedFactor into an integer with a range limited to the minimum and maximum values we have previously defined.

This way, we use only 5 bits to send the value without any floating-point data. Next, we define *streamReadSpeedFactor()* which reads from the stream the value that the mower's rotor speedFactor should be. We use the network utility to automatically convert the unsigned integer back into a Lua number.

Lastly, we register the mower's particle effect to the type defined by the attributes in our .i3d material holder with the particle system manager utility. Let us continue through the contents of the script:

```
function RotateMower.prerequisitesPresent(specializations)
    return SpecializationUtil.hasSpecialization
    (TurnOnVehicle, specializations)
end
```

Like in the previous mod, we must ensure that the prerequisite specializations for the mod have been loaded before we try to use them. Attempting to use them before they have loaded will result in an error. To do this, we add the prerequisitesPresent() function which uses the internal SpecializationUtil to ensure all the specializations used by the mod have been loaded. In this case, TurnOnVehicle must be loaded.

```
function RotateMower.registerEventListeners(vehicleType)
    SpecializationUtil.registerEventListener(vehicleType,
    "onLoad", RotateMower)
    SpecializationUtil.registerEventListener(vehicleType,
    "onDelete", RotateMower)
    SpecializationUtil.registerEventListener(vehicleType,
    "onReadStream", RotateMower)
    SpecializationUtil.registerEventListener(vehicleType,
    "onWriteStream", RotateMower)
    SpecializationUtil.registerEventListener(vehicleType,
    "onUpdateTick", RotateMower)
    SpecializationUtil.registerEventListener(vehicleType,
    "onRegisterActionEvents", RotateMower)
    SpecializationUtil.registerEventListener(vehicleType,
    "onTurnedOn", RotateMower)
    SpecializationUtil.registerEventListener(vehicleType,
    "onTurnedOff", RotateMower)
end
```

The *registerEventListeners()* function is a very important function of our specialization as it registers the events associated with player input to our functions which update mower attributes that should be triggered by the base vehicle script. Events for both the custom functions we defined as well as default events associated with the base Vehicle class specialization are registered in this function. More specifically, it forces the vehicle script to call some of the Vehicle base class events, such as *onLoad()*

when the vehicle is loaded and *onDelete()* where the vehicle is removed from the game. Additionally, *onReadStream()* and *onWriteStream()* if a player joins a multiplayer game. The *onUpdateTick()* function will be called with a more or less constant tick rate for 30 FPS (~33 ms), and *onRegisterActionEvents()* will be called if the input context changes, such as it would if the player gets in or out of a tractor. The function will also register a listener to the *onTurnedOn* and *onTurnedOff* events defined by the TurnOnVehicle specialization, allowing us to be notified if the mower is turned on or off.

```
function RotateMower.registerFunctions(vehicleType)
    SpecializationUtil.registerFunction(vehicleType,
            "getRotorSpeedFactor",
            RotateMower.getRotorSpeedFactor)
    SpecializationUtil.registerFunction(vehicleType,
            "setRotorSpeedFactor",
            RotateMower.setRotorSpeedFactor)
    SpecializationUtil.registerFunction(vehicleType,
            "getRotorSpeedScale",
            RotateMower.getRotorSpeedScale)
    SpecializationUtil.registerFunction(vehicleType,
            "processRotateMowerArea",
            RotateMower.processRotateMowerArea)
end
```

The *registerFunctions()* function associates our custom defined functions in our specialization with the vehicle type. This is required because the functions are custom and will not be an included functionality of the vehicle by default.

```
function RotateMower.registerOverwrittenFunctions(vehicleType)
    SpecializationUtil.registerOverwrittenFunction
    (vehicleType, "getRawSpeedLimit",
              RotateMower.getRawSpeedLimit)
    SpecializationUtil.registerOverwrittenFunction
    (vehicleType, "doCheckSpeedLimit",
              RotateMower.doCheckSpeedLimit)
end
```

Lastly, the *registerOverwrittenFunctions()* function will overwrite the inherited functions from the vehicle specialization with those we have redefined for our vehicle. With these functions implemented, let us continue through the contents of the file:

```
function RotateMower.initSpecialization()
    g_workAreaTypeManager:addWorkAreaType("rotateMower",
    false)

    local schema = Vehicle.xmlSchema
    schema:setXMLSpecializationType("RotateMower")
    AnimationManager.registerAnimationNodesXMLPaths(schema,
              "vehicle.rotateMower.animationNodes")
    EffectManager.registerEffectXMLPaths(schema, "vehicle.
    rotateMower.effects")
    SoundManager.registerSampleXMLPaths(schema,
              "vehicle.rotateMower.sounds", "start")
    SoundManager.registerSampleXMLPaths(schema,
              "vehicle.rotateMower.sounds", "stop")
    SoundManager.registerSampleXMLPaths(schema,
              "vehicle.rotateMower.sounds", "work")
    schema:setXMLSpecializationType()
```

```
    local schemaSavegame = Vehicle.xmlSchemaSavegame
    schemaSavegame:register(XMLValueType.FLOAT,
            "vehicles.vehicle(?)."..modName..".rotateMower
            #rotorSpeedFactor",
             "Current rotor speed factor")
end
```

initSpecialization() is a function that loads and registers relevant information from our .xml files with our vehicle and Lua script. Particularly, it adds the xml-element-paths from the .xml files for the mower's sounds, its effects, and animation nodes. We also want the state of the mower to be loaded in from when the player last played the game. This is used at the end of the function where we load the saved rotor speed factor:

```
function RotateMower:onLoad(savegame)
    local spec = self[RotateMower.SPEC_TABLE_NAME]
    spec.rotorSpeedFactor = 1
    spec.isEffectDirty = false
    if self.isClient then
        spec.animationNodes =
        g_animationManager:loadAnimations(self.xmlFile,
                "vehicle.rotateMower.animationNodes",
                self.components,
                self, self.i3dMappings)
        spec.effects = g_effectManager:loadEffect
        (self.xmlFile,
                "vehicle.rotateMower.effects", self.
                components, self, self.i3dMappings)
        for _, effect in ipairs(spec.effects) do
            effect.currentFillType = nil
        end
```

```
            g_effectManager:setFillType(spec.effects, FillType.
            UNKNOWN)
            for _, effect in ipairs(spec.effects) do
                 effect.defaultSpeed = ParticleUtil.
                 getParticleSystemSpeed(effect.particleSystem)
            end
            spec.samples = {}
            spec.samples.start =
            g_soundManager:loadSampleFromXML(self.xmlFile,
                        "vehicle.rotateMower.sounds", "start",
                        self.baseDirectory,
                        self.components, 1, AudioGroup.VEHICLE,
                        self.i3dMappings, self)
            spec.samples.stop  =
            g_soundManager:loadSampleFromXML(self.xmlFile,
                        "vehicle.rotateMower.sounds", "stop",
                        self.baseDirectory,
                        self.components, 1, AudioGroup.VEHICLE,
                        self.i3dMappings, self)
            spec.samples.work  =
            g_soundManager:loadSampleFromXML(self.xmlFile,
                        "vehicle.rotateMower.sounds", "work",
                        self.baseDirectory,
                        self.components, 0, AudioGroup.VEHICLE,
                        self.i3dMappings, self)
        end
if savegame ~= nil then
     local rotKey = savegame.key..".."..modName..".rotateMower#
     rotorSpeedFactor"
     local rotorSpeedFactor =
     savegame.xmlFile:getValue(rotKey)
```

```
        if rotorSpeedFactor ~= nil then
            self:setRotorSpeedFactor(rotorSpeedFactor, true)
        end
end
if self.addAIGroundTypeRequirements ~= nil then
        self:addAIGroundTypeRequirements
        (Mulcher.AI_REQUIRED_GROUND_TYPES)
end
if self.addAIFruitRequirement ~= nil then
        self:clearAIFruitRequirements()
        for _, fruitType in ipairs(g_fruitTypeManager:getFruitT
        ypes()) do
            self:addAIFruitRequirement(fruitType.index, 2,
            fruitType.cutState-1)
        end
        local weedSystem = g_currentMission.weedSystem
        if weedSystem ~= nil then
        local weedTerrainDataPlaneId, weedStartChannel,
        weedNumChannels =
                weedSystem:getDensityMapData()
            local factors = weedSystem:getFactors()
            local minFactor = math.huge
            local maxFactor = 0
            for state, _ in pairs(factors) do
                minFactor = math.min(state, minFactor)
                maxFactor = math.max(state, maxFactor)
            end
            self:addAIFruitRequirement(nil, minFactor,
                    maxFactor,
```

```
                              weedTerrainDataPlaneId,
                              weedStartChannel, weedNumChannels)
            end
        end
end
```

The *onLoad()* function first references the namespace of our specialization and defines our *rotorSpeedFactor* field. This field is what will actually be modified when the updating functions we implemented earlier are called. We additionally include *isEffectDirty* as a field which we use to determine whether the effect should be updated.

Next, we load the mower's *animations* and add its *effects*. We must also set the *currentFillType* field of each effect to nil manually for them to appear. With the effects loaded, we want to cache the *default particle speed* of each effect as a point of reference as we will be changing it as the mower operates. Following this, we will load the three *sounds* for the mower and store them so that they can be easily referenced later.

If the game is being loaded from a save file, we will want to set the attributes of the mower to those that were saved previously. The *savegame. xmlFile* field holds a reference to the savegame instance's vehicle.xml file and *savegame.key* in the xml element of the current vehicle. This allows us to easily read saved data for our mower.

Next, we will want to confine the mower to fields if it is operating autonomously as part of the *field worker* functionality. Furthermore, we want the worker to only move after fruits and weeds rather than all crops in a field area. Note that we also consider the cut state of the crop so that we do not revisit field areas which have already been mowed. We will now look at more of the script's contents:

```
function RotateMower:onDelete()
    local spec = self[RotateMower.SPEC_TABLE_NAME]
    g_animationManager:deleteAnimations(spec.animationNodes)
    g_effectManager:deleteEffects(spec.effects)
    g_soundManager:deleteSamples(spec.samples)
end
```

The *onDelete()* function manages the case where the mower is deleted in the scope of our specialization. In particular, we do not want a memory leak to occur, so we delete the loaded animations, effects, and sounds.

```
function RotateMower:saveToXMLFile(xmlFile, key, usedModNames)
    xmlFile:setValue(key .. "#rotorSpeedFactor",
    self:getRotorSpeedFactor())
end
```

The *saveToXMLFile()* function will save the state of the mower (more specifically the *rotorSpeedFactor*) to an .xml file so that it can be loaded in when the player next joins the game.

```
function RotateMower:onReadStream(streamId, connection)
    local rotorSpeedFactor = RotateMower.streamReadSpeedFactor
    (streamId)
    self:setRotorSpeedFactor(rotorSpeedFactor, true)
end
```

The *onReadStream()* function is used to synchronize the current speed factor with new players who join the game by way of the *setRotorSpeedFactor()* function. We will implement the latter function later in this section.

```
function RotateMower:onWriteStream(streamId, connection)
    local spec = self[RotateMower.SPEC_TABLE_NAME]
    RotateMower.streamWriteSpeedFactor(streamId, spec.
    rotorSpeedFactor)
end
```

Similarly, the *onWriteStream()* function is called on the server if a player joins the game to sync the speed factor. Let us continue through the file:

```
function RotateMower:onUpdateTick(dt, isActiveForInput,
                              isActiveForInputIgnoreSelection,
                              isSelected)
    if self.isClient then
        if self:getIsTurnedOn() then
            local spec = self[RotateMower.SPEC_
            TABLE_NAME]
            if spec.isEffectDirty then
                local scale = MathUtil.lerp(0.05, 1,
                self:getRotorSpeedScale())
                for _, effect in ipairs(spec.
                effects) do
                    ParticleUtil.
                    setEmitCountScale(effect.
                    particleSystem, scale + 2
                    * scale)
                    ParticleUtil.
                    setParticleSystemSpeed(effect.
                    particleSystem,
                        effect.defaultSpeed
                        * scale)
                end
                spec.isEffectDirty = false
            end
            local workArea = self:getWorkAreaByIndex(1)
            if workArea ~= nil and workArea.
            requiresGroundContact then
```

```
                        local hasGroundContact = workArea.
                        groundReferenceNode ~= nil and
                        workArea.groundReferenceNode.isActive
                        if hasGroundContact then
                                g_effectManager:
                                startEffects(spec.effects)
                        else
                                g_effectManager:stopEffects(spec.
                                effects)
                        end
                end
            end
        end
end
```

The first function of this section of the script is *onUpdateTick()*. This
function is used to make frequent checks regarding the mower's state
and changes that should occur as the mower operates. We first check if
the mower is *turned on* and that the *isEffectDirty* flag is true – if so, we
update the speed of the particles based on the current *rotorSpeedScale* and
either enable or disable the particle effects based on whether the mower
attachment is lowered. The value range for rotor speed scale is 0–1, but we
always want to spawn a few particles. So, if the speed scale is 0, we use the
MathUtil.lerp() function to bring the value to a new range (0.05 to 1). We
then use this scale value for particle speed and emit count.

```
function RotateMower:getRawSpeedLimit(superFunc)
      local speedLimit = superFunc(self)
      if self:getIsTurnedOn() and (self.getIsLowered == nil or
      self:getIsLowered()) then
            local scale = MathUtil.lerp(0.05, 1,
            self:getRotorSpeedScale())
```

```
        speedLimit = speedLimit * scale
    end
    return speedLimit
end
```

Next, the *getRawSpeedLimit()* function gets the current speed limit of the vehicle. This function is needed as we want the vehicle's maximum speed to change based on whether it is currently mowing. That is, if the mower attachment is not lowered, the maximum speed of the tractor should be set to its default value.

```
function RotateMower:doCheckSpeedLimit(superFunc)
    if self:getIsTurnedOn() and (self.getIsLowered == nil or
    self:getIsLowered()) then
        return true
    end
    return superFunc(self)
end
```

Finally, the *doCheckSpeedLimit()* function returns whether the speed limit should be checked; if the mower is on and the mower attachment is lowered, we want to check that the maximum speed has been limited. Let us continue:

```
function RotateMower:getRotorSpeedScale()
    local spec = self[RotateMower.SPEC_TABLE_NAME]
    return MathUtil.inverseLerp(RotateMower.MIN_SPEED_FACTOR,
            RotateMower.MAX_SPEED_FACTOR, spec.
            rotorSpeedFactor)
end
```

```
function RotateMower:getRotorSpeedFactor()
      local spec = self[RotateMower.SPEC_TABLE_NAME]
      return spec.rotorSpeedFactor
end

function RotateMower:setRotorSpeedFactor(factor, noEventSend)
      local spec = self[RotateMower.SPEC_TABLE_NAME]
      factor = MathUtil.clamp(factor,
      RotateMower.MIN_SPEED_FACTOR,
                RotateMower.MAX_SPEED_FACTOR)
      if math.abs(spec.rotorSpeedFactor - factor) > 0.0001 then
           spec.rotorSpeedFactor = factor
           spec.isEffectDirty = true
           RotorSpeedFactorEvent.sendEvent(self, factor,
           noEventSend)
           local actionEvent =
           spec.actionEvents[InputAction.CHANGE_ROTOR_SPEED]
           if actionEvent ~= nil then
                g_inputBinding:setActionEventText
                (actionEvent.actionEventId,
                     string.format(g_i18n:getText("input_
                     CHANGE_ROTOR_SPEED"),
                     self:getRotorSpeedFactor()*100 + 0.1))
           end
      end
end
```

The *getRotorSpeedFactor()* function similarly returns the value of the *rotorSpeedFactor* field. The *setRotorSpeedFactor()* function is critical as it ensures the passed factor value is constrained by the minimum and maximum value constants we defined at the beginning of the script.

We check if the set value is different to the old value with the *math. abs()* function and a subtraction. If so, it sets the new value of the *rotorSpeedFactor* field and sends the event that the factor has changed. Notably, we set the *isEffectDirty* field to true to force an update from *onUpdateTick()*.

Lastly, we update the custom text displayed to the user for the input action. Let us continue through more of the file's contents:

```
function RotateMower:processRotateMowerArea(workArea, dt)
    local startWorldX, _, startWorldZ =
    getWorldTranslation(workArea.start)
    local widthWorldX, _, widthWorldZ =
    getWorldTranslation(workArea.width)
    local heightWorldX, _, heightWorldZ =
    getWorldTranslation(workArea.height)
    FSDensityMapUtil.updateRotateMowerArea
                (startWorldX, startWorldZ,
                widthWorldX, widthWorldZ, heightWorldX,
                heightWorldZ)
    return 0, 0
end
```

The *processRotateMowerArea()* function is called when we need to mow an area of land. We are passed the work area which contains the needed *start, width,* and *height* .i3d nodes (transformGroups) for use with our density map utility. By calling the internal *getWorldTranslation()* function, we can translate these into the six values passed to the *updateRotateMowerArea()* function of *FSDensityMapUtilExtension.lua*. Once this function is called, we do not need to do anything further. The work area specialization does expect to receive information about the total area worked, but this is not returned to us by the function, so we can simply return 0 without issue.

```
function RotateMower:onTurnedOn()
    if self.isClient then
        local spec = self[RotateMower.SPEC_TABLE_NAME]
        g_animationManager:startAnimations
            (spec.animationNodes)
        g_effectManager:setFillType(spec.effects,
            FillType.UNKNOWN)
        g_effectManager:startEffects(spec.effects)
        g_soundManager:stopSamples(spec.samples)
        g_soundManager:playSample(spec.samples.start)
        g_soundManager:playSample(spec.samples.work, 0,
        spec.samples.start)
    end
end
```

Next, the *onTurnedOn()* function handles behavior for when the mower is turned on. By using the animation, effect, and sound managers, we begin playing the mower's animations, enable its effects, and start playing the appropriate sounds. We begin by playing the *start* sound and play the idle *work* sound immediately after. Note that the work sound call has two additional parameters: a value (0) and another sample (start). This means that the sound is played 0 ms after start has finished.

```
function RotateMower:onTurnedOff()
    if self.isClient then
        local spec = self[RotateMower.SPEC_TABLE_NAME]
        g_animationManager:stopAnimations
            (spec.animationNodes)
        g_effectManager:stopEffects(spec.effects)
        g_soundManager:stopSamples(spec.samples)
        g_soundManager:playSample(spec.samples.stop)
    end
end
```

When the mower is turned off, the onTurnedOff event is fired by the TurnOnVehicle specialization which calls the *onTurnedOff()* function. Here, we do the reverse of the previous function and use the managers to stop the animations, disable the effects, and play the *stop* sound.

Let us now cover the final section of the script:

```
function RotateMower:onRegisterActionEvents(isActiveForInput,
                isActiveForInputIgnoreSelection)
    if self.isClient then
        local spec = self[RotateMower.SPEC_TABLE_NAME]
        self:clearActionEventsTable(spec.actionEvents)
        if isActiveForInputIgnoreSelection then
            local _, actionEventId =
            self:addActionEvent(spec.actionEvents,
                    InputAction.CHANGE_ROTOR_
                    SPEED, self,
                    RotateMower.
                    actionEventChangeRotorSpeed,
                    false, true,
                    false, true, nil)
            g_inputBinding:setActionEventText
            (actionEventId,
                    string.format
                    (g_i18n:getText
                    ("input_CHANGE_ROTOR_SPEED"),
                self:getRotorSpeedFactor()*100 + 0.1))
            g_inputBinding:setActionEventTextPriority
            (actionEventId, GS_PRIO_HIGH)
        end
    end
end
```

The *onRegisterActionEvents()* function is called when the player enters the vehicle or connects or disconnects an attachment to the tractor. The purpose of the function is to set the current available or enabled input actions a user can trigger. In our case, we first clear the old registered action events and check if our input action is possible. For example, if the tool is not selected by the user, we do not want to register the input action. If it is selected, we call the *addActionEvent()* function of the Vehicle base class. The function takes as arguments our specialization *actionEvents* table that holds all registered inputActions for our specialization, the new input action (*InputAction.CHANGE_ROTOR_SPEED*), a callback target object (*self*), and a callback function *RotateMower. actionEventChangeRotorSpeed.*

The next three bool values define if the callback should be called *triggerUp*, *triggerDown*, or *triggerAlways*. The last bool value defines if the action should be enabled by default. The last parameter can be ignored for now, and so we simply pass nil.

Next, we set the text that should be displayed in the input help menu Head Up Display (HUD) and also set a priority of this input that is used to sort the registered input actions to display in this part of the HUD.

```
function RotateMower.actionEventChangeRotorSpeed(self,
actionName, inputValue, callbackState, isAnalog)
      local spec = self[RotateMower.SPEC_TABLE_NAME]
      local step = inputValue * RotateMower.STEP_SIZE
      local newFactor = spec.rotorSpeedFactor + step
      self:setRotorSpeedFactor(newFactor, false)
end
```

The *actionEventChangeRotorSpeed()* function is important as it updates the vehicle in response to player input. The function is passed the directional value associated with the player's input which is 1, 0, or −1 corresponding to increase, do nothing, and decrease. Depending on the bind input device, the *inputValue* can also be a float in ranging between −1 and 1. For example, if we bind a joystick axis to the input, we get analog input values. The function then calls upon *setRotorSpeedFactor()* to change the *speedFactor* field based on the input and by the amount specified by the *STEP_SIZE* constant we define at the beginning of the script.

```
function RotateMower.getDefaultSpeedLimit()
        return 20
end
```

The last function we will define is *getDefaultSpeedLimit()* which simply returns a default value for the speed limit when the mower is attached.

```
g_soundManager:registerModifierType(
        "ROTOR_RPM",
        RotateMower.getRotorSpeedScale
)
```

Finally, we register a new sound modifier with the sound manager so that the pitch or volume can be altered in response to changes in the RPM of the mower's rotor. In the XML config file, there is the rotateMower element. It contains a sound element with start, stop, and work children elements. There we use a modifier of type *ROTOR_RPM* to modify the pitch and volume of the sound. This line in the Lua code creates this modifier type.

You have now finished writing all of the .xml and .lua files and have completed your first complex mod! Take a moment to look at the progress you've made from when you started the book to where you are now. Where you may have had no programming knowledge before, you are now implementing behaviors and effects for full Farming Simulator mods. In the next section, we'll test the completed mod!

Testing the Mod

We will follow the testing procedure from the previous chapter. From the GIANTS Studio, you can run the game without debugging from the Debug application menu. After you begin a new game on the map of your choice, you should open the vehicle shop. Go to the Tools tab and select the Mowers category. You will find the rotate mower and be able to purchase it. Attach the mower to a tractor of your choice and turn it on and off and drive over a field or meadow. Don't forget to test the mod in multiplayer with your friends. To do this, include the mod files in a .zip file and send the .zip file to your friends. Note that mods in multiplayer need to be zip files, not folders!

Summary

In this chapter, you made your first complex mod which allows players to attach a mower to tractors and clear foliage from the map. You were introduced to the concept of density maps when we made extensions onto an existing utility for the first time. By saving the state of the mower, you also learned how to create persistence in the player's world. Importantly, you also learned how to add multiplayer support to your mod.

In the next chapter, we will be taking a step back and making a simpler mod. In this new mod, we will explore using AI and vehicles to add more life to your Farming Simulator world.

CHAPTER 7

Speed Trap Trailer Mod

Speed Trap Trailer Mod

This chapter will explore making a speed trap trailer which will detect and fine a vehicle exceeding the speed limit (see Figure 7-1). This will require you to learn methods for detecting vehicles, displaying certain effects with shaders, and deducting currency from a player's balance. Let's get started!

Figure 7-1. *Be aware, speeders will be fined!*

© GIANTS Software GmbH 2024
Z. Brumbaugh and M. Leithner, *Scripting Farming Simulator with Lua*,
https://doi.org/10.1007/979-8-8688-0060-3_7

Technical Requirements

Like the previous chapter, you will be working entirely in the GIANTS Editor and Studio and must meet the requirements mentioned in the "Technical Requirements" section of Chapter 2, "Getting Started with the GIANTS Editor." Make sure you are always using the most recent version of the GIANTS Editor. This will ensure that you are able to take advantage of any new features. You can find all the code and assets used in this chapter in the book's code repository on the GDN at the following link:

https://gdn.giants-software.com/lp/scriptingBook.php

Creating Mod Scripts

This section will explore all of the scripts necessary for this mod. We will start by looking at the .xml files and then cover the .Lua files. Please see the "Preparing the Mod Folder Structure" section of Chapter 5, "Making a Diner with a Rotating Sign," on how to set up a mod project and use the sample files provided on GDN.

Creating XML Files

We start by creating the *modDesc.xml* for the mod. As with the previous mods, we define a title, description, and icon along with other basic properties. Let us now look at its contents:

```xml
<?xml version="1.0" encoding="utf-8" standalone="no" ?>
<modDesc descVersion="72">
    <Author>GIANTS Software</author>
    <version>1.0.0.0</version>
    <multiplayer supported="true" />
    <title>
        <en>Sample Mod - Speed Trap Trailer</en>
    </title>
    <description>
        <en>A sample mod</en>
    </description>
    <iconFilename>icon_speedTrapTrailer.png</iconFilename>
    <extraSourceFiles>
        <sourceFile
            filename="scripts/events/SpeedTrapEvent.Lua"/>
    </extraSourceFiles>
    <specializations>
        <specialization name="speedTrap"
                className="SpeedTrap"
                filename="scripts/SpeedTrap.Lua" />
    </specializations>
    <vehicleTypes>
        <type name="speedTrapTrailer"
                parent="baseAttachable"
                filename="$dataS/scripts/vehicles/
                Vehicle.Lua">
            <specialization name="speedTrap" />
        </type>
    </vehicleTypes>
```

```
<storeItems>
    <storeItem
        xmlFilename="vehicle/speedTrapTrailer.xml"/>
</storeItems>
<l10n filenamePrefix="l10n/l10n" />
</modDesc>
```

In the *extraSourceFiles* field, we include *SpeedTrapEvent.Lua*, and in the *specialization* field, we include the *speedTrap* specialization which will use the *SpeedTrap.Lua* file we will cover in the next section. Through the *vehicleTypes* field, we add a new *speedTrapTrailer* vehicle type which uses our specialization and the functionality from the base Vehicle class.

Next, the *storeItems* field defines one or more placeables of the mod with the path of the .xml file for the item. Lastly, we use the l10n field to reference the folder containing the translation files for the mod.

Now we will define the configuration file for the trailer item itself, *speedTrapTrailer.xml*. Let us take a look at the file:

```
<?xml version="1.0" encoding="utf-8" standalone="no" ?>
<vehicle type="speedTrapTrailer" xmlns:xsi="http://www.
w3.org/2001/XMLSchema-instance" xsi:noNamespaceSchemaLoca
tion="https://validation.gdn.giants-software.com/xml/fs22/
vehicle.xsd">
    <annotation>
        Copyright (C) GIANTS Software GmbH, All Rights
        Reserved.
    </annotation>
    <storeData>
        <name>Speed Trap Trailer</name>
        <functions>
            <function>$l10n_function_speedTrapTrailer
            </function>
        </functions>
```

```
<image>vehicle/store_speedTrapTrailer.png</image>
<price>3500</price>
<lifetime>600</lifetime>
<rotation>0</rotation>
<brand>LIZARD</brand>
<category>misc</category>
<shopTranslationOffset>0 0.05 0
</shopTranslationOffset>
<shopRotationOffset>0 -1.102 0</shopRotationOffset>
<vertexBufferMemoryUsage>0
</vertexBufferMemoryUsage>
<indexBufferMemoryUsage>0</indexBufferMemoryUsage>
<textureMemoryUsage>0</textureMemoryUsage>
<instanceVertexBufferMemoryUsage>0
</instanceVertexBufferMemoryUsage>
<instanceIndexBufferMemoryUsage>0
</instanceIndexBufferMemoryUsage>
```

```
</storeData>
```

We start the file by defining a *storeData* field which holds the *price*, *brand*, and *description* of the item which will be displayed in the shop. This part of the file should be familiar, as we defined this same field and its elements in the "Creating XML Files" sections of Chapter 5, "Making a Diner with Rotating Element," and Chapter 6, "Rotating Mower Mod." Let us continue through the file:

```
<base>
<typeDesc>$l10n_typeDesc_speedTrapTrailer</typeDesc>
<filename>vehicle/speedTrapTrailer.i3d</filename>
<size width="2.2" height="2.5" length="4"
    lengthOffset="0.1" />
```

```
<components maxMass="1850">
     <component centerOfMass="0 0.45 0"
                    solverIterationCount="10" mass="306" />
</components>
<schemaOverlay attacherJointPosition="0 0"
name="IMPLEMENT" />
<mapHotspot type="TRAILER" />
</base>
```

The *base* field defines the base settings for the speed trap tool. In this field, we reference the path to the .i3d file containing the speed trap trailer, set a *size* which is used for determining the required store area when buying the tool, and make sure it shows on the in-game map as a trailer via the *mapHotspot* field. We additionally get the description of the trailer from the appropriate translation file. We will now continue through the file:

```
<wheels>
     <wheelConfigurations>
          <wheelConfiguration name="$l10n_configuration_
          valueDefault" price="0"
                    brand="MITAS" saveId="MITAS_DEFAULT">
               <wheels>
                    <wheel filename="$data/shared/wheels/
                    tires/mitas/FL02/6_R9.xml"
                              isLeft="true"
                              hasTireTracks="true"
                              hasParticles="true">
                         <physics tipOcclusionArea
                         GroupId="1" restLoad="0.13"
                              repr="wheelLeft"
                              forcePointRatio="0.15"
                              initialCompression="10"
```

```
                    suspTravel="0.05"
                    spring="21" damper="10"
                    yOffset="0.015"/>
            <innerRim filename="$data/shared/
            wheels/rims/rimsCar.i3d"
                    node="3|0" scale="0.28 0.32
                    0.32" offset="0.01"/>
        </wheel>
        <wheel filename="$data/shared/wheels/
        tires/mitas/FL02/6_R9.xml"
                    isLeft="false"
                    hasTireTracks="true"
                    hasParticles="true">
            <physics tipOcclusionAreaGroupId=
            "1" restLoad="0.13"
                    repr="wheelRight"
                    forcePointRatio="0.15"
                    initialCompression="10"
                    suspTravel="0.05"
                    spring="21" damper="10"
                    yOffset="0.015"/>
            <innerRim filename="$data/shared/
            wheels/rims/rimsCar.i3d"
                    node="3|1" scale="0.28 0.32
                    0.32" offset="0.01"/>
        </wheel>
        </wheels>
    </wheelConfiguration>
    </wheelConfigurations>
    <rimColor material="18">SHARED_SILVER</rimColor>
</wheels>
```

The *wheels* field contains information about the wheels of the trailer. It references the wheel components of the physical model and sets the relevant physics information. Let us now look at the next portion of the file:

```
<attachable>
    <inputAttacherJoints>
        <inputAttacherJoint node="attacherJoint"
        jointType="trailer" attacherHeight="0.48" />
    </inputAttacherJoints>
    <!-- support animation if trailer is detached -->
    <support animationName="moveSupport" />
    <brakeForce force="0.03" maxForce="0.15"
        maxForceMass="1850"/>
</attachable>
```

Like in previous attachable tools, we define the attachment point for the tool via an attachable field. We also include the moveSupport animation if the trailer is detached via the support field.

```
<animations>
    <animation name="moveSupport">
        <part node="supportFeet" startTime="0.35"
            endTime="0.70"
            startTrans="0.108 0.250 1"
            endTrans="0.108 0.110 1" />
    </animation>
</animations>
```

This *animation* is then defined in the *animations* field where we associate the *supportFeet* node of the model with the animation.

```
<ai>
    <allowTurnBackward value="false"/>
    <turningRadiusLimitation radius="8"/>
    <agentAttachment jointNode="attacherJoint"
        rotCenterWheelIndices="1 2"
        width="1.6" height="1.1" length="3.2"
        lengthOffset="0.55"/>
</ai>
```

Following this, the *ai* field configures behaviors for when the tool is being operated autonomously.

```
<foliageBending>
    <bendingNode minX="-0.8" maxX="0.8" minZ="-1.75"
        maxZ="0.85" yOffset="0.3" />
    <bendingNode minX="-0.15" maxX="0.15" minZ="0.85"
        maxZ="1.7" yOffset="0.3" />
</foliageBending>
```

The *foliageBending* field creates behavior for how foliage should bend when run over by the attachment.

```
<wearable wearDuration="480" workMultiplier="5"
    fieldMultiplier="2"/>
<washable dirtDuration="90" washDuration="1"
    workMultiplier="3" fieldMultiplier="2"/>
```

The *wearable* and *washable* fields are used for calculating repair costs and visual effects on the tool. More specifically, *wearDuration* and *dirtDuration* define the time it takes until the vehicle is completely dirty or worn. The *workMultiplier* and *fieldMultiplier* fields are factors that speed up this process. The *washDuration* field is the time it takes to fully clean the vehicle. The repair costs are based on the initial price, age, and the current wear factor. Let us continue through the file:

```
<speedTrap maxSpeedKmh="30" fine="1000" cooldownDuration="20">
     <raycast node="raycastNode" maxDistance="35"
          detectionRadius="2"
          numDetectionSamples="10"/>
     <flash node="flashNode" duration="0.15" />
     <sounds>
          <trap file="sounds/speedTrap.wav" innerRadius="5.0"
                    outerRadius="65.0"
                    fadeOut="0.1"
                    linkNode="speedTrapTrailer_main_
                    component1">
               <volume indoor="2" outdoor="4.1" />
               <pitch indoor="1.00" outdoor="1" />
               <lowpassGain indoor="0.50" outdoor="1.00" />
          </trap>
     </sounds>
</speedTrap>p>
```

In this section of the file, we define a custom XML element called
speedTrap. In this element, we declare custom attributes such as
maxSpeedKmh, *fine*, and *cooldownDuration*.

The *maxSpeedKmh* field defines the maximum speed permitted along
the road in kilometers per hour. The *fine* field is how much a violator
will be fined. The fine will not be paid to any user, simply deducted from
the violator's farm. The *cooldownDuration* field determines how much
time there is between a vehicle being able to be fined again. Inside the
speedTrap element, we include a *raycast* element. A **raycast** is a construct
used in many game engines in which a ray is a line in space with a start
point but no fixed endpoint. With raycasts, we can get information about
intersections with the ray, making them very useful for hit detection.
We define a maximum length for our raycast by defining *maxDistance*,
which is set to 35 meters. A ray does not have any width, so we define

detectionRadius to do some tricks internally to widen our hit detection. We then assign a flash effect to the *flashNode* on the tool. We also include sounds for the tool, which are defined via a sounds field like in previous chapters.

```
<i3dMappings>
    <i3dMapping id="speedTrapTrailer_main_component1"
        node="0>" />
    <i3dMapping id="speedTrapTrailer_vis" node="0>0" />
    <i3dMapping id="attacherJoint" node="0>0|0|0" />
    <i3dMapping id="supportFeet" node="0>0|0|1|0" />
    <i3dMapping id="supportCol" node="0>0|0|1|0|0" />
    <i3dMapping id="wheelLeft" node="0>0|1|0" />
    <i3dMapping id="wheelRight" node="0>0|1|1" />
    <i3dMapping id="raycastNode" node="0>0|2|0" />
    <i3dMapping id="flashNode" node="0>0|2|1" />
</i3dMappings>
</vehicle>
```

Finally, we define .i3d mappings via an *i3dMappings* element which references points on the tool model.

With speedTrapTrailer.xml now complete, we are ready to create the next file, *flashShader.xml*. This file contains code written in the High-Level Shader Language (HLSL) which interacts with the part of the engine responsible for graphics rendering. You are not expected to fully understand the code written here, but your knowledge of Lua should be helpful in being able to follow the general work being done by the code. Let us now explore the file's contents:

```
<?xml version="1.0" encoding="utf-8"?>
<CustomShader version="5">
    <Parameters>
```

```
            <Parameter name = "flashFactor"
                   target = "flashFactor" type = "float"
                   defaultValue = "1" minValue = "0.0"
                   maxValue = "1"/>
        </Parameters>
        <UvUsages/>
        <LodLevel startDistance="0">
            <CodeInjections>
                <CodeInjection position="CONFIG_DEFINES">
                    <![CDATA[
                    #if defined( ALPHA_BLENDED )
                    // only for alpha blended materials
                        #undef FOG_INSCATTERING
                        // only apply the fog extinction
                        #undef SPECULAR
                        // also remove specular
                    #endif
                    ]]>
                </CodeInjection>
                <CodeInjection position = "OBJECT_
                PARAMETERS">
                    <![CDATA[
                        float flashFactor;
                    ]]>
                </CodeInjection>
```

This first section starts by specifying the shader *parameters* that can be changed and set by the script. We include the parameter *flashFactor* which is a float value between 0 and 1 used to determine the light level of the flash. Following this, we use the *CodeInjections* field to inject two blocks of HLSL code into the shader. The first block in this case changes the base configurations of the shader, while the second block defines our custom variable. Let us continue:

```
<CodeInjection position="LIB_FUNCTION_VS">
    <![CDATA[
    float4x3 getBillboardMatrix( float3 centerPosition,
    VS_INPUT In,
        ObjectParameters& object )
    {
        float3 pos = mul(object.modelMatrix,
        float4(centerPosition, 1)).xyz;
        float3 negDirVector = normalize(pos);
        float3 upVector = float3(invViewMatrix[0][1],
            invViewMatrix[1][1],
            invViewMatrix[2][1]);
        float3 sideVector = normalize(cross(negDirVector,
        upVector));
        upVector = cross(sideVector, negDirVector);
        float4x3 billboardMatrix = float4x3(pos,
        sideVector, upVector, negDirVector);
        return billboardMatrix;
    }
    float3 transformBillboardPoint(float3 centerPosition,
    VS_INPUT In, ObjectParameters& object)
    {
        float4x3 billboardMatrix = getBillboardMatrix
        (centerPosition,In,object);
        float3 pos          = billboardMatrix[0];
        float3 sideVector   = billboardMatrix[1];
```

```
            float3 upVector     = billboardMatrix[2];
            float3 negDirVector = billboardMatrix[3];
            return (pos + sideVector*In.position.x +
                  upVector*In.position.y);
}
float3 transformBillboardVector(float3 centerPosition,
      float3 inputVector, VS_INPUT In, ObjectParameters& object)
{
      float4x3 billboardMatrix = getBillboardMatrix(
            centerPosition,In,object);
      float3 pos           = billboardMatrix[0];
      float3 sideVector    = billboardMatrix[1];
      float3 upVector      = billboardMatrix[2];
      float3 negDirVector = billboardMatrix[3];
      return (sideVector*inputVector.x +
            upVector*inputVector.y -
            negDirVector*inputVector.z);
}
]]>
</CodeInjection>
```

This section of the file injects additional HLSL code. Here, we define custom functions for the vertex shader which is responsible for manipulating the vertices of the mesh the material is applied to.

So you can assume that all these lines are applied on each single vertex. We need these functions to create a **billboard**. A billboard in computer games is a simple two-dimensional plane that always faces the player's camera. These helper functions are later used to recalculate the position, normal, and tangent of a vertex to face the player's camera.

We could alternatively rotate the physical mesh in Lua with the setRotation() function, but it is much faster creating this effect with a shader.

We will now cover the next section of the file:

```
<CodeInjection position="GET_TANGENT_VS">
    <![CDATA[
    {
        return transformBillboardVector(
        float3(0.0,0.0,0.0), In.tangent.xyz, In, object);
    }
    ]]>
</CodeInjection>
<CodeInjection position="GET_NORMAL_VS">
    <![CDATA[
    {
        return transformBillboardVector(
        float3(0.0,0.0,0.0), In.normal.xyz, In, object);
    }
    ]]>
</CodeInjection>
<CodeInjection position="GET_POSITION_VS">
    <![CDATA[
        return transformBillboardPoint(float3(0.0,0.0,0.0),
        In, object);
    ]]>
</CodeInjection>
<CodeInjection position="POST_GET_WORLD_POSE_VS">
    <![CDATA[
    {
        worldPosition = position;
        prevWorldPosition = worldPosition; // no motion blur
```

```
        worldTangent   = normalize(getTangent(In, object));
        worldBitangent = normalize(getBitangent(In, object));
        worldNormal    = normalize(getNormal(In, object));
    }
    ]]>
</CodeInjection>
```

This section of the file begins by injecting three lines which change the *tangent, normal,* and *position* in the vertex shader. It then injects code to customize some data after the vertex world data has been calculated in the vertex shader. Let us now look at the final section of the file:

```
<CodeInjection position="LIB_FUNCTION_FS">
    <![CDATA[
    float getDepthFade(FS_INPUT In, FS_GLOBALS globals,
    ObjectParameters& object, float fadeDistance)
    {
        float screenDepth = In.vs.screenPosZ / In.vs.
            screenPosW;
        float screenDepthLinear = convertDepthToEyeZ(
            screenDepth);
        float sceneDepthLinear = getLinearSceneDepth(In,
            globals,object);
        return saturate((sceneDepthLinear -
            screenDepthLinear)/fadeDistance);
    }
    ]]>
</CodeInjection>
<CodeInjection position="ALPHA_FS">
    <![CDATA[
    #if defined(ALPHA_BLENDED) || defined(ALPHA_TESTED)
```

```
        // increase emissive color, in order to enable
        // bloom post process
        float scaler = 5.0;
        // for low pec profile bloom post process is
        // disabled
        #if GPU_PROFILE < GPU_PROFILE_MEDIUM
              scaler = 1.0;
        #endif
        alpha *= scaler*object.flashFactor;
    #endif
    #if defined( ALPHA_BLENDED )
        // with high gpu profile add soft blending to
        // the contact
        // of the alpha blended mesh
        #if GPU_PROFILE >= GPU_PROFILE_HIGH
              alpha *= getDepthFade(In, globals,
              object,0.1);
        #endif
        reflectingLightingScale = alpha;
    #endif
    ]]>
</CodeInjection>
<CodeInjection position="FINAL_POS_FS">
    <![CDATA[
    #if defined(ALPHA_BLENDED)
        oColor.a = 0.0; // enable additive blending
    #endif
    ]]>
    </CodeInjection>
</CodeInjections>
</LodLevel>
</CustomShader>>
```

We conclude the file with additional injections. The first code injection defines custom functions in the fragment shader (see www.khronos. org/opengl/wiki/Fragment_Shader for more information). We then inject code to customize the alpha value in the fragment shader. Finally, we customize data at the end of the fragment shader with another code injection and close off the customShader element.

We have now covered the bulk of the .xml content for this mod. We must now include some simple translation files as we have for previous chapters so that players who speak different languages can interact with the mod more easily. Let us start with the contents of the English translation file, *l10n_en.xml*:

```xml
<?xml version="1.0" encoding="UTF-8" standalone="yes" ?>
<l10n>
    <elements>
        <e k="function_speedTrapTrailer"
            v="Speed Trap Trailer"/>
        <e k="typeDesc_speedTrapTrailer"
            v="Speed Trap Trailer"/>
    </elements>
</l10n>
```

In this file, we only include an element which holds text for the description and function of the tool in the shop. For both, we simply set the text to *Speed Trap Trailer*.

Let us now look at *l10n_de.xml* which will hold the same translations but for the German language:

```xml
<?xml version="1.0" encoding="UTF-8" standalone="yes" ?>
<l10n>
    <elements>
        <e k="function_speedTrapTrailer"
            v="Mobile Radar-Kontrolle"/>
```

```
    <e k="typeDesc_speedTrapTrailer"
         v="Radar-Kontrolle"/>
    </elements>
</l10n>
```

Like in the English file, we have two elements corresponding to the description and function of the tool for the shop. That concludes all of the .xml files needed for the mod. In the next section, we will explore the Lua files required for the mod.

Creating Lua Files

The first Lua file we will create is *SpeedTrapEvent.Lua*. Like in previous chapters, this script will implement some new behavior for the base Event class. Let us begin:

```
SpeedTrapEvent = {}
local SpeedTrapEvent_mt = Class(SpeedTrapEvent, Event)
InitEventClass(SpeedTrapEvent, "SpeedTrapEvent")
function SpeedTrapEvent.emptyNew()
    local self = Event.new(SpeedTrapEvent_mt)
    return self
end

function SpeedTrapEvent.new(vehicle)
    local self = SpeedTrapEvent.emptyNew()
    self.vehicle = vehicle
    return self
end

function SpeedTrapEvent:writeStream(streamId, connection)
    NetworkUtil.writeNodeObject(streamId, self.vehicle)
end
```

```
function SpeedTrapEvent:readStream(streamId, connection)
      self.vehicle = NetworkUtil.readNodeObject(streamId)
      self:run(connection)
end

function SpeedTrapEvent:run(connection)
      assert(connection:getIsServer(), "SpeedTrapEvent is
      server to client only")
      if self.vehicle ~= nil and
      self.vehicle:getIsSynchronized() then
            self.vehicle:activateSpeedTrapFlash()
      end
end
```

After creating a new event from the Event base class, we create two constructors with one that takes no arguments and one that takes a *vehicle*. If a *vehicle* is passed to the constructor, then that vehicle is assigned to the *vehicle* field of the class. We then define the *writeStream()* function and, like in previous chapters, it will write updates to the network stream. The *readStream()* function similarly reads updates from the network stream like in previous chapters. In our case, we only have to sync the speed trap trailer object that should activate its flash. Finally, the *run()* function executes the event. In our case, we require that the trap flash is activated locally only if the trailer is fully synchronized on the client side. If so, then the *activateSpeedTrapFlash()* function of the specialization we will define in *SpeedTrap.Lua* is called.

The SpeedTrap.Lua script defines our specialization and is the main Lua component of the mod. Let us start covering its contents:

```
local modName = g_currentModName
SpeedTrap = {}
SpeedTrap.SPEC_TABLE_NAME = "spec_"..modName..".speedTrap"
```

```
function SpeedTrap.prerequisitesPresent(specializations)
    return true
end

function SpeedTrap.registerEventListeners(vehicleType)
    SpecializationUtil.registerEventListener(vehicleType,
        "onLoad", SpeedTrap)
    SpecializationUtil.registerEventListener(vehicleType,
        "onDelete", SpeedTrap)
    SpecializationUtil.registerEventListener(vehicleType,
        "onUpdate", SpeedTrap)
end

function SpeedTrap.registerFunctions(vehicleType)
    SpecializationUtil.registerFunction(vehicleType,
        "activateSpeedTrapFlash",
        SpeedTrap.activateSpeedTrapFlash)
    SpecializationUtil.registerFunction(vehicleType,
        "onSpeedTrapRaycastCallback",
        SpeedTrap.onSpeedTrapRaycastCallback)
end
```

After defining the namespace for the mod, we include the default functions like in previous chapters. This mod has no prerequisites, so we simply return true in the *prerequisitesPresent()* function. Following this, we register the *onLoad()*, *onDelete()*, and *onUpdate()* base functions in the *registerEventListeners()* function. Lastly, we define two new functions in *registerFunctions()* called *activateSpeedTrapFlash()* and *onSpeedTrapRayc astCallback()*. We will define these functions later in this section.

Let us continue through the script:

```
function SpeedTrap.initSpecialization()
    local schema = Vehicle.xmlSchema
    schema:setXMLSpecializationType("SpeedTrap")
```

```
schema:register(XMLValueType.NODE_INDEX,
    "vehicle.speedTrap.raycast#node",
    "Raycast start node")
schema:register(XMLValueType.FLOAT,
    "vehicle.speedTrap.raycast#maxDistance",
    "Max. raycast distance")
schema:register(XMLValueType.INT,
    "vehicle.speedTrap.raycast#detectionRadius",
    "Detection sample radius at max raycast distance")
schema:register(XMLValueType.INT,
    "vehicle.speedTrap.raycast#numDetectionSamples",
    "Number of sample for detection")
schema:register(XMLValueType.FLOAT,
    "vehicle.speedTrap#maxSpeedKmh",
    "Max. speed in km/h")
schema:register(XMLValueType.FLOAT,
    "vehicle.speedTrap#fine", "The fine for speeding")
schema:register(XMLValueType.TIME,
    "vehicle.speedTrap#cooldownDuration",
    "Cooldown time in seconds")
schema:register(XMLValueType.NODE_INDEX,
    "vehicle.speedTrap.flash#node", "Flash node")
schema:register(XMLValueType.TIME,
    "vehicle.speedTrap.flash#duration",
    "Flash duration in seconds")
SoundManager.registerSampleXMLPaths(schema,
    "vehicle.speedTrap.sounds", "trap")
schema:setXMLSpecializationType()
end
```

The *initSpecialization()* function works like those implemented in previous chapters, registering all of the XML elements and attributes associated with our mod in the script. Additionally, we register the path to the sound for the tool. We will now continue:

```
function SpeedTrap:onLoad(savegame)
    local spec = self[SpeedTrap.SPEC_TABLE_NAME]
    if self.isServer then
        local rayKey = "vehicle.speedTrap.raycast"
        local node = self.xmlFile:getValue(rayKey ..
        "#node", nil, self.components, self.i3dMappings)
        if node ~= nil then
            spec.raycastNode = node
            spec.maxRaycastDistance =
                self.xmlFile:getValue(rayKey ..
                "#maxDistance", 25)
            spec.detectionRadius =
                self.xmlFile:getValue(rayKey ..
                "#detectionRadius", 2)
            spec.numDetectionSamples =
                self.xmlFile:getValue(rayKey ..
                "#numDetectionSamples", 10)
            spec.currentDetectionSample = 0
            spec.raycastCollisionMask = 2 ^ 13 -- bit 13
            -- identifies a vehicle
            spec.ignoredVehicles = {}
            spec.cooldownDuration =
                self.xmlFile:getValue("vehicle.
                speedTrap#cooldownDuration", 30)
```

```
                spec.maxSpeedKmh =
                     self.xmlFile:getValue("vehicle.
                     speedTrap#maxSpeedKmh", 20)
                spec.fine = self.xmlFile:getValue("vehicle.
                     speedTrap#fine", 500)
          else
                Logging.xmlWarning(self.xmlFile, "Trigger
                node missing for speed trap!")
          end
     end
     spec.flashDuration =
          self.xmlFile:getValue("vehicle.speedTrap.
          flash#duration", 0.5)
     spec.flashTimeRemaining = 0
     if self.isClient then
          spec.flashNode = self.xmlFile:getValue(
                "vehicle.speedTrap.flash#node", nil,
                self.components, self.i3dMappings)
          spec.samples = {}
          spec.samples.trap = g_soundManager:loadSample
          FromXML(self.xmlFile,
                "vehicle.speedTrap.sounds", "trap",
                self.baseDirectory,
                self.components, 1, AudioGroup.VEHICLE,
                self.i3dMappings, self)
     end
end
```

The *onLoad()* function also works like in previous chapters. For each field we need to define for the specialization, we get these values from the relevant XML files. We define the *raycastNode, maxRaycastDistance, detectionRadius, numDetectionSamples, currentDetectionSample,* and *raycastCollisionMask* fields for use with raycasting. Most of these fields were previously explained in the "Creating XML Files" section. Two newly defined fields are *raycastCollisionMask* and *currentDetectionSample*. The *currentDetectionSample* field keeps track of the sample we are currently collecting.

Because a raycast has no width, we shoot **numDetectionSamples + 1 raycasts** in a cone. The target of each raycast is determined using the *currentDetectionSample* field. The *raycastCollisionMask* defines a collision mask for detecting objects with the raycast. A collision mask is a **32-bit unsigned integer**. Two objects *collide* or *interact* if they have at least one matching bit. This concept is used for raycasts, collisions, and triggers. You can use the system to include or exclude objects from physical interaction. A similar system called *Object masks* is also used for rendering.

Next, we define *ignoredVehicles*, which holds a list of vehicles that have already been detected by the speed trap. Next, *cooldownDuration* is used to determine how much time must elapse before a vehicle can be removed from the *ignoredVehicles* list and be trapped again. As explained in the previous section, the *maxSpeedKmh* and *fine* fields determine the maximum allowed speed and the fine for speeding. The *flashDuration* field sets the duration of the flash on the tool. The *flashTimeRemaining* is used internally to track how much time there is remaining for the flash animation. If the specialization is being run on the client, then we include the *flashNode* field as well as a table for samples called samples. In the *samples* table, we also load the trap sound under the *trap* index. Let us now continue through the script:

```
function SpeedTrap:onDelete()
    local spec = self[SpeedTrap.SPEC_TABLE_NAME]
    if self.isClient then
        g_soundManager:deleteSamples(spec.samples)
    end
end
```

In the *onDelete()* function, we simply delete the recorded samples if we are on the client:

```
function SpeedTrap:onUpdate(dt, isActiveForInput,
        isActiveForInputIgnoreSelection, isSelected)
    local spec = self[SpeedTrap.SPEC_TABLE_NAME]
    if self.isServer and
            (self.getAttacherVehicle == nil or
            self:getAttacherVehicle() == nil) then
        for vehicle, lastTrappedTime in pairs(spec.
        ignoredVehicles) do
            if g_time - lastTrappedTime > spec.
            cooldownDuration then
                -- remove vehicle from ignore list again
                spec.ignoredVehicles[vehicle] = nil
            end
        end
    end
    local x, y, z = getWorldTranslation(spec.
    raycastNode)
    local tx = 0
    local ty = 0
    local tz = spec.maxRaycastDistance
    if spec.currentDetectionSample > 0 then
        local factor = spec.currentDetectionSample
        / spec.numDetectionSamples
        tx = spec.detectionRadius * math.cos(factor *
        2 * math.pi)
        ty = spec.detectionRadius * math.sin(factor *
        2 * math.pi)
    end
```

```
            tx, ty, tz = localToWorld(spec.raycastNode,
            tx, ty, tz)
            local dirX, dirY, dirZ = MathUtil.
            vector3Normalize(tx - x, ty - y, tz - z)
    raycastAll(x, y, z, dirX, dirY, dirZ,
            "onSpeedTrapRaycastCallback",
            spec.maxRaycastDistance, self, spec.
            raycastCollisionMask, false, true)
            spec.currentDetectionSample = spec.
            currentDetectionSample + 1
            if spec.currentDetectionSample > spec.
            numDetectionSamples then
                    spec.currentDetectionSample = 0
            end
    end
    if self.isClient then
            if spec.flashNode ~= nil and spec.
            flashTimeRemaining > 0 then
                    spec.flashTimeRemaining = math.max(spec.
                    flashTimeRemaining - dt, 0)
                    local factor = spec.flashTimeRemaining /
                    spec.flashDuration
                    local alpha = math.sin(factor * math.pi)
                    setShaderParameter(spec.flashNode,
                    "flashFactor", alpha, 0, 0, 0, false)
            end
    end

    self:raiseActive()
end
```

The *onUpdate()* function is responsible for frequent updates of our tool as well as raycasting. Client physics are not super accurate as they are interpolated based on the data received from the server. Therefore, we do vehicle detection on the server only and then send an event to the clients to show the flash animation if we detect speeding.

If the specialization is being run on the server and the tool is not attached to a vehicle, then we start by iterating over the *ignoredVehicles* list. If any of the vehicles have been in the list for longer than *cooldownDuration* value, then they are removed from the list so that they may be trapped again.

Next, we get the position of the *raycast node* and calculate the direction our raycast should go. We want the raycast to come out of the forward-facing direction of the raycast node. The direction is a 3D vector that is a unit vector, meaning its magnitude is 1. This is important as having a vector with a magnitude not equal to one can cause odd behavior for our raycast, particularly in the distance we want to cast.

We use sine and cosine functions to calculate the target point of the vector. If the *currentDetectionSample* field is greater than 0, the target point should be on a circle around the *raycastNode* with the given *detectionRadius*. After the vector is normalized, we shoot the raycast at the specified position, in the specified direction, for the distance set by *maxRaycastDistance*.

We then increment *currentDetectionSample* by 1 and reset it to 0 if it exceeds the *numDetectionSamples* value. Continuing through the function, if the specialization is being run on the client, we need to update the visual of the flash. We use the *flashTimeRemaining* field to record how far along in the animation we are, then using a sine wave, we can create an effect of the flash smoothly transitioning between off and on. After calculating the *flashFactor* for the flash, we set it via the internal *setShaderParameter()* function which passes the value to our custom shader.

Lastly, we call *raiseActive()* to call *onUpdate()* for the next cycle. Let us now cover the final section of the script:

```
function SpeedTrap:activateSpeedTrapFlash()
    local spec = self[SpeedTrap.SPEC_TABLE_NAME]
    g_soundManager:playSample(spec.samples.trap)
    spec.flashTimeRemaining = spec.flashDuration
end
```

In this section, we define our custom functions *activateSpeedTrapFlash()* and *onSpeedTrapRaycastCallback()*. The *activateSpeedTrapFlash()* function is called when a violating vehicle is detected. It simply plays the trap sound and sets the *flashTimeRemaining* field to *flashDuration* to begin a new flash animation.

```
function SpeedTrap:onSpeedTrapRaycastCallback(hitActorId, x, y,
z, distance, nx, ny, nz, subShapeIndex, shapeId, isLast)
    local spec = self[SpeedTrap.SPEC_TABLE_NAME]
    local vehicle =
    g_currentMission:getNodeObject(hitActorId)
    if vehicle ~= nil and spec.ignoredVehicles[vehicle] ==
    nil then
        local isActiveDrivable = vehicle.getIsControlled
        ~= nil and vehicle:getIsControlled()
        if isActiveDrivable then
            local speedKmh = vehicle:getLastSpeed()
            if speedKmh > spec.maxSpeedKmh then
                local farmId = vehicle:getOwnerFarmId()
                g_currentMission:addMoney(-spec.fine,
                farmId, MoneyType.OTHER, true, true)
```

```
                        spec.ignoredVehicles[vehicle] = g_time
                        g_server:broadcastEvent(SpeedTrapEvent.
                        new(self), true)
                   end
              end
         end
         return true
end
```

The *onSpeedTrapRaycastCallback()* function is passed the entity ID of a hit vehicle's collision shape. If the vehicle exists and is not contained in the *ignoredVehicles* list, then we check that the vehicle is *driveable* and being actively driven. If so, then we get the speed of the vehicle via the *getLastSpeed()* function. If the last speed of the vehicle exceeds the value of *maxSpeedKm*h, then we get the farm ID of the driver and remove the fine amount from their balance. We then add their vehicle to the *ignoredVehicles* list and broadcast the event to the network.

This concludes all of the programming for the mod. Take a moment to review what you have accomplished and the new concepts you have learned.

Testing the Mod

With all of the XML and Lua files for the mod created, we are ready to begin testing. Start by running the game without debugging from the Debug application menu of the GIANTS Studio. After you begin a new game on the map of your choice with your mod selected, buy the trailer and buy a tractor. Attach the trailer to the tractor and drive to a road. Place the trailer so its camera is facing oncoming traffic and detach it from the tractor. Next, drive your tractor at full speed toward the trap, and you should be fined for exceeding the speed limit.

Summary

In this chapter, you learned how to use raycasting to create a tool that gauges the speed of passing vehicles and charges a fine accordingly. You also saw how the mods can change rendering behavior by injecting HLSL code into the engine.

In the next chapter, you will learn to create a mileage counter to record how far a vehicle has been driven and sync these values with elements of a player's user interface.

205

CHAPTER 8

Mileage Counter HUD Mod

In this chapter, you will create a mod that displays a mileage counter user interface (UI) element to players when they are seated in a vehicle (see Figure 8-1). This will teach you to not only create UI elements and the networking that is required to update them but also how to add additional functionality to existing specializations and systems. Let us begin!

Figure 8-1. *Track your mileage with a UI element next to the speedometer*

© GIANTS Software GmbH 2024
Z. Brumbaugh and M. Leithner, *Scripting Farming Simulator with Lua*,
https://doi.org/10.1007/979-8-8688-0060-3_8

Technical Requirements

Like the previous chapter, you will be working entirely in the GIANTS Editor and Studio and must meet the requirements mentioned in the "Technical Requirements" section of Chapter 2, "Getting Started with the GIANTS Editor." Make sure you are always using the most recent version of the GIANTS Editor. This will ensure that you are able to take advantage of any new features. You can find all the code and assets used in this chapter in the book's code repository on the GDN at the following link:

https://gdn.giants-software.com/lp/scriptingBook.php

Creating Mod Scripts

This section will explore all of the scripts necessary for this mod. We will start by looking at the .xml files and then cover the .lua files. Please see the "Preparing the Mod Folder Structure" section of Chapter 5, "Making a Diner with a Rotating Sign," on how to set up a mod project and use the sample files provided on GDN.

Creating XML Files

We start by defining the *modDesc.xml* file for the mod. We do not introduce any new fields for the file in this mod, so you should be familiar with each of them. Let us now look at the contents of the file:

```xml
<?xml version="1.0" encoding="utf-8" standalone="no" ?>
<modDesc descVersion="72">
    <Author>GIANTS Software</author>
    <version>1.0.0.0</version>
    <multiplayer supported="true" />
    <title>
        <en>Sample Mod - Mileage Counter</en>
    </title>
    <description>
        <en>A sample mod</en>
    </description>
    <iconFilename>icon_mileageCounter.png</iconFilename>
    <extraSourceFiles>
        <sourceFile filename=
            "scripts/InjectSpecialization.lua"/>
        <sourceFile filename="scripts/MileageDisplay.lua"/>
        <sourceFile filename=
            "scripts/MileageHUDExtension.lua"/>
    </extraSourceFiles>
    <specializations>
        <specialization name="mileageCounter"
            className="MileageCounter"
            filename="scripts/MileageCounter.lua" />
    </specializations>
</modDesc>
```

In the *extraSourceFiles* field, we include *InjectSpecialization.lua,*
MileageDisplay.lua, and *MileageHUDExtension.lua.* These three files
are in the *scripts* subdirectory of the mod directory. In the specialization
field, we include the *mileageCounter* specialization which will use the
MileageCounter.lua file we will create in the next section.

Creating Lua Files

The first Lua file we will create is InjectSpecialization.lua. This script is used to add the mileage counter to vehicles that use the *driveable* specialization. Let us explore the file's contents:

```lua
local modName = g_currentModName

TypeManager.finalizeTypes = Utils.prependedFunction(
    TypeManager.finalizeTypes,
    function(self, ...)
        if self.typeName == "vehicle" then
            for typeName, typeEntry in
            pairs(self:getTypes()) do
                for name, _ in pairs(typeEntry.
                specializationsByName) do
                    if name == "motorized" then
                        self:addSpecialization(
                        typeName,
                        modName..".mileageCounter")
                        break
                    end
                end
            end
        end
    end
)
```

We start by prepending a new function to the *finalizeTypes()* function of the *TypeManager* class. To prepend a function to another function, is to have the function we are prepending be called first whenever the function we are prepending to is called. The function we are prepending takes self as an argument, which refers to an instance of some class. There are two

210

typeManagers in the game: one is responsible for placeable types and the other for vehicle types. We use *self.typeName* to identify the manager and ensure we are working with one of the vehicle type – that is, the object we are interacting with is a vehicle. If so, we will loop over all registered vehicle types by using the *getTypes()* method of self. For each vehicle type, we will check if it uses the *motorized* specialization. If the vehicle is motorized, then we will add the *mileageCounter* specialization to the vehicle via the *addSpecialization()* method.

Next, we will create *MileageCounter.lua.* This file is the core Lua script of the mod. Let us now cover its contents:

```
local modName = g_currentModName
MileageCounter = {}
MileageCounter.SPEC_TABLE_NAME = "spec_"..
modName..".mileageCounter"

function MileageCounter.prerequisitesPresent(specializations)
    return true
end

function MileageCounter.registerEventListeners(vehicleType)
    SpecializationUtil.registerEventListener(vehicleType,
        "onLoad", MileageCounter)
    SpecializationUtil.registerEventListener(vehicleType,
        "onReadStream", MileageCounter)
    SpecializationUtil.registerEventListener(vehicleType,
        "onWriteStream", MileageCounter)
    SpecializationUtil.registerEventListener(vehicleType,
        "onReadUpdateStream", MileageCounter)
    SpecializationUtil.registerEventListener(vehicleType,
        "onWriteUpdateStream", MileageCounter)
    SpecializationUtil.registerEventListener(vehicleType,
        "onUpdate", MileageCounter)
end
```

```
function MileageCounter.registerFunctions(vehicleType)
    SpecializationUtil.registerFunction(vehicleType,
        "getDrivenDistance", MileageCounter.
        getDrivenDistance)
end

function MileageCounter.initSpecialization()
    local schemaSavegame = Vehicle.xmlSchemaSavegame
    schemaSavegame:register(XMLValueType.FLOAT,
        "vehicles.vehicle(?).".. modName..".mileageCounter
        #drivenDistance",
        "Driven distance in meters")
end
```

Like in previous mods, there are some functions we must define for every specialization we create. After defining the namespace for the specialization, we include the *prerequisitesPresent()* function. This mod does not depend on any other specializations, so we only need to return true.

Next, we add the *registerEventListeners()* function which will create the event listeners associated with the *vehicle* specialization. In *registerFunctions()*, we register a custom *getDrivenDistance()* function, which we will define later in this file. Lastly, in the *initSpecialization()* function, we register the path to the saved value for the mileage counter.

For more details on required functions of specializations, refer to the "Creating Lua Files" section of Chapter 6, "Rotating Mower Mod," where we cover RotateMower.lua. We will now continue through the file:

```
function MileageCounter:onLoad(savegame)
    local spec = self[MileageCounter.SPEC_TABLE_NAME]
    spec.drivenDistance = 0
    if savegame ~= nil then
        spec.drivenDistance = savegame.xmlFile:getValue(
            savegame.key .. "."..modName..".mileageCounte
            r#drivenDistance", 0)
```

```
end
spec.drivenDistanceNetworkThreshold = 10
spec.drivenDistanceSent = spec.drivenDistance
spec.dirtyFlag = self:getNextDirtyFlag()
end
function MileageCounter:saveToXMLFile(xmlFile, key,
usedModNames)
    local spec = self[MileageCounter.SPEC_TABLE_NAME]
    xmlFile:setValue(key .. "#drivenDistance",
    spec.drivenDistance)
end
```

In the *onLoad()* function, we set the value for the *drivenDistance* field of the class. If the player is joining a game they have saved previously, then the *drivenDistance* field is set to the saved value; otherwise, it is set to 0. The *drivenDistanceNetworkThreshold* field specifies the distance the driven distance must change before a signal to update the distance display is sent to the client. In the HUD, we display the distance in kilometers with 100 meters of precision; thus, the threshold needs to be 10 meters because of rounding in the display. The *drivenDistanceSent* field records the value of *drivenDistance* when the counter was last updated and is used to determine whether an update should be sent to the client. Lastly, the *dirtyFlag* field is used by the network to determine if the specialization is in need of an update. Next, we create the *saveToXML()* function, which will save the value of *drivenDistance* to the saved .xml file.

```
function MileageCounter:onReadStream(streamId, connection)
    local spec = self[MileageCounter.SPEC_TABLE_NAME]
    spec.drivenDistance = streamReadInt32(streamId)
end

function MileageCounter:onWriteStream(streamId, connection)
    streamWriteInt32(streamId, spec.drivenDistance)
end
```

213

The *onReadStream()* function is used to synchronize the value of *drivenDistance* with new players that join the game. The *onWriteStream()* function is called on the server if a player joins the game to sync the *drivenDistance* value.

```
function MileageCounter:onReadUpdateStream(streamId, timestamp,
connection)
    if connection:getIsServer() then
        if streamReadBool(streamId) then
            local spec = self[MileageCounter.SPEC_
            TABLE_NAME]
            spec.drivenDistance = streamReadInt32(streamId)
        end
    end
end

function MileageCounter:onWriteUpdateStream(streamId,
connection, dirtyMask)
    if not connection:getIsServer() then
        local spec = self[MileageCounter.SPEC_TABLE_NAME]
        if streamWriteBool(streamId, bitAND(dirtyMask,
        spec.dirtyFlag) ~= 0) then
            streamWriteInt32(streamId,
            spec.drivenDistance)
        end
    end
end
```

The *onReadUpdateStream()* function is used by the client to read values written to the stream and update the *driveDistance* field accordingly. The *onWriteUpdateStream()* function is used by the server to tell the client the new value for the *drivenDistance* field only if the mileage counter has changed.

Let us now continue through the file:

```
function MileageCounter:onUpdate(dt, isActiveForInput,
        isActiveForInputIgnoreSelection, isSelected)
    local spec = self[MileageCounter.SPEC_TABLE_NAME]
    if self:getIsMotorStarted() then
        if self.isServer then
            if self.lastMovedDistance > 0.001 then
                spec.drivenDistance = spec.
                drivenDistance + self.lastMovedDistance
                if math.abs(spec.drivenDistance -
                spec.drivenDistanceSent) >
                spec.drivenDistanceNetworkThreshold then
                    self:raiseDirtyFlags(spec.
                    dirtyFlag)
                    spec.drivenDistanceSent = spec.
                    drivenDistance
                end
            end
        end
    end
end
```

The *onUpdate()* function will update the state of the mileage counter. We first check that the vehicle is turned on, and then if the vehicle has moved more than *0.001* meters, we increase the *drivenDistance* field by that distance. If the difference between the *drivenDistance* and *drivenDistanceSent* fields is greater than the *drivenDistanceNetworkThreshold* value, then the *dirtyFlag* is raised to mark the vehicle for a network update in the next network package. We also set *drivenDistanceSent* to *drivenDistance* so we do not send multiple updates.

Note that we have this system in place as sending an update signal whenever the vehicle moves in the slightest would be a waste of resources and risk overloading the network.

```
function MileageCounter:getDrivenDistance()
      -- first get the specialization namespace
      local spec = self[MileageCounter.SPEC_TABLE_NAME]
      return spec.drivenDistance
end
```

Finally, the *getDrivenDistance()* function simply returns the value of the *drivenDistance* field.

The next script we will create is *MileageDisplay.lua*. This script is responsible for creating and managing the actual HUD UI element which will display the driven distance to the player. Let us now look at the script:

```
local modDirectory = g_currentModDirectory
MileageDisplay = {}

local MileageDisplay_mt = Class(MileageDisplay,
HUDDisplayElement)

function MileageDisplay.new()
      local backgroundOverlay = MileageDisplay.
      createBackground()
      local self = MileageDisplay:superClass().
            new(backgroundOverlay,
            nil, MileageDisplay_mt)
      self.vehicle = nil
      self:applyValues(1)
      return self
end
```

We begin by creating the constructor for the class, *MileageDisplay.
new()*. The constructor will create a background element, create a
HUDDisplayElement from the background, and apply a default UI scale
value of 1. We create the background by calling the *createBackground()*
function, which we will define later in the script.

```
function MileageDisplay:setVehicle(vehicle)
    if vehicle ~= nil and
    vehicle.getDrivenDistance == nil then
        vehicle = nil
    end

    self.vehicle = vehicle
end
```

Next, the *setVehicle()* function will set the *vehicle* field of the class to the
passed vehicle reference.

```
function MileageDisplay:draw()
    if self.vehicle == nil then
        return
    end
    MileageDisplay:superClass().draw(self)
    local drivenDistance = self.vehicle:getDrivenDistance()
    local distanceInKM = drivenDistance / 1000
    distanceInKM = distanceInKM % 999999.9
    local distance = g_i18n:getDistance(distanceInKM)
    local unit = g_i18n:getMeasuringUnit()
    local textBG = string.format("%08.1f %s", distance, unit)
    local text = string.format("%.1f %s", distance, unit)
    local textColor = MileageDisplay.COLOR.TEXT
    local textColorBG = MileageDisplay.COLOR.TEXT_BACKGROUND
    local textSize = self.textSize
    local posX, posY = self:getPosition()
```

```
posX = posX + self.textOffsetX
posY = posY + self.textOffsetY
setTextBold(false)
setTextAlignment(RenderText.ALIGN_RIGHT)
setTextColor(textColorBG[1], textColorBG[2],
        textColorBG[3], textColorBG[4])
renderText(posX, posY, textSize, textBG)
setTextColor(textColor[1], textColor[2], textColor[3],
        textColor[4])
renderText(posX, posY, textSize, text)
setTextAlignment(RenderText.ALIGN_LEFT)
setTextColor(1, 1, 1, 1)
end
```

The *draw()* method is used to "draw" the mileage display. That is, this function will render the UI element and set its contents such as text. After rendering the element via the *draw()* function of the overlay's superclass, we retrieve the *drivenDistance* value via the *getDrivenDistance()* function we defined earlier. The *drivenDistance* value is in meters, and we want the mileage counter to display in kilometers, so we must simply divide by 1000. The largest value we want to display on the mileage counter is 999999.9, so using a modulo operation, it will flip over back to 0 just like a real-life odometer!

Because not everyone in the world uses the metric system, we will use the il8n utility to convert the value to the appropriate unit of kilometers or miles and get the corresponding abbreviations (km or mi).

Next, we format these values in a string before updating the element's text. Now we have all of the information to render on the screen.

We first calculate the x and y positions on the screen. We then disable the bold text rendering mode with *setTextBold(false)*. Our mileage counter display should be right aligned, so we set the global text rendering alignment to *RenderText.ALIGN_RIGHT*. Before rendering, we set the correct text color for the background text.

We can now render the background text. The text is used to always show eight digits. So, if our mileage counter is 100 miles, we render the text with five leading zeros. After rendering the background, we need to set the text color for the foreground and render the text.

Finally, we need to reset our changes to the global text rendering (alignment, color) to make sure that our changes do not affect other text rendering scripts. Let us continue through the program:

```
function MileageDisplay:setScale(uiScale)
    MileageDisplay:superClass().setScale(self, uiScale,
    uiScale)
    local posX, posY =
        MileageDisplay.getBackgroundPosition(uiScale)
    self:setPosition(posX, posY)
    self:applyValues(uiScale)
end

function MileageDisplay:applyValues(uiScale)
    local textOffsetX, textOffsetY =
        getNormalizedScreenValues(unpack(MileageDisplay.
        POSITION.TEXT_OFFSET))
    local _, textSize = getNormalizedScreenValues(0,
        MileageDisplay.SIZE.TEXT)
    self.textOffsetX = textOffsetX*uiScale
    self.textOffsetY = textOffsetY*uiScale
    self.textSize = textSize*uiScale
end
```

The *setScale()* method will scale the mileage counter element as a whole and adjust its position to fit different screens and devices. This function then calls *applyValues()* which will adjust the *scale* and *offset* of the text element within the background.

```
function MileageDisplay.getBackgroundPosition(uiScale)
    local width, _ = getNormalizedScreenValues(unpack(Mileage
        Display.SIZE.SELF))
    local offsetX, offsetY =
        getNormalizedScreenValues(unpack(MileageDisplay.
        POSITION.OFFSET))
    local posX = 1 - width*uiScale + offsetX*uiScale
    local posY = offsetY*uiScale

    return posX, posY
end
```

Next, we include the *getBackgroundPosition()* function which will return the absolute position of the mileage counter element in pixels. Note that it accounts for the current *uiScale* value.

```
function MileageDisplay.createBackground()
    local posX, posY =
        MileageDisplay.getBackgroundPosition(1)
    local width, height =
        getNormalizedScreenValues(unpack(MileageDisplay.
        SIZE.SELF))
    local filename = Utils.getFilename(
        "hud/mileageCounterBackground.png",
        modDirectory)
    local overlay = Overlay.new(filename, posX, posY,
        width, height)

    return overlay
end

MileageDisplay.SIZE = {
    SELF = {128, 32},
    TEXT = 17
}
```

```
MileageDisplay.POSITION = {
     OFFSET = {-35, 280},
     TEXT_OFFSET = {115, 10}
}

MileageDisplay.COLOR = {
     TEXT = {1, 1, 1, 1},
     TEXT_BACKGROUND = {0.15, 0.15, 0.15, 1}
}
```

The last function we define is *createBackground()* which uses the background image in the *hud* subdirectory of our mod and creates a new overlay instance, which it then returns.

Finally, we set an initial size, position, and color for the text background and text element.

The last script is *MileageHUDExtension.lua*. This program will add our mileage display UI element to the game's interface. Let us look at its contents:

```
HUD.createDisplayComponents =
     Utils.appendedFunction(HUD.createDisplayComponents,
     function(self, uiScale)
          self.mileageDisplay = MileageDisplay.new()
          self.mileageDisplay:setScale(uiScale)
          table.insert(self.displayComponents, self.
          mileageDisplay)
     end)

HUD.drawControlledEntityHUD =
     Utils.appendedFunction(HUD.drawControlledEntityHUD,
     function(self)
          if self.isVisible then
               self.mileageDisplay:draw()
          end
```

```
        end)

HUD.setControlledVehicle = Utils.appendedFunction(
    HUD.setControlledVehicle,
    function(self, vehicle)
          self.mileageDisplay:setVehicle(vehicle)
    end)
```

In this script, we append three new functions to existing internal HUD system functions. The first we define is appended to the *createDisplayComponents()* function of the HUD. In the new function, we call the constructor for the mileage display, set its scale to the current *uiScale* value, and insert the display into the UI components currently displayed.

Next, we append a function onto the *drawControlledEntityHUD()* function of the HUD. This function is responsible for drawing HUD elements, and the function we append will call the *draw()* function we defined earlier for the mileage counter.

Lastly, we append a new function to the *setControlledVehicle()* function of the HUD. As the name implies, this function is used to associate a vehicle with a HUD element. The function we append will call the *setVehicle()* function of the mileage counter we defined earlier, passing along the vehicle reference.

You have now finished creating all of the scripts for the mod. You should take some time to do a high-level review of everything we have implemented in this chapter and what you have learned from it.

Testing the Mod

We will follow the testing procedure from the previous chapter. From the GIANTS Studio, you can run the game without debugging from the Debug application menu. After you begin a new game on the map of your choice, you should open the vehicle shop. After spawning any motorized vehicle, sit in it, and you should see the mileage counter displayed to you. If everything is working, the mileage reading should increase as you drive and be displayed in the units of your preference.

Summary

In this chapter, you created a mileage counter that displays the distance that has been driven by a motorized vehicle to players. This mod taught you how to create UI elements and have them use existing systems as well as injecting additional functionality into existing specializations.

In the next chapter, you will work on another UI-oriented mod where players will be able to spawn bales of different shapes and types.

CHAPTER 9

Multibale Spawner Mod

In this chapter, we will be creating a mod that allows players to spawn bales of shapes and types specified by the player (see Figure 9-1). You will work to tie GUI elements into your Lua programs to create new objects the player can interact with on their farm. Let's jump into it!

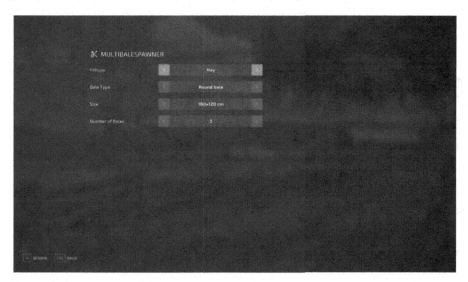

Figure 9-1. *Spawn bales through a new GUI menu*

© GIANTS Software GmbH 2024
Z. Brumbaugh and M. Leithner, *Scripting Farming Simulator with Lua*,
https://doi.org/10.1007/979-8-8688-0060-3_9

Technical Requirements

Like the previous chapter, you will be working entirely in the GIANTS Editor and Studio and must meet the requirements mentioned in the "Technical Requirements" section of Chapter 2, "Getting Started with the GIANTS Editor." Make sure you are always using the most recent version of the GIANTS Editor. This will ensure that you are able to take advantage of any new features. You can find all the code and assets used in this chapter in the book's code repository on the GDN at the following link:

https://gdn.giants-software.com/lp/scriptingBook.php

Creating Mod Scripts

This section will explore all of the scripts necessary for this mod. We will start by looking at the .xml files and then cover the .lua files. Please see the "Preparing the Mod Folder Structure" section of Chapter 5, "Making a Diner with a Rotating Sign," on how to set up a mod project and use the sample files provided on GDN.

Creating XML Files

The first step of making our mod is creating the modDesc.xml file. Let us now cover its contents:

```xml
<?xml version="1.0" encoding="utf-8" standalone="no" ?>
<modDesc descVersion="72">
    <Author>GIANTS Software</author>
    <version>1.0.0.0</version>
    <multiplayer supported="true" />
    <title>
        <en>Sample Mod - Multi Bale Spawner</en>
    </title>
    <description>
        <en>A sample mod</en>
    </description>
    <iconFilename>icon_multiBaleSpawner.png</iconFilename>
    <extraSourceFiles>
        <sourceFile
            filename="scripts/AdditionalGuiProfiles.lua"/>
        <sourceFile
            filename="scripts/MultiBaleSpawnerUtil.lua"/>
        <sourceFile
            filename="scripts/MultiBaleSpawnerScreen.lua"/>
        <sourceFile
            filename="scripts/events/MultiBaleSpawner
            Event.lua"/>
        <sourceFile
            filename="scripts/PlayerExtension.lua"/>
    </extraSourceFiles>
    <actions>
        <action name="OPEN_MULTI_BALE_SPAWNER"
            axisType="HALF" />
    </actions>
```

```
<inputBinding>
    <actionBinding action="OPEN_MULTI_BALE_SPAWNER">
        <binding device="KB_MOUSE_DEFAULT"
                input="KEY_b" />
    </actionBinding>
</inputBinding>
<l10n filenamePrefix="l10n/l10n" />
</modDesc>
```

After defining the basic information about our mod, we include five source files in the *extraSourceFiles* field. These scripts will be created in the following "Creating Lua Files" section.

We also define a new action in the actions field called *OPEN_MULTI_BALE_SPAWNER* and mark it as a *HALF* axis. This action will be used by the player to open the GUI menu they will use to make selections and spawn bales. Then, via the *inputBinding* field, we bind the event to the *B key* on the keyboard.

Lastly, we create a reference for translation files in the l10n field.

The next file we need to create is guiProfiles.xml. The purpose of the file is to define the appearance of the GUI menu. Let us now look at its contents:

```
<?xml version="1.0" encoding="utf-8" standalone="no" ?>
<GUIProfiles>
    <Profile name="baleSpawnerBox" extends="baseReference"
                with="anchorTopCenter">
        <Value name="imageColor" value="0 0 0 0" />
        <Value name="size" value="1258px 698px"/>
        <Value name="position" value="0px 0px"/>
        <Value name="fitFlowToElements" value="true"/>
        <Value name="flowDirection" value="vertical" />
    </Profile>
```

```
<Profile name="baleIcon" extends="baseIcon">
     <Value name="imageUVs"
          value="384px 96px 48px 48px" />
</Profile>
<Profile name="multiTextOptionBaleSpawner"
          extends="multiTextOption">
     <Value name="margin" value="0 12px 0 12px"/>
     <Value name="size" value="1258px 48px"/>
</Profile>

<Profile name="multiTextOptionLeftBaleSpawner"
          extends="multiTextOptionLeft"
          with="anchorMiddleLeft">
     <Value name="position" value="300px 0px" />
</Profile>
<Profile name="multiTextOptionRightBaleSpawner"
          extends="multiTextOptionRight"
          with="anchorMiddleLeft">
     <Value name="position" value="700px 0" />
</Profile>
<Profile name="multiTextOptionTextBaleSpawner"
          extends="multiTextOptionText"
          with="anchorMiddleLeft">
     <Value name="position" value="350px 0px" />
     <Value name="size" value="350px 48px"/>
     <Value name="textSize" value="20px"/>
     <Value name="textMaxWidth" value="340px" />
     <Value name="textAlignment" value="center"/>
</Profile>
```

```
<Profile name="multiTextOptionBgBaleSpawner"
         extends="multiTextOptionBg"
         with="anchorMiddleLeft">
    <Value name="size" value="352px 48px" />
    <Value name="position" value="348px 0" />
</Profile>
<Profile name="multiTextOptionTitleBaleSpawner"
         extends="textDefault"
         with="anchorMiddleLeft">
    <Value name="textSize" value="20px" />
    <Value name="textMaxWidth" value="400px" />
    <Value name="size" value="0 48px" />
    <Value name="textMaxNumLines" value="2" />
    <Value name="textVerticalAlignment"
           value="middle" />
    <Value name="textAutoWidth" value="true" />
</Profile>
</GUIProfiles>
```

The file consists of a *GUIProfiles* element. The *profile* elements are used to define some basic settings of the GUI element. Functionally, they are similar to CSS in web development. The **GUI's xml file defines the structure**, and the **profiles define the look and feel of the UI**.

Some elements of this GUI make use of *predefined profiles* used already in the base game. Some other elements use custom styles – these styles are defined by this file.

GUIProfiles also support inheritance and traits so we can easily reuse existing profiles from the base game and only change a few configurations relating to their style for use with our mod.

You should be made aware that some traits like *anchorMiddleLeft* or *anchorTopCenter* are used in the with attribute. They simply define the alignment of the objects within the parent space. Most of the other fields and attributes for the profiles are intuitive.

Let us now cover the contents of *multiBaleSpawnerScreen.xml*:

```xml
<?xml version="1.0" encoding="utf-8" standalone="no" ?>
<GUI onOpen="onOpen" onClose="onClose" onCreate="onCreate">
    <GuiElement type="dynamicFadedBitmap"
        profile="uiFullBlurBG"/>
    <GuiElement type="bitmap" profile="bgVignette"/>
    <GuiElement type="bitmap" profile="bgGlow" />
    <GuiElement type="bitmap"
        profile="uiElementContainerFullScreen">
        <GuiElement type="bitmap"
        profile="uiElementCenter">
            <GuiElement type="bitmap"
            profile="headerBoxDocked" >
                <GuiElement type="bitmap"
                profile="baleIcon"/>
                <GuiElement
                type="text"    profile="headerText"
                    text="$l10n_multiBaleSpawner_ui_
                    title"/>
            </GuiElement>
            <GuiElement type="boxLayout"
            profile="baleSpawnerBox">
            <GuiElement type="multiTextOption"
                    profile="multiTextOptionBale
                    Spawner" onClick="onClickFillType"
                    id="fillTypes" focusInit="onOpen">
                <GuiElement type="button" profile=
                "multiTextOptionLeftBaleSpawner" />
```

```xml
            <GuiElement type="button" profile=
            "multiTextOptionRightBaleSpawner"/>
            <GuiElement type="text"    profile=
            "multiTextOptionTextBaleSpawner" />
            <GuiElement type="text"    profile=
            "multiTextOptionTitleBaleSpawner"
                text="$l10n_multiBaleSpawner_ui_
                fillType"/>
            <GuiElement type="bitmap" profile=
            "multiTextOptionBgBaleSpawner" />
        </GuiElement>
        <GuiElement type="multiTextOption" profile=
        "multiTextOptionBaleSpawner"
                onClick="onClickBaleType"
                id="baleTypes">
            <GuiElement type="button" profile=
            "multiTextOptionLeftBaleSpawner" />
            <GuiElement type="button" profile=
            "multiTextOptionRightBaleSpawner"/>
            <GuiElement type="text"    profile=
            "multiTextOptionTextBaleSpawner" />
            <GuiElement type="text"    profile=
            "multiTextOptionTitleBaleSpawner"
                text="$l10n_multiBaleSpawner_ui_
                baleType"/>
            <GuiElement type="bitmap" profile=
            "multiTextOptionBgBaleSpawner" />
        </GuiElement>
        <GuiElement type="multiTextOption" profile=
        "multiTextOptionBaleSpawner"
                id="baleSizes">
```

```
    <GuiElement type="button" profile=
    "multiTextOptionLeftBaleSpawner" />
    <GuiElement type="button"
    profile="multiTextOptionRight
    BaleSpawner"/>
    <GuiElement type="text"    profile=
    "multiTextOptionTextBaleSpawner" />
    <GuiElement type="text"    profile=
    "multiTextOptionTitleBaleSpawner"
        text="$l10n_multiBaleSpawner_ui_
        baleSize"/>
    <GuiElement type="bitmap" profile=
    "multiTextOptionBgBaleSpawner" />
</GuiElement>
<GuiElement type="multiTextOption" profile=
"multiTextOptionBaleSpawner"
    id="numBales">

    <GuiElement type="button" profile=
    "multiTextOptionLeftBaleSpawner" />
    <GuiElement type="button" profile=
    "multiTextOptionRightBaleSpawner"/>
    <GuiElement type="text"    profile=
    "multiTextOptionTextBaleSpawner" />
    <GuiElement type="text"    profile=
    "multiTextOptionTitleBaleSpawner"
        text="$l10n_multiBaleSpawner_ui_
        numBales"/>
    <GuiElement type="bitmap" profile=
    "multiTextOptionBgBaleSpawner" />
</GuiElement>
</GuiElement>
```

```
        </GuiElement>
</GuiElement>
<GuiElement type="flowLayout" profile="buttonBoxDockedOnScreen">
        <GuiElement type="button" profile="buttonOK"
            text="$l10n_multiBaleSpawner_ui_spawn_button"
            onClick="onClickOk" />
        <GuiElement type="button" profile="buttonBack"
        text="$l10n_button_back"
            onClick="onClickBack" />
</GuiElement>
</GUI>
```

This file is for managing multiple *GuiElement* fields within our mod. The most common elements include **button, slider, text, textInput, bitmap, multiTextOption, checkedOption, smoothList, listItem, boxLayout, flowLayout**, and **scrollingLayout**.

Each of these elements can be customized or stylized using XML syntax or by using profiles. The GUI layout is done in **full HD** (1920 x 1080px). When the game is loaded, the GUI elements are rescaled and repositioned to adjust for the player's game resolution.

We use background elements from the base game to get the class Farming Simulator 2022 look. Then, we create a container that centers the GUI and optimizes it for full HD screens with a 16:9 aspect ratio. In the *container*, we include a header that holds an *icon* and *text* label element.

Next, we include a *boxLayout* element which automatically adjusts the positions of its child elements. Inside of this layout, we include *multiTextOption* elements. These elements are similar to a dropdown menu in other UI frameworks but include a left or right toggle. We define these *multiTextOption* elements for the *baleType*, *fillType*, and *numBales* selections. The id attribute is later used in the code to access the element and set or get its associated values.

Lastly, we include a button at the bottom to close the menu and spawn the bales with the current selections.

Now we will define translation files for text we want to display to the user. We will start by defining *l10n_en.xml* which is the file for English. Let us look at its contents:

```
<?xml version="1.0" encoding="UTF-8" standalone="yes" ?>
<l10n>
    <elements>
        <e k="input_OPEN_MULTI_BALE_SPAWNER"
            v="Open MultiBaleSpawner"/>
        <e k="multiBaleSpawner_ui_baleType" v="Bale Type"/>
        <e k="multiBaleSpawner_ui_numBales"
            v="Number of Bales"/>
        <e k="multiBaleSpawner_ui_title"
            v="MultiBaleSpawner"/>
        <e k="multiBaleSpawner_ui_spawn_button" v="Spawn"/>
        <e k="multiBaleSpawner_ui_fillType" v="Filltype"/>
        <e k="multiBaleSpawner_ui_baleSize" v="Size"/>
    </elements>
</l10n>
```

We see that we define seven text elements in the file. The first is for the custom *OPEN_MULTI_BALE_SPAWNER* action we defined earlier and will show *Open* to the player. Next, when the bale types are shown to the user, we will want to display *Bale Type* at the beginning of the list. For the number of bales to be spawned, we want to display *Number of Bales*. Next, for the title of the mod, we include *MultiBaleSpawner*. For the spawn button, we want it to read as *Spawn*. For the fill type, which determines the type of bale (straw, hay, cotton, etc.), we set the text to *Filltype*. Lastly, for bale size we display *Size* to the user.

To provide a better experience to players who speak other languages, we will provide translations. In this case, we will provide a translation into German in *l10n_de.xml*:

```
<?xml version="1.0" encoding="UTF-8" standalone="yes" ?>
<l10n>
    <elements>
        <e k="input_OPEN_MULTI_BALE_SPAWNER"
            v="MultiBaleSpawner öffnen"/>
        <e k="multiBaleSpawner_ui_baleType"
            v="Ballen Typ"/>
        <e k="multiBaleSpawner_ui_numBales"
            v="Anzahl der Ballen"/>
        <e k="multiBaleSpawner_ui_title"
            v="MultiBaleSpawner"/>
        <e k="multiBaleSpawner_ui_spawn_button"
            v="Erzeugen"/>
        <e k="multiBaleSpawner_ui_fillType" v="Fruchttyp"/>
        <e k="multiBaleSpawner_ui_baleSize" v="Größe"/>
    </elements>
</l10n>
```

Like previous chapters, we provide the same keys for each element but a different text value in the language associated with the file.

In the next section, we will create the .lua files needed for the mod.

Creating Lua Files

The first Lua file we will create is *MultiBaleSpawnerUtil.lua*. This program serves as a helper for spawning bales at a given position. Let us look at the file:

```
MultiBaleSpawnerUtil = {}
MultiBaleSpawnerUtil.MAX_NUM_BALES = 4
MultiBaleSpawnerUtil.SEND_NUM_BITS = 3

function MultiBaleSpawnerUtil.spawnBales(baleTypeIndex,
fillTypeIndex, numBales, x, y, z, dirX, dirZ, farmId)
    -- bale creation is only allowed on server and afterwards
    -- synched to the client
    if not g_currentMission:getIsServer() then
        Logging.error("This is function is only allowed on
        server!")
        return
    end
    local baleInfo = g_baleManager.bales[baleTypeIndex]
    if baleInfo == nil then
        Logging.error("Could not find bale info for
        baleTypeIndex '%s'", tostring(baleTypeIndex))
        return
    end
    local baleToBaleOffset = 0.2
    local yOffset = baleInfo.height * 0.5
    local zOffset = baleInfo.length
    if baleInfo.isRoundbale then
        yOffset = baleInfo.diameter * 0.5
        zOffset = baleInfo.width
    end
    local ry = MathUtil.getYRotationFromDirection(dirX, dirZ)
    x = x + dirX * zOffset*0.5
    z = z + dirZ * zOffset*0.5
    for i=1, numBales do
```

```
        local baleObject = Bale.new(
            g_currentMission:getIsServer(),
            g_currentMission:getIsClient())
    y = math.max(y,
            getTerrainHeightAtWorldPos(g_currentMission.
            terrainRootNode, x, y, z) +
            yOffset)
    if baleObject:loadFromConfigXML(
            baleInfo.xmlFilename, x, y, z, 0, ry, 0) then
            baleObject:setFillType(fillTypeIndex, true)
            baleObject:setWrappingState(0)
            baleObject:setOwnerFarmId(farmId, true)
            baleObject:register()
            x = x + dirX * (zOffset + baleToBaleOffset)
            z = z + dirZ * (zOffset + baleToBaleOffset)
    else
            baleObject:delete()
    end
    end
end
```

We first define two fields, *MAX_NUM_BALES* and *SEND_NUM_
BITS*. The *MAX_NUM_BALES* field determines the maximum number of
bales a player can spawn at a time. The *SEND_NUM_BITS* is the number of
bits required to represent *MAX_NUM_BALES* in binary.

You may remember from Chapter 6, "Rotating Mower Mod," that we
want to send as little data across the network as possible – thus, using the
binary representation of this value saves on bandwidth. The only function
we implement in this program is *spawnBales()*.

This function will spawn a specified number of bales at a given
position. Notably, bale creation is only allowed on the server and is later
synchronized with the client. After ensuring the function is being called

by the server, we get the information about the bale based on the passed *baleTypeIndex*. Critically, there must be information associated with the passed bale index; otherwise, we will produce an error. We define an *offset* for how high off the ground and how far away from the player the bale should spawn.

Next, we spawn the number of bales specified by creating new Bale objects and configure them based on the player's selection. The call of the **register()** method registers the object as a network object on the server. The server will then sync the bale to the clients on the next update. If for some unknown reason an error occurs in configuring the bale, we delete it and move to the next bale.

The next script we need to add is *MultiBaleSpawnerEvent.lua*. You should be familiar with what functions are required by the Event base class. Try to see if you can recall each of them before you continue. Let us continue:

```
MultiBaleSpawnerEvent = {}
local MultiBaleSpawnerEvent_mt =
Class(MultiBaleSpawnerEvent, Event)
InitEventClass(MultiBaleSpawnerEvent, "MultiBaleSpawnerEvent")

function MultiBaleSpawnerEvent.emptyNew()
      local self = Event.new(MultiBaleSpawnerEvent_mt)
      return self
end

function MultiBaleSpawnerEvent.new(baleTypeIndex,
fillTypeIndex, numBales, x, y, z, dirX, dirZ, farmId)
      local self = MultiBaleSpawnerEvent.emptyNew()
      self.baleTypeIndex = baleTypeIndex
      self.fillTypeIndex = fillTypeIndex
      self.numBales = numBales
```

```
    self.x = x
    self.y = y
    self.z = z
    self.dirX = dirX
    self.dirZ = dirZ
    self.farmId = farmId

    return self
end
```

For our new event, we include two instructors: one that takes no
arguments and one that takes a *baleTypeIndex, fillTypeIndex,* the number
of bales, and information about the spawn position. If the constructor with
arguments is used, then each argument is assigned to a corresponding
field in the event class.

```
function MultiBaleSpawnerEvent:writeStream(streamId,
connection)
    streamWriteUInt8(streamId, self.baleTypeIndex)
    streamWriteUIntN(streamId, self.fillTypeIndex,
        FillTypeManager.SEND_NUM_BITS)
    streamWriteUIntN(streamId, self.numBales,
        MultiBaleSpawnerUtil.SEND_NUM_BITS)
    streamWriteFloat32(streamId, self.x)
    streamWriteFloat32(streamId, self.y)
    streamWriteFloat32(streamId, self.z)
    streamWriteFloat32(streamId, self.dirX)
    streamWriteFloat32(streamId, self.dirZ)
    streamWriteUIntN(streamId, self.farmId,
        FarmManager.FARM_ID_SEND_NUM_BITS)
end
```

Next, we include the *writeStream()* function which writes the event data to the network stream. Note we use the *SEND_NUM_BITS* field defined in the previous program when writing to the network.

```
function MultiBaleSpawnerEvent:readStream(streamId, connection)
    self.baleTypeIndex = streamReadUInt8(streamId)
    self.fillTypeIndex = streamReadUIntN(streamId,
        FillTypeManager.SEND_NUM_BITS)
    self.numBales = streamReadUIntN(streamId,
        MultiBaleSpawnerUtil.SEND_NUM_BITS)
    self.x = streamReadFloat32(streamId)
    self.y = streamReadFloat32(streamId)
    self.z = streamReadFloat32(streamId)
    self.dirX = streamReadFloat32(streamId)
    self.dirZ = streamReadFloat32(streamId)
    self.farmId = streamReadUIntN(streamId,
        FarmManager.FARM_ID_SEND_NUM_BITS)

    self:run(connection)
end
```

The *readStream()* function will read the event data from the network stream, updating the fields of the class with the data previously written to the network.

```
function MultiBaleSpawnerEvent:run(connection)
    assert(not connection:getIsServer(),
        "MultiBaleSpawnerEvent is client to server only")

    MultiBaleSpawnerUtil.spawnBales(self.baleTypeIndex, self.
    fillTypeIndex, self.numBales, self.x, self.y, self.z,
        self.dirX, self.dirZ, self.farmId)
end
```

Once the fields are updated, we call the *run()* function. The *run()* function executes the event by calling the *spawnBales()* function of *MultiBaleSpawnerUtil.lua*, passing along the relevant information about the bales and the spawn position.

With the utility and event scripts created, we are ready to create the main component program of the mod, *MultiBaleSpawnerScreen.lua*. Let us now explore the script:

```
MultiBaleSpawnerScreen = {}
MultiBaleSpawnerScreen.MOD_DIRECTORY = g_currentModDirectory

MultiBaleSpawnerScreen.CONTROLS = {
      "baleTypes",
      "numBales",
      "fillTypes",
      "baleSizes"
}

local MultiBaleSpawnerScreen_mt = Class(MultiBaleSpawnerScreen,
          ScreenElement)
function MultiBaleSpawnerScreen.register()
      local screen = MultiBaleSpawnerScreen.new()
      if g_gui ~= nil then
            -- load the xml layout and assign it to the
            -- controller
            local filename = Utils.getFilename("gui/
            MultiBaleSpawnerScreen.xml",
                MultiBaleSpawnerScreen.MOD_DIRECTORY)
            g_gui:loadGui(filename,
                "MultiBaleSpawnerScreen", screen)
      end
      MultiBaleSpawnerScreen.INSTANCE = screen
end
```

We start by defining a list of GUI elements that should be accessible via the script in a field named *CONTROLS*. We then create the *register()* function, which registers and loads our custom GUI. In this function, we create a new instance of the GUI controller and load the appearance from *MultiBaleSpawnerScreen.xml* into this object. This page is then assigned to the *INSTANCE* field of the class.

```
function MultiBaleSpawnerScreen.show(callbackFunc,
callbackTarget)
    if MultiBaleSpawnerScreen.INSTANCE ~= nil then
        local screen = MultiBaleSpawnerScreen.INSTANCE
        screen:setCallback(callbackFunc, callbackTarget)
        g_gui:changeScreen(nil, MultiBaleSpawnerScreen)
    end
end
```

The show() function is a helper function to open the GUI while in-game.

```
function MultiBaleSpawnerScreen.new(custom_mt)
    local self = ScreenElement.new(nil, custom_mt or
        MultiBaleSpawnerScreen_mt)
    self:registerControls(MultiBaleSpawnerScreen.CONTROLS)
    self.callbackFunc = nil
    self.callbackTarget = nil
    self.numBalesTexts = {}
    for i=1, MultiBaleSpawnerUtil.MAX_NUM_BALES do
        table.insert(self.numBalesTexts, tostring(i))
    end
    return self
end
```

The *new()* constructor of the class registers the GUI elements that should be accessible via the script and then creates the list of options for the number of bales that can be spawned by the player. Let us continue through the contents of the file:

```
function MultiBaleSpawnerScreen.createFromExistingGui(gui,
guiName)
    MultiBaleSpawnerScreen.register()
    local callbackFunc = gui.callbackFunc
    local callbackTarget = gui.callbackTarget
    MultiBaleSpawnerScreen.show(callbackFunc, callbackTarget)
end

function MultiBaleSpawnerScreen:setCallback(callbackFunc,
callbackTarget)
    self.callbackFunc = callbackFunc
    self.callbackTarget = callbackTarget
end
```

The *createFromExistingGui()* function creates a GUI from an existing one. This is used to support in-game GUI hot reloading via the *gsGuiReloadCurrent* console command. The *setCallback()* function sets the callback data for the screen, assigning the passed callback function and target to *callbackFunc* and *callbackTarget* fields.

```
function MultiBaleSpawnerScreen:onOpen()
    MultiBaleSpawnerScreen:superClass().onOpen(self)
    self.numBales:setTexts(self.numBalesTexts)
    local fillTypeTexts = {}
    self.textIndexToFillTypeIndex = {}
    self.fillTypeToBales = {}
    for k, baleType in ipairs(g_baleManager.bales) do
        baleType.baleTypeIndex = k
```

```
        for _, fillTypeData in ipairs(baleType.
        fillTypes) do
                local fillTypeIndex = fillTypeData.
                fillTypeIndex
                local added = table.addElement(self.
                textIndexToFillTypeIndex, fillTypeIndex)
                if added then
                        local fillTypeTitle = g_fillTypeManager
                        :getFillTypeTitleByIndex(fillTypeIndex)
                        table.insert(fillTypeTexts,
                        fillTypeTitle)
                end
                if self.fillTypeToBales[fillTypeIndex] ==
                nil then
                        self.fillTypeToBales[fillTypeIndex] = {}
                end
                table.insert(self.fillTypeToBales
                [fillTypeIndex], baleType)
        end
    end
    self.fillTypes:setTexts(fillTypeTexts)
    self.baleTypes:setTexts({
        g_i18n:getText("fillType_roundBale"),
        g_i18n:getText("fillType_squareBale")})
    self:updateBaleTypes()
end
```

The *onOpen()* function handles the event of the GUI opening. In this function, we set the text for the options for the number of bales that can be spawned by the player. The options for the bale type and fill type depend on the map chosen and the mods being used by the player. Because these options are not fixed, we need to set them when the page is

245

opened. Once the list of options for bale and fill types is created, the text for the corresponding GUI elements is set. We will now continue through the script:

```
function MultiBaleSpawnerScreen:updateBaleTypes()
    local hasRoundBale = false
    local hasSquareBale = false
    local index = self.fillTypes:getState()
    local fillTypeIndex =
        self.textIndexToFillTypeIndex[index]
    local bales = self.fillTypeToBales[fillTypeIndex]
    for _, bale in ipairs(bales) do
        if bale.isRoundbale then
            hasRoundBale = true
        else
            hasSquareBale = true
        end
    end
    self.baleTypes:setState(hasRoundBale and 1 or 2)
    self.baleTypes:setDisabled(not hasRoundBale or not
    hasSquareBale)
    self:updateBaleSizes()
end
```

The *updateBaleTypes()* function updates the text for the available bale types. The function checks if round and square bale types are available for the current fill type. If so, we select the round bale – we always select the round bale if it's available; otherwise, we select the square bale. We disable the multi-option menu if only one bale type can be selected. At the end of the function, we call *updateBaleSizes()*.

```lua
function MultiBaleSpawnerScreen:updateBaleSizes()
    local index = self.fillTypes:getState()
    local fillTypeIndex =
        self.textIndexToFillTypeIndex[index]
    local bales = self.fillTypeToBales[fillTypeIndex]
    local useRoundBale = self.baleTypes:getState() == 1
    local baleSizeTexts = {}
    self.baleSizeIndexToBale = {}
    for _, bale in ipairs(bales) do
        if useRoundBale == bale.isRoundbale then
            local size
            if bale.isRoundbale then
                size = string.format("%dx%d cm",
                    bale.diameter*100, bale.width*100)
            else
                size = string.format("%dx%dx%d cm",
                    bale.length*100, bale.width*100,
                    bale.height*100)
            end
            table.insert(baleSizeTexts, size)
            table.insert(self.baleSizeIndexToBale, bale)
        end
    end
    self.baleSizes:setTexts(baleSizeTexts)
    self.baleSizes:setDisabled(#baleSizeTexts < 2)
end
```

The *updateBaleSizes()* function is used to update the text for the available bale sizes. The function checks the available bales for the selected fill type and iterates over them. If a given bale matches the bale type selection, then its size option is included in the list of bale size options. Finally, the relevant text GUI elements are updated with the list of

available bale sizes. We again disable the option menu if only one bale size
is available. Let us look at the final section of the script:

```
function MultiBaleSpawnerScreen:onClickOk()
     g_gui:changeScreen(nil)
     local numBales = tonumber(self.numBales:getState())
     local fillTypeIndex =
          self.textIndexToFillTypeIndex[
          self.fillTypes:getState()]
     local bale =
          self.baleSizeIndexToBale[self.baleSizes:getState()]
     local baleTypeIndex = bale.baleTypeIndex
     if self.callbackFunc ~= nil then
          if self.callbackTarget ~= nil then
               self.callbackFunc(self.callbackTarget,
                    baleTypeIndex, fillTypeIndex, numBales)
          else
               self.callbackFunc(baleTypeIndex,
                    fillTypeIndex, numBales)
          end
     end
end

function MultiBaleSpawnerScreen:onClickBack()
     g_gui:changeScreen(nil)
end

function MultiBaleSpawnerScreen:onClickBaleType()
     self:updateBaleSizes()
end

function MultiBaleSpawnerScreen:onClickFillType()
     self:updateBaleTypes()
end

MultiBaleSpawnerScreen.register()
```

The *onClickOk()* function handles the click event for the interaction with the GUI. When pressed, the GUI is closed and the player's selections are recorded. We then perform the callback function, passing along the player's selections so the bales can be spawned. The *onClickBack()* function simply closes the GUI. The *onClickBaleType()* will call the *updateBaleSizes()* function to ensure the options displayed to the player are accurate. The *onClickFileType()* function will call the *updateBaleTypes()* function to similarly make sure the list of available bale types is accurate. Finally, we call the *register()* function we implemented earlier to register the GUI and make it available to the player.

We now only have two shorter scripts to add for the mod. We will start with *PlayerExtension.lua*:

```
Player.registerActionEvents = Utils.appendedFunction(
     Player.registerActionEvents,
     function(self)
          g_inputBinding:beginActionEventsModification(
               Player.INPUT_CONTEXT_NAME)
          local inputAction =
               InputAction.OPEN_MULTI_BALE_SPAWNER
          local callbackTarget = self
          local callbackFunc = self.openMultiBaleSpawner
          local triggerUp = false
          local triggerDown = true
          local triggerAlways = false
          local startActive = true
          local _, eventId =
               g_inputBinding:registerActionEvent(inputAction,
               callbackTarget, callbackFunc, triggerUp,
               triggerDown, triggerAlways,
               startActive)
```

```
    g_inputBinding:setActionEventText(eventId,
        g_i18n:getText("input_OPEN_MULTI_BALE_
        SPAWNER"))
    g_inputBinding:setActionEventTextVisibility(
        eventId, true)
    g_inputBinding:endActionEventsModification()
end)
```

This script is responsible for appending an anonymous function to the *registerActionEvents()* function of the player class. Much like prepending functions to existing library functions, causing our function to run before the library code, we can add functionality after a library function by appending it.

The function we are appending registers the new input action to open the multibale spawner menu. We register this action event for the player context without switching – this is important when called from within the UI context. The input action is then registered in the player context.

The first value returned by the *registerActionEvent()* function is *isActive* which tells you whether the action was registered successfully. We do not need this value, so we will use the underscore (_) as traditionally used to ignore values in a tuple return. The second value returned by the function is the *eventId*. We will use this value later to set the help text and activate the input in the upper-left help box. Lastly, we reset registration context, which updates event data in the input system.

```
function Player:openMultiBaleSpawner(actionName, inputValue,
callbackState, isAnalog, isMouse, deviceCategory)
    local callback = function(baleTypeIndex, fillTypeIndex,
    numBales)
        local x, y, z = getWorldTranslation(self.rootNode)
```

```
    local dirX, dirZ = -math.sin(self.rotY),
        -math.cos(self.rotY)
    x = x + dirX * 4
    z = z + dirZ * 4
    local farmId = self.farmId
    g_client:getServerConnection():sendEvent(
        MultiBaleSpawnerEvent.new(
            baleTypeIndex, fillTypeIndex, numBales, x, y,
            z, dirX, dirZ, farmId))
    end

    MultiBaleSpawnerScreen.show(callback)
end
```

The last function we add in this program is *openMultiBaleSpawner()* which handles user input of clicking the button and opening the GUI. In this function, we define a callback function which sends the event to spawn the bales with the player's current selections. This callback is passed to the *show()* function of *MultiBaleSpawnerScreen.lua* which binds the function to the spawn button.

Our final script, *AdditionalGuiProfiles.lua*, loads an additional GUI profiles file. This is needed to access our mod-defined profiles in the multiBaleSpawnerScreen.xml:

```
if g_gui ~= nil then
    g_gui:loadProfiles(g_currentModDirectory ..
        "gui/guiProfiles.xml")
end
```

With this small program, you have finished creating all of the XML and Lua files required for the multibale spawner mod. As always, you should take some time to review what you have learned and accomplished in this chapter.

Testing the Mod

With the scripts for your mod now created, you are ready to begin testing. Start by running the game without debugging from the Debug application menu of the GIANTS Studio. After you begin a new game on the map of your choice with your mod selected, press the *B key* on your keyboard while controlling your character. This should open the GUI and allow you to select the bale type, size, and fill type. Once you have made your selections, the bale should appear in front of you after clicking the *Spawn* button.

Summary

In this chapter, you gained experience working with GUI elements and giving players the ability to interactively spawn items. Additionally, you learned how to generally create behavior in the environment with GUI buttons.

In the next chapter, you will learn how to create a machine that gives players money based on their own numeric input.

253

CHAPTER 10

Money Cheat Mod

This chapter will explore making a *money cheat* which will allow players to give themselves unlimited amounts of in-game money (see Figure 10-1). This mod may also be useful for testing other mods you make as you will be able to make any purchases from the shop or upgrades without concern for money. Furthermore, you will need to learn how to make it so players can interact with placeable objects in the environment. Let's start!

Figure 10-1. *Running out of money? Fear no more!*

© GIANTS Software GmbH 2024
Z. Brumbaugh and M. Leithner, *Scripting Farming Simulator with Lua*,
https://doi.org/10.1007/979-8-8688-0060-3_10

Technical Requirements

Like the previous chapter, you will be working entirely in the GIANTS Editor and Studio and must meet the requirements mentioned in the "Technical Requirements" section of Chapter 2, "Getting Started with the GIANTS Editor." Make sure you are always using the most recent version of the GIANTS Editor. This will ensure that you are able to take advantage of any new features. You can find all the code and assets used in this chapter in the book's code repository on the GDN at the following link:

https://gdn.giants-software.com/lp/scriptingBook.php

Creating Mod Scripts

This section will explore all of the scripts necessary for this mod. We will start by looking at the .xml files and then cover the .lua files. Please see the "Preparing the Mod Folder Structure" section of Chapter 5, "Making a Diner with a Rotating Sign," on how to set up a mod project and use the sample files provided on GDN.

Creating XML Files

As always, we begin the mod by creating modDesc.xml. Let us explore its contents:

```xml
<?xml version="1.0" encoding="utf-8" standalone="no" ?>
<modDesc descVersion="72">

    <Author>GIANTS Software</author>
    <version>1.0.0.0</version>
    <multiplayer supported="true" />
    <title>
        <en>Sample Mod - Money Cheat</en>
    </title>
    <description>
        <en>A sample mod</en>
    </description>
    <iconFilename>icon_moneyCheat.png</iconFilename>
    <placeableSpecializations>
        <specialization name="atm" className="PlaceableATM"
            filename="scripts/PlaceableATM.lua" />
    </placeableSpecializations>
    <placeableTypes>
        <type name="atm" parent="simplePlaceable"
                filename="$dataS/scripts/placeables/
                Placeable.lua">
            <specialization name="atm" />
        </type>
    </placeableTypes>
    <extraSourceFiles>
        <sourceFile
            filename="scripts/events/ATMEvent.lua"/>
    </extraSourceFiles>
    <storeItems>
        <storeItem xmlFilename="placeable/atm.xml"/>
    </storeItems>
    <l10n filenamePrefix="l10n/l10n" />
</modDesc>
```

After defining the basic fields of the mod, we define a specialization in the *placeableSpecializations* field called *PlaceableATM*. In our mod, players will be able to get the money from a physical ATM, so they will need to buy the ATM and place it down.

We will define the *PlaceableATM* specialization in the "Creating Lua Files" section of this chapter. Following this, we set the ATM to be placeable by using the *placeableTypes* field and using the functionality of the *Placeable* base class.

Additionally, we add our previous defined specialization to add the features of the ATM script. In the *extraSourceFiles* field, we also include *ATMEvent.lua*, which will also be defined in the next section. In the *storeItems* field, we include a reference to *atm.xml*, which we will define later in this section.

Finally, we define the l10n element which is used for referencing translation files.

Next, we will define the atm.xml file which holds the configurations for the ATM. We will now look at the contents of the file:

```
<?xml version="1.0" encoding="utf-8" standalone="no" ?>
<placeable type="atm" xmlns:xsi="http://www.w3.org/2001/
XMLSchema-instance" xsi:noNamespaceSchemaLocation="https://
validation.gdn.giants-software.com/fs22/placeable.xsd">
    <storeData>
        <name>ATM</name>
        <functions>
            <function>An ATM to get Money</function>
        </functions>
        <image>placeable/store_atm.png</image>
        <price>1500</price>
        <lifetime>1000</lifetime>
        <rotation>0</rotation>
        <brand>NONE</brand>
        <species>placeable</species>
```

```
    <category>decoration</category>
    <brush>
        <type>placeable</type>
        <category>decoration</category>
        <tab>uncategorized</tab>
    </brush>
    <vertexBufferMemoryUsage>0</
    vertexBufferMemoryUsage>
    <indexBufferMemoryUsage>0</indexBufferMemoryUsage>
    <textureMemoryUsage>0</textureMemoryUsage>
    <instanceVertexBufferMemoryUsage>0</
    instanceVertexBufferMemoryUsage>
    <instanceIndexBufferMemoryUsage>0</
    instanceIndexBufferMemoryUsage>
</storeData>
```

We again start with the XML declaration of the placeable root element. We define ATM to be of the *placeable* type, so the system knows the feature set of the object. In the *storeData* field, we include the information relevant to the item being displayed in the store. This includes the *price, image, function,* and other basic information about the ATM. You can refer to the "Creating XML Files" section of Chapter 5, "Making a Diner with a Rotating Sign," where we first use this field. Let us continue:

```
<base>
    <filename>placeable/atm.i3d</filename>
</base>
<placement useRandomYRotation="false"
    useManualYRotation="true" >
    <testAreas>
        <testArea startNode="testArea1Start"
        endNode="testArea1End" />
    </testAreas>
</placement>
```

In the base element, we include the relative path from the mod directory to the .i3d file containing the ATM. Next, we configure placement for the ATM via the placement field. In this field, we reference nodes on the model to determine whether an object obstructs the area the player wants to put the ATM.

```
<clearAreas>
      <clearArea startNode="clearArea1Start"
           widthNode="clearArea1Width"
           heightNode="clearArea1Height"/>
</clearAreas>

<leveling requireLeveling="true" maxSmoothDistance="10"
     maxSlope="75"
     maxEdgeAngle="30" >
     <levelAreas />
</leveling>
<indoorAreas />
```

In the clearAreas field, we set the area the ATM is placed to be clear of foliage and other environmental objects.

```
<ai>
      <updateAreas>
            <updateArea startNode="testArea1Start"
                  endNode="testArea1End" />
      </updateAreas>
</ai>
```

In the ai field, we mark the area as blocked so autonomous equipment and other AI will avoid the ATM. We will now cover the remaining portion of the file:

```
<atm moneyPerAction="15000">
      <trigger node="playerTrigger" />
      <sounds>
```

```
        <action file="sounds/cashRegistry.wav"
            innerRadius="5.0" outerRadius="15.0"
            fadeOut="0.1" linkNode="playerTrigger">
            <volume indoor="0.45" outdoor="1.1" />
            <pitch indoor="1.0" outdoor="1.0" />
        </action>
    </sounds>
</atm>
<i3dMappings>
    <i3dMapping id="playerTrigger" node="0>0|0" />
    <i3dMapping id="clearArea1Start" node="0>1|0" />
    ...
</i3dMappings>
</placeable>
```

The file concludes with a custom element for the mod called atm. In
this element, we define the amount of money the player receives when
they interact with the ATM via the *moneyPerAction* field, which holds
a value of 15000. You can change this value to however much you want
players to receive. The *trigger* element references a trigger shape in our
i3d file. It is later used to notify a script if a player is close to the ATM. We
also include a satisfying sound when the ATM is used by the player and
they receive their money. Lastly, we include the i3d mappings inside of the
i3dMappings field.

We will now create translation files for text we want to display to the
user about the ATM. For English, we will define a file called *l10n_en.xml*.
Let us now look at the file:

```
<?xml version="1.0" encoding="UTF-8" standalone="yes" ?>
<l10n>
    <elements>
        <e k="action_atmRequest" v="Draw Money"/>
    </elements>
</l10n>
```

In the file, we simply include the text that should be associated with the ATM interaction. In this case, we want to tell the player that by interacting with the ATM they will *Draw Money*.

Let us now look at the contents of the German translation file, *l10n_de.xml*:

```
<?xml version="1.0" encoding="UTF-8" standalone="yes" ?>
<l10n>
     <elements>
          <e k="action_atmRequest" v="Geld abheben"/>
     </elements>
</l10n>
```

Like in the file for English, we include the text that describes the action with the ATM. This concludes all of the .xml files for the mod. In the next section, we will look at the .lua files we need to create.

Creating Lua Files

The first file we will create is *ATMEvent.lua*, which builds on the base Event class. Let us now cover the file's contents:

```
ATMEvent = {}
local ATMEvent_mt = Class(ATMEvent, Event)
InitEventClass(ATMEvent, "ATMEvent")

function ATMEvent.emptyNew()
     local self = Event.new(ATMEvent_mt)
     return self
end

function ATMEvent.new(placeable, farmId)
     local self = ATMEvent.emptyNew()
     self.placeable = placeable
     self.farmId = farmId
     return self
end
```

We start by creating two constructors with one that takes no arguments and one that takes a placeable object and farm ID. If the object and ID are passed to the constructor, then they are assigned to placeable and farmId fields within the class.

```
function ATMEvent:writeStream(streamId, connection)
    NetworkUtil.writeNodeObject(streamId, self.placeable)
    streamWriteUIntN(streamId, self.farmId,
        FarmManager.FARM_ID_SEND_NUM_BITS)
end

function ATMEvent:readStream(streamId, connection)
    self.placeable = NetworkUtil.readNodeObject(streamId)
    self.farmId = streamReadUIntN(streamId, FarmManager.
        FARM_ID_SEND_NUM_BITS)
    self:run(connection)
end
```

Like in other chapters, the *readStream()* and *writeStream()* functions are used to send and process updates to the network stream. In the *readStream()* function, we update the *placeable* and *farmId* fields with what has been written to the stream.

```
function ATMEvent:run(connection)
    assert(not connection:getIsServer(),
    "ATMEvent is client to server only")
    if self.placeable ~= nil then
        self.placeable:requestMoney(self.farmId)
    end
end
```

Lastly, the *run()* function calls the *requestMoney()* function of the *placeable* object associated with the event. This function will be implemented in the *PlaceableATM* specialization, which we will define in this section.

With *ATMEvent.lua* complete, we are ready to define *PlaceableATM. lua*, the main component of the mod. Let us now look through its contents:

```
local modName = g_currentModName
PlaceableATM = {}
PlaceableATM.SPEC_TABLE_NAME = "spec_"..modName..".atm"

function PlaceableATM.registerXMLPaths(schema, basePath)
    schema:setXMLSpecializationType("ATM")
    schema:register(XMLValueType.NODE_INDEX,
        basePath .. ".atm.trigger#node",
        "Node index or i3d mapping name of the
        trigger shape")
    schema:register(XMLValueType.INT,
        basePath .. ".atm#moneyPerAction",
        "The amount of money a player gets", 100000)
    SoundManager.registerSampleXMLPaths(schema,
        basePath .. ".atm.sounds", "action")
    schema:setXMLSpecializationType()
end

function PlaceableATM.prerequisitesPresent(specializations)
    return true
end
```

We begin the specialization by defining the default functions. After defining the namespace for the mod, we include the *registerXMLPaths()* function which registers elements from the XML files with the placeable schema. Next, we add the *prerequisitesPresent()* function. Because we do not require any prerequisites, we simply return *true*.

```
function PlaceableATM.registerEventListeners(placeableType)
    SpecializationUtil.registerEventListener(placeableType,
        "onLoad", PlaceableATM)
```

```
SpecializationUtil.registerEventListener(placeableType,
        "onDelete", PlaceableATM)
end

function PlaceableATM.registerFunctions(placeableType)
    SpecializationUtil.registerFunction(placeableType,
        "onATMTriggerCallback",
        PlaceableATM.onATMTriggerCallback)
    SpecializationUtil.registerFunction(placeableType,
        "requestMoney",
        PlaceableATM.requestMoney)
end
```

The *registerEventListeners()* function registers the *onLoad()* and *onDelete()* functions of the mod. These functions will be implemented later in the script. Lastly, the *registerFunctions()* function registers our custom *onATMTriggerCallback()* and *requestMoney()* functions, which will be added later in the file. Let us continue through the script:

```
function PlaceableATM:onLoad(savegame)
local spec = self[PlaceableATM.SPEC_TABLE_NAME]
local node = self.xmlFile:getValue("placeable.atm.
        trigger#node", nil, self.components, self.i3dMappings)
if node ~= nil then
        addTrigger(node, "onATMTriggerCallback", self)
        spec.triggerNode = node
        spec.activatable = ATMActivatable.new(self, node)
        spec.moneyPerAction = self.xmlFile:getValue(
            "placeable.atm#moneyPerAction", 100000)
        spec.samples = {}
        spec.samples.action =
            g_soundManager:loadSampleFromXML(self.xmlFile,
            "placeable.atm.sounds", "action", self.
            baseDirectory, self.components, 1,
            AudioGroup.VEHICLE, self.i3dMappings, self)
```

```
    else
        Logging.xmlWarning(self.xmlFile, "Missing atm
        trigger!")
    end
end
```

The *onLoad()* function starts by referencing the node the player triggers to receive the money. If the node exists, then we add an *interaction* trigger that calls the *onATMTriggerCallback()* function when triggered. A shape within the i3d can be marked as a trigger shape in the editor.

Triggers are a part of the physics system, so this shape also has to be a physics shape. Normally, it should have the rigidbody type *STATIC* or *KINEMATIC*. It is also important to set the correct *collisionMask* of the shape; otherwise, the script may not fire any trigger callback because the physics engine does not detect any collisions.

The node is then assigned to the *triggerNode* field of the class. We also assign an **Activatable** object to the *activatable* field of the class. Activatable objects are script objects that are handled by the *ActivatableObjectsSystem* and used to tell the system that the player is within a given area where they can activate or trigger a specific action. From *atm.xml*, we retrieve the value for how much money the player should get per interaction and assign it to the *moneyPerAction* field. Finally, we load the interaction sound into the *samples* field of the class.

```
function PlaceableATM:onDelete()

local spec = self[PlaceableATM.SPEC_TABLE_NAME]
if spec.triggerNode ~= nil then
    removeTrigger(spec.triggerNode)
    local system = g_currentMission.activatableObjectsSystem
    system:removeActivatable(spec.activatable)
    g_soundManager:deleteSamples(spec.samples)
end

end
```

The *onDelete()* function will clean up the class when the ATM is deleted by checking that the trigger node exists and if so removing the trigger *callback*, the *activatable object*, and the trigger *sound*.

Let us now explore our custom functions:

```
function PlaceableATM:onATMTriggerCallback(triggerId, otherId,
onEnter, onLeave, onStay, otherShapeId)
    if onEnter or onLeave then
        if g_currentMission.player ~= nil and
            otherId == g_currentMission.player.
            rootNode and
            g_currentMission.player.farmId ~=
            FarmManager.SPECTATOR_FARM_ID
        then
            local spec =
                self[PlaceableATM.SPEC_TABLE_NAME]
            local activatableSystem =
                g_currentMission.activatableObjectsSystem
            if onEnter then
                activatableSystem:addActivatable(
                    spec.activatable)
            else
                activatableSystem:removeActivatable(
                    spec.activatable)
            end
        end
    end
end
```

The *onATMTriggerCallback()* function is passed whether the player is entering or leaving the trigger area. If the player is *leaving* or *entering* the area, then we check that the player is actually present and display or *remove* the trigger accordingly. The second parameter of the callback holds the *entity ID* of the colliding physics shape. We can use it to determine if the shape is a player or not by simply comparing it with the player *rootNode*. Let us continue:

```
function PlaceableATM:requestMoney(farmId)
    local spec = self[PlaceableATM.SPEC_TABLE_NAME]
    g_soundManager:playSample(spec.samples.action)
    if not self.isServer then
        g_client:getServerConnection():sendEvent(
            ATMEvent.new(self, farmId))
        return
    end
    local amount = spec.moneyPerAction
    local moneyType = MoneyType.OTHER
    local addChange = true
    local forceShow = true
    g_currentMission:addMoney(amount, farmId, moneyType,
        addChange, forceShow)
end
```

The requestMoney() function will play the trigger sound and, if we are on the client, send a request to the server to dispense money. The handling and syncing of money are done on the server only, and the balance is not allowed to be changed on the client. As such, we need to tell the server that we requested money.

We do so by sending the *ATMEvent* to the server and leave the function by calling return afterward. So, if this function is being run on the server, then it will add the specified amount of money to the player's balance. The *addMoney()* function takes the amount of money that should be added or subtracted and the ID of the farm that the change should be applied to.

The money type is mostly used for the statistics of the game. The *addChange* and *forceShow* flags tell the system if the money change should be shown immediately using the **in-game notifications** in the top-right corner of the HUD or if the system should sum all calls up until an explicit call with *forceShow* = *true* occurs. We will now cover the remaining contents of the file:

```
ATMActivatable = {}
local ATMActivatable_mt = Class(ATMActivatable)

function ATMActivatable.new(placeable, triggerNode)
    local self = setmetatable({}, ATMActivatable_mt)
    self.placeable = placeable
    self.triggerNode = triggerNode
    self.activateText = g_i18n:getText("action_atmRequest")
    return self
end

function ATMActivatable:getIsActivatable()
    if g_gui.currentGui ~= nil then
        return false
    end
    return g_currentMission.player.farmId ~= FarmManager.
        SPECTATOR_FARM_ID
end

function ATMActivatable:getDistance(x, y, z)
    local tx, ty, tz = getWorldTranslation(self.triggerNode)
    return MathUtil.vector3Length(x-tx, y-ty, z-tz)
end

function ATMActivatable:run()
    self.placeable:requestMoney(g_currentMission.
    player.farmId)
end
```

We create *ATMActivatable* to be a new class. For this class, we include a constructor that takes a *placeable* object and *trigger* node. The placeable object and trigger node are respectively assigned to the *placeable* and *triggerNodes* fields of the *ATMActivatable* class. We also set the *activateText* field to the action text defined in the translation file. The *getIsActivatable()* function checks whether the player can currently request money.

The *getDistance()* function returns the distance to the activatable object and is used to prioritize actions if multiple activatables are in range.

Finally, we define the *run()* function which will call the *requestMoney()* function of the object held in the placeable field. This concludes all of the programming required for this mod. Like with the other chapters, take a moment to review what you have accomplished and written and how these concepts may apply to future mods.

Testing the Mod

With the scripts for your mod now created, you are ready to begin testing. First, start a new game and select a map of your choice. Make sure that you have your mod selected to be used in the game. Once the game had loaded, open the Construction screen. Go to the miscellaneous category and place the ATM. If your mod has been created correctly, you should be prompted to withdraw money in the amount you set in the configuration file.

Summary

In this chapter, you learned how to create an ATM that dispenses a predetermined amount of money to the player. Importantly, you learned how to use activatable objects to trigger functions when a player interacts with an object within a certain distance.

In the next chapter, you will learn to make your mods available to other players and members of the Farming Simulator community by publishing your creations to the ModHub.

CHAPTER 11

Publishing on the ModHub

You have now successfully created six mods and should feel confident in bringing your own ideas for mod creations to life. In this chapter, we will explore how to publish your creations to the ModHub for others to download and play while potentially earning revenue with your mod's success.

Technical Requirements

You will not need any software or additional materials for this chapter as it will mostly cover information. However, you will need an Internet connection and web browser available to you to search any topics covered in further detail or visit any websites mentioned.

What Is the ModHub?

The ModHub is where you will publish your mods for all players to be able to use. The ModHub has different categories including maps, many different types of vehicles, and different buildings or farm technologies for players to include in their game.

© GIANTS Software GmbH 2024
Z. Brumbaugh and M. Leithner, *Scripting Farming Simulator with Lua*,
https://doi.org/10.1007/979-8-8688-0060-3_11

The best-performing and highest-quality mods can appear in several algorithmic categories, including *Latest* and *Top Downloaded*. These categories are then featured to players on the front page of the ModHub. We will be referencing the ModHub website often, which can be found at the following link:

`https://www.farming-simulator.com/mods.php`

When users download your mod, they can leave a review on a five-star scale. Naturally, mods with a higher rating are more likely to be downloaded by other players and find their way into the sorts shown earlier. With dedication, your mods can also see wide usage and be shown at the top of these sorts. To get started, you will need to create an account, which we will do in the next section.

Creating an Account

To create your ModHub account, go to the ModHub website and click the *login* button highlighted in Figure 11-1.

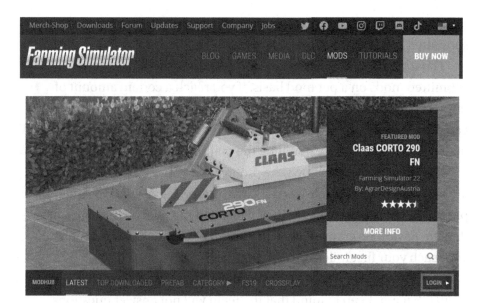

Figure 11-1. *You can log in to your ModHub account by clicking the login button on the front page*

Note that this account is different from the account you use to access the GDN. Once on the login page, click the *Register new account here* button and follow the instructions presented to you. Make sure you accept the "Terms of Use" checkbox. Once you enter your basic information, your login information will be sent to the email you provided. Log in to your account once you receive this information, and you should arrive on your personal *Mods* page. The link to this page can be found here:

```
https://www.farming-simulator.com/modHubBEMain.php
```

On this page, you will find several different sections shown by tabs.

The first tab is the *Mods* page, which shows you a list of all your submitted mods.

The *Rewards* tab shows the rewards you have earned for your submitted mods on a per mod basis. If you reach a certain amount of rewards, you can enter your bank details to receive the rewards, or **you can decide to donate them to a charity**. If donated, GIANTS Software will match your contribution, doubling the amount.

The *Awards* section shows the progress on your awards of which there are four types: the Console (red) award, Bronze, Silver, and Gold. On this page, you can see if you have already reached the milestone and request that the reward be granted. Note that this tab will not become visible until you reach your first milestone.

The *Messenger* tab is where you can get in touch with the GIANTS ModHub team. Keep in mind that the team will not answer questions about modding itself but will assist with questions and issues with the submission process and other inquiries directly related to the ModHub.

Lastly, the *Help* section provides you with resources regarding the ModHub, Farming Simulator, and the GDN.

In the next section, we will cover the content guidelines of the ModHub.

ModHub Creation Guidelines

Not all types of content are allowed on the ModHub. In this section, we will explore what type of content is and is not permitted on the ModHub as well as the potential consequences of violating these restrictions. Throughout this section, we will reference the official ModHub guideline document, which can be found at the following link. The most current version of the guidelines can always be found in the *Data* subsection of the *Upload* page:

`https://farming-simulator.com/modhub-guidelines`

After passing all of the tests of the TestRunner tool (see the next section), you are ready to submit your mod for manual review. We will cover the submission process in more detail in the "Uploading Your First Mod" section of this chapter. Your mod will again be checked against the TestRunner, and if all tests are passed, your mod will be tested in game. If all tests are passed, the mod will be ready for release on PC. Mods must go through additional tests to be made available on the console. After the in-game test on PC, your mod will be tested on the console. If all tests are passed, your mod is ready for console release, and you will receive the red Console award once it is downloaded 250K times. You can see this whole process outline in the diagram shown in Figure 11-2.

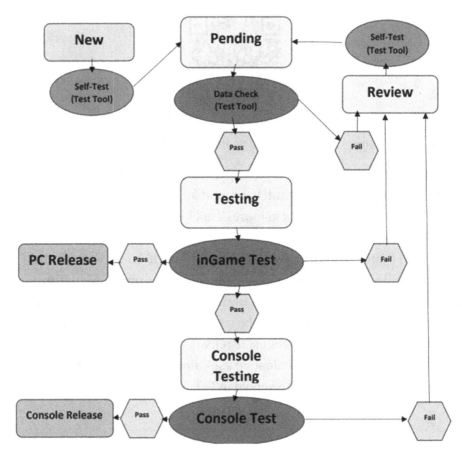

Figure 11-2. *Your mod must go through a manual review process to be approved for the ModHub*

Remember to read all of the requirements set by the guidelines carefully to ensure that your mod is able to be approved quickly.

In the next section, you will learn how to ensure your mod is ready to be uploaded to ModHub.

Using the TestRunner

The TestRunner is a piece of software created by GIANTS Software used to verify that your mod is in a state that is ready to be uploaded. For example, it will check for issues such as duplicate files, texture formats, XML validation, and more. To download the TestRunner, navigate to the Downloads page of the GDN and search for the *Farming Simulator 22 Test Runner* download link. For convenience, you can find the Downloads page of the GDN at the following link:

https://gdn.giants-software.com/downloads.php

After downloading, unzip the folder and put the *TestRunner_public.exe* executable in the directory containing all of your mods. To test a specific mod, grab the mod directory for a single mod and release it while hovering over the executable as shown in Figure 11-3. The TestRunner will then be executed on your selected folder.

Name	Date modified	Type	Size
mileageCounter	2/28/2023 11:43 PM	File folder	
moneyCheat	3/14/2023 9:33 PM	File folder	
multiBaleSpawner	3/14/2023 9:33 PM	File folder	
myMod	1/17/2023 3:27 PM	File folder	
restaurant	1/21/2023 7:09 PM	File folder	
rotateMower	2/13/2023 10:06 PM	File folder	
speedTrapTrailer	3/13/2023 10:58 PM	File folder	
TestRunner_public.exe	4/3/2023 7:51 PM	Application	6,611 KB

+ Open with Farming Simulator 22 Test Runner

Figure 11-3. *You can execute the TestRunner on a mod by dragging the mod folder to the executable*

Note that your mod folder does not need to be in the same directory as the TestRunner, but it may be convenient for this interaction. A command-line window will open displaying the current progress, and if something went wrong, an error message is displayed giving details on the problem. All outputs from the TestRunner are saved in the "TestRunner.log". An XML and HTML file will be generated in the same directory as the TestRunner. The files are named after the directory name of the tested mod and contain the results of the test. The HTML file only contains all the found errors (per module), and the XML contains all errors and more detailed (meta) information. The generated HTML report should be automatically opened in your web browser. Errors are outlined in red, explanations are in italics, and instructions for correcting the errors are colored green.

For more general information about the TestRunner and troubleshooting, you can view the announcement thread linked here:

https://forum.giants-software.com/viewtopic.php?t=187502

In the next section, you will upload your first mod to the ModHub.

Uploading Your First Mod

When you are ready to upload your first mod, navigate to the Mods tab of the ModHub once you have logged in. Click the *Add New* button and select the new *Untitled Mod* option that appears. At the top of the page, you can see the status of your submission which will show whether you have uploaded the required materials to submit your mod for review.

If you encounter an issue uploading your mod, you can create a ticket from this page to get in contact with the GIANTS ModHub team. The ModHub team can neither answer mod requests nor help you with modding questions in a private ticket. If you have questions about modding, please visit the forum and send your questions to other members of the modding community.

You can see this section of the page in Figure 11-4.

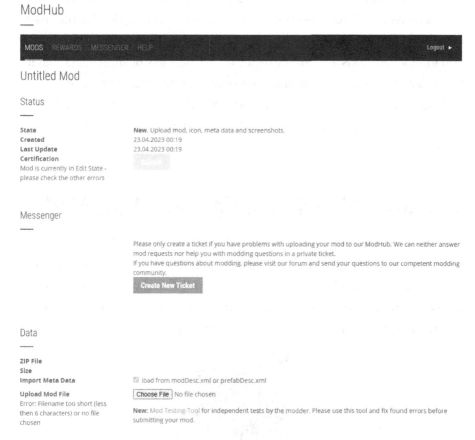

Figure 11-4. *You will need to upload files and information about your mod for it to be submitted*

You are first asked to upload the files for your mod. At this point, you will be asked to confirm that your mod passes the TestRunner application and is compliant with the modding rules set out in the "ModHub Creation Guidelines" section of this chapter. Next, you are asked to include metadata for your mod including the icon, mod version, and the title and description in English, German, and French. Most or all of this information can be automatically extracted if you select the *load from modDesc.xml or prefabDesc.xml* option seen in Figure 11-4. Lastly, you must include at least three screenshots of your mod for the team to review. Once all materials have been uploaded, you are ready to return to the top of the page and submit your mod for review. Mods are usually reviewed within a few business days, but it depends on the amount of mod submissions currently being processed.

Note that you should not upload any of the mods you created in this book as they are not original and will be denied by the GIANTS ModHub test team.

Getting Feedback and Updating Your Mod

Once your mod is accepted, it will be released by the ModHub team and millions of players will be able to see and download your mod. This also means there will be a lot of feedback. This feedback may come from the official forum, Facebook, Discord, or other social platforms. You can find the link to the English-speaking section of the forum here:

https://forum.giants-software.com/viewforum.php?f=478

Feedback can be helpful when considering how to improve your mod. Do keep in mind that you may sometimes receive negative feedback, but you should not be discouraged. If feedback is not constructive, do your best to ignore it and continue doing what you enjoy as a creator.

By updating your mod, you may see an increase in positive feedback from the community who are happy to see new content and their suggestions incorporated into the mod. By creating more content, you will also become more notable in the community and gain the recognition of other creators. And of course, with more mods and consistent updates, your mod will become more popular, resulting in more downloads and additional rewards. Note that mods that are updated are more visible on the in-game ModHub and as well as on the ModHub website. In the next section, we will look in more detail at rewards and awards you can earn as a mod creator.

Rewards and Awards

As mentioned in Chapter 1, "Introduction," there are ways to earn money by creating mods and making them available for all Farming Simulator players to use. Once you create a quality mod, it must go through a manual approval process. This process ensures that the mod does what it claims to do and that it is free of any prohibited content. This content can vary, but copyrighted material, such as specific brands or companies, are generally not permitted to appear in your mod. If your mod is approved to be published on the ModHub, you may be eligible to receive payouts from GIANTS Software based on how many times your mod is downloaded. Remember, quality mods that receive the best reviews are more likely to appear in certain categories of the ModHub. When your mod is featured, more users will be able to see it and download, allowing you to earn more money from your mod.

Your mod can also earn awards depending on its performance and content. If your mod is made compatible with consoles, you are eligible for the red *Console* award. If your mod is widely downloaded, you can also earn the *Bronze, Silver,* and *Gold* awards (see Figure 11-5).

Figure 11-5. *The red ModHub award is given if your mod achieves 250K downloads on the console*

In the next section, we will review what you have learned in this chapter and the book as a whole.

Summary

In this chapter, you learned how to use the ModHub to make your mod available to thousands of other Farming Simulator players. Additionally, you learned how you can earn money by making successful mods.

This brings us to the end of this modding guide. At the beginning, you may have had little to no programming experience but now are able to create and manage complex systems using Lua and XML. You learned about networks, the client-server relationship, and how to efficiently make use of the bandwidth and other limited resources available to you. From your first sample mod to the first mod of your own design you uploaded to the ModHub, you have taken a great leap in your journey as a mod developer. I hope you find these learned skills valuable as you continue creating and approach new technical challenges throughout your life. I wish you the best on your journey!

CHAPTER 12

Documentation and Appendix

Throughout the tutorial chapters of the book, we used many internally defined functions in the systems of the mods. While the purpose and function of these mods were explained in context, you may find official use and documentation for each of them useful in your own projects. In this chapter, you will find the official engine API documentation used by GIANTS Software engineers. Please note that you can find the latest version of the documentation on the GDN:

```
https://gdn.giants-software.com/documentation.php
```

Debugging

print

Prints given arguments to the console.

© GIANTS Software GmbH 2024
Z. Brumbaugh and M. Leithner, *Scripting Farming Simulator with Lua*,
https://doi.org/10.1007/979-8-8688-0060-3_12

Arguments

any arg1 – [optional]
any arg2 – [optional]
any arg3 – [optional]
any arg4 – [optional]
any arg5 – [optional]
any arg6 – [optional]
any arg7 – [optional]
any arg8 – [optional]

printCallstack

Prints the current application callstack.

Position, Orientation, and Size

getWorldTranslation

Gets world translation of a transform object.

Arguments

integer entityId – ID of the entity (transformGroup, shape, etc.).

Returns

float x – x position in entityId's world space.
float y – y position in entityId's world space.
float z – z position in entityId's world space.

setWorldTranslation

Sets world translation of a transform object.

Arguments

integer entityId – ID of the entity (transformGroup, shape, etc.).
float x – x position in entityId's world space.
float y – y position in entityId's world space.
float z – z position in entityId's world space.

setTranslation

Sets local translation of a transform object.

Arguments

integer entityId – ID of the entity (transformGroup, shape, etc.).
float x – x position in entityId's local space.
float y – y position in entityId's local space.
float z – z position in entityId's local space.

getTranslation

Gets local translation of a transform object.

Arguments

integer entityId – ID of the entity (transformGroup, shape, etc.).

Returns

float x – x position in entityId's local space.
float y – y position in entityId's local space.
float z – z position in entityId's local space.

worldToLocal

Converts the world position into entityId's local space.

Arguments

integer entityId – ID of the entity (transformGroup, shape, etc.).
float x – x position in entityId's world space.
float y – y position in entityId's world space.
float z – z position in entityId's world space.

Returns

float x – x position in entityId's local space.
float y – y position in entityId's local space.
float z – z position in entityId's local space.

localToWorld

Converts the given position from entityId's local space to world space.

Arguments

integer entityId – ID of the entity (transformGroup, shape, etc.).
float x – x position in entityId's local space.
float y – y position in entityId's local space.
float z – z position in entityId's local space.

Returns

float x – x position in entityId's world space.
float y – y position in entityId's world space.
float z – z position in entityId's world space.

localToLocal

Converts the given position from entityId's local space to targetEntityId's local space.

Arguments

integer entityId – ID of the entity (transformGroup, shape, etc.).
integer targetEntityId – ID of the target entity (transformGroup, shape, etc.).
float x – x position in entityId's local space.
float y – y position in entityId's local space.
float z – z position in entityId's local space.

Returns

float x – x position in targetEntityId's local space.
float y – y position in targetEntityId's local space.
float z – z position in targetEntityId's local space.

setRotation

Sets the local rotation of the given transform object.

Arguments

integer entityId – ID of the entity (transformGroup, shape, etc.).

Returns

float x – x rotation (radians) in entityId's local space.

float y – y rotation (radians) in entityId's local space.

float z – z rotation (radians) in entityId's local space.

getRotation

Gets the local rotation of the given transform object.

Arguments

integer entityId – ID of the entity (transformGroup, shape, etc.).

Returns

float x – x rotation (radians) in entityId's local space.

float y – y rotation (radians) in entityId's local space.

float z – z rotation (radians) in entityId's local space.

getWorldRotation

Gets world rotation of a transform object.

Arguments

integer entityId – ID of the entity (transformGroup, shape, etc.).

Returns

float x – x rotation (radians) in entityId's world space.

float y – y rotation (radians) in entityId's world space.

float z – z rotation (radians) in entityId's world space.

setWorldRotation

Sets world rotation of a transform object.

Arguments

integer entityId – ID of the entity (transformGroup, shape, etc.).
float x – x rotation (radians) in entityId's world space.
float y – y rotation (radians) in entityId's world space.
float z – z rotation (radians) in entityId's world space.

localRotationToWorld

Converts the rotation in entityId's local space to world space.

Arguments

integer entityId – ID of the entity (transformGroup, shape, etc.).
float x – x rotation (radians) in entityId's local space.
float y – y rotation (radians) in entityId's local space.
float z – z rotation (radians) in entityId's local space.

Returns

float x – x rotation (radians) in entityId's world space.
float y – y rotation (radians) in entityId's world space.
float z – z rotation (radians) in entityId's world space.

worldRotationToLocal

Converts the world rotation into entityId's local space.

Arguments

integer entityId – ID of the entity (transformGroup, shape, etc.).
float x – x rotation (radians) in entityId's world space.
float y – y rotation (radians) in entityId's world space.
float z – z rotation (radians) in entityId's world space.

Returns

float x – x rotation (radians) in entityId's local space.
float y – y rotation (radians) in entityId's local space.
float z – z rotation (radians) in entityId's local space.

worldDirectionToLocal

Converts a world direction vector into entityId's local space.

Arguments

integer entityId – ID of the entity (transformGroup, shape, etc.).
float x – x component of direction vector in world space.
float y – y component of direction vector in world space.
float z – z component of direction vector in world space.

Returns

float x – x component of direction vector in entityId's local space.
float y – y component of direction vector in entityId's local space.
float z – z component of direction vector in entityId's local space.

localDirectionToLocal

Converts a direction vector in entityId's local space to targetEntityId's local space.

Arguments

integer entityId – ID of the entity (transformGroup, shape, etc.).
integer targetEntityId – ID of the target entity (transformGroup, shape, etc.).
float x – x component of direction vector in entityId's local space.
float y – y component of direction vector in entityId's local space.
float z – z component of direction vector in entityId's local space.

Returns

float x – x component of direction vector in targetEntityId's local space.
float y – y component of direction vector in targetEntityId's local space.
float z – z component of direction vector in targetEntityId's local space.

localDirectionToWorld

Converts a local space direction vector into world space.

Arguments

integer entityId – ID of the entity (transformGroup, shape, etc.).
float x – x component of direction vector in entityId's local space.
float y – y component of direction vector in entityId's local space.
float z – z component of direction vector in entityId's local space.

Returns

float x – x component of direction vector in world space.
float y – y component of direction vector in world space.
float z – z component of direction vector in world space.

setDirection

Sets the direction of an object; the positive Z axis points toward the given direction. The Y axis lies in the direction-up-plane.

Arguments

integer entityId – ID of the entity (transformGroup, shape, etc.).
float x – x component of direction vector (z axis) in entityId's local space.
float y – y component of direction vector (z axis) in entityId's local space.
float z – z component of direction vector (z axis) in entityId's local space.
float upX – x component of up vector (y axis) in entityId's local space.
float upY – y component of up vector (y axis) in entityId's local space.
float upZ – z component of up vector (y axis) in entityId's local space.

setScale

Sets scale of a transform object.

Arguments

integer entityId – ID of the entity (transformGroup, shape, etc.).
float x – x scale of entityId in local space.
float y – y scale of entityId in local space.
float z – z scale of entityId in local space.

getScale

Gets the scale of a transform object.

Arguments

integer entityId – ID of the entity (transformGroup, shape, etc.).

Returns

float x – x scale of entityId in local space.
float y – y scale of entityId in local space.
float z – z scale of entityId in local space.

Entities

clone

Clones a scenegraph object (transformGroup, shape, etc.).

Arguments

integer entityId – ID of the entity (transformGroup, shape, etc.).
boolean groupUnderParent – If the cloned entity should be parented to the same parent.
boolean callOnCreate – If script callbacks (onCreate) should be called.
boolean addPhysics – If the cloned entity should be added to physics.

Returns

integer clonedEntityId – ID of the cloned entity (transformGroup, shape, etc.).

createTransformGroup

Creates a transform group.

Arguments

string transformName – Name of the transform group.

Returns

integer entityId – ID of the transformGroup entity.

setName

Sets the name of an entity.

Arguments

integer entityId – ID of the entity (transformGroup, shape, etc.).
string transformName – Name of the object.

getName

Gets the name of an entity.

Arguments

integer entityId – ID of the entity (transformGroup, shape, etc.).

Returns

string objectName – Name of the object.

setVisibility

Sets transform object visibility.

Arguments

integer entityId – ID of the entity (transformGroup, shape, etc.).
boolean visibility – Visibility state of the object.

getVisibility

Gets transform object visibility.

Arguments

integer entityId – ID of the entity (transformGroup, shape, etc.).

Returns

boolean visibility – Visibility state of the object.

setUserAttribute

Sets user attribute value.

Arguments

integer entityId – ID of the entity (transformGroup, shape, etc.).
string attributeName – Name of the attribute.
string typeName – Name of the attribute type (Float, Integer, String).
any value – Value of the attribute.

getUserAttribute

Gets the user attribute value.

Arguments

integer entityId – ID of the entity (transformGroup, shape, etc.).
string attributeName – Name of the attribute.

Returns

any attributeValue – Value of the attribute.

getHasClassId

Gets if an entity has the given class id.

Arguments

integer entityId – ID of the entity (transformGroup, shape, etc.).
integer classId – The class ID. See ClassIds enum.

Returns

boolean hasClassId – True if the entity has the classId.

ClassIds Enum

ClassIds.OVERLAY
ClassIds.IMAGE_OVERLAY
ClassIds.VIDEO_OVERLAY
ClassIds.TERRAIN_TRANSFORM_GROUP
ClassIds.FOLIAGE_TRANSFORM_GROUP
ClassIds.TERRAIN_DETAIL_TRANSFORM_GROUP
ClassIds.TERRAIN_LAYER_TRANSFORM_GROUP
ClassIds.SHAPE
ClassIds.LIGHT_SOURCE

ClassIds.AUDIO_SOURCE

ClassIds.CAMERA

ClassIds.NAVIGATION_MESH

ClassIds.MESH_SPLIT_SHAPE

ClassIds.GEOMETRY

ClassIds.TRANSFORM_GROUP

ClassIds.PARTICLE_SYSTEM

ClassIds.SPLINE

Entity Relations

link

Links a transform object to another transform object.

Arguments

integer parentEntityId – ID of the parent entity (transformGroup, shape, etc.).

integer childEntityId – ID of the child entity (transformGroup, shape, etc.).

integer index – [optional] Position of the child among children.

unlink

Unlinks a transform object from the parent.

Arguments

integer entityId – ID of the entity (transformGroup, shape, etc.).

getParent

Gets the entity id of the parent.

Arguments

integer entityId – ID of the entity (transformGroup, shape, etc.).

Returns

integer parentEntityId – ID of the parent entity (transformGroup, shape, etc.).

getChild

Gets the id of the first child that matches the given name.

Arguments

integer entityId – ID of the child entity (transformGroup, shape, etc.).
string childName – Name of the child.

Returns

integer childEntityId – ID of the child entity (transformGroup, shape, etc.).

getChildAt

Gets the entity id at a given child index.

Arguments

integer entityId – ID of the entity (transformGroup, shape, etc.).
integer childIndex – Index (zero based) of the child

Returns

integer childEntityId – ID of the child entity (transformGroup, shape, etc.).

getNumOfChildren

Gets the number of children.

Arguments

integer entityId – ID of the entity (transformGroup, shape, etc.).

Returns

integer numOfChildren – Number of children.

getRootNode

Gets the root node of the scenegraph.

Returns

integer entityId – ID of the entity (transformGroup, shape, etc.).

Camera
getCamera

Gets the active camera.

Returns

integer entityId – ID of the camera entity.

setCamera

Sets the active camera.

Arguments

integer entityId – ID of the camera entity.

I3D

loadI3DFile

Loads the I3D file (blocking).

Arguments

string filename – The I3D file name.
boolean addPhysics – If entities should be added to physics.
boolean callOnCreate – If script callbacks (onCreate) should be called.
boolean verbose – [optional] If the loading info should be displayed in the log file.

Returns

integer rootNodeId – ID of the root entity (transformGroup, shape, etc.) of the loaded file.
integer failedReason – The failed reason. See LoadI3dFailedReason enum.

loadSharedI3DFile

Loads a shared I3D file (blocking). If the file is already in cache, the system clones the objects. If another shared stream request is still pending for the same i3d, the call blocks until this request is finished.

Arguments

string filename – The I3D file name.

boolean addPhysics – If the objects should be added to physics.

boolean callOnCreate – If script callbacks (onCreate) should be called.

boolean verbose – [optional] If the loading info should be displayed in the log file.

Returns

integer rootNodeId – ID of the root entity (transformGroup, shape, etc.) of the loaded file.

integer requestId – The ID of the load request (used to cancel or release files).

integer failedReason – A specific reason why the loading failed.

LoadI3dFailedReason Enum

LoadI3DFailedReason.NONE

LoadI3DFailedReason.CANCELLED

LoadI3DFailedReason.FILE_NOT_FOUND

LoadI3DFailedReason.UNKNOWN

streamI3DFile

Streams the I3D file (non-blocking).

Arguments

string filename – The I3D file name.

string callbackFunctionName – [optional] Callback function if the loading is done.

object target – [optional] Target object of the callback function.

object args – [optional] Arguments for callback function.

boolean addPhysics – If the objects should be added to physics.

boolean callOnCreate – If script callbacks (onCreate) should be called.

boolean verbose – [optional] If the loading info should be displayed in the log file.

Returns

integer requestId – Request id for streaming, used to cancel the stream request.

cancelStreamI3DFile

Cancels streaming the I3D file.

Arguments

integer requestId – Request id of the streamed load request.

streamSharedI3DFile

Streams the shared I3D file (non-blocking). Can call the callback in the same callstack when the file is already loaded.

Arguments

string filename – The I3D file name.
string callbackFunctionName – [optional] Callback function if the loading is done.
object target – [optional] Target object of the callback function.
object args – [optional] Arguments for the callback function.
boolean addPhysics – If the objects should be added to physics.
boolean callOnCreate – If script callbacks (onCreate) should be called.
boolean verbose – [optional] If the loading info should be displayed in the log file.

Returns

integer requestId – Request id for streaming, used to cancel the stream request.

releaseSharedI3DFile

Reduces the ref count of the given shared i3d. Must be called for every successfull loadSharedI3DFile and streamSharedI3DFile call to avoid memory leaks.

Arguments

integer requestId – Stream I3D request ID.
integer warnIfInvalid – [optional, default=false] Print a warning if the request ID is invalid.

Physics
getRigidBodyType

Gets the rigid body type of a physics shape entity.

Arguments

integer entityId – ID of the physics shape entity.

Returns

integer RIGID_BODY_TYPE – Type of the rigid body (see RigidBodyType Enum).

RigidBodyType Enum

RigidBodyType.NONE
RigidBodyType.STATIC
RigidBodyType.DYNAMIC
RigidBodyType.KINEMATIC

setRigidBodyType

Sets the rigid body type of a physics shape entity.

Arguments

integer entityId – ID of the physics shape entity.
integer rigidBodyType – Type of the rigid body (see RigidBody Enum).

getCenterOfMass

Gets the center of mass of a physics shape entity.

Arguments

integer entityId – ID of the physics shape entity.

Returns

float x – x position of the center of mass in entityId's local space.
float y – y position of the center of mass in entityId's local space.
float z – z position of the center of mass in entityId's local space.

setCenterOfMass

Sets the center of mass of a physics shape entity.

Arguments

integer entityId – ID of the physics shape entity.
float x – x position of the center of mass in entityId's local space.
float y – y position of the center of mass in entityId's local space.
float z – z position of the center of mass in entityId's local space.

getMass

Gets the mass of a physics shape entity.

Arguments

integer entityId – ID of the physics shape entity.

Returns

float mass – Mass in tons.

setMass

Sets the mass of a physics shape entity.

Arguments

integer entityId – ID of the physics shape entity.
float mass – Mass in tons.

raycastAll

Raycast objects.

Arguments

float x – x position in world space.
float y – y position in world space.
float z – z position in world space.
float nx – x component of direction vector in world space.
float ny – y component of direction vector in world space.
float nz – z component of direction vector in world space.
string raycastFunctionCallback – See raycastCallback documentation.
float maxDistance – Max distance of the raycast.
object targetObject – [optional] Target object of the callback function.
integer collisionMask – [optional] The collision mask of the raycast.
boolean generateNormal – [optional, default=false] If a normal should be
generated for each hit.

boolean async – [optional, default=false] If true, callback will be called in the next frame and calculations will be done in a background thread. In Async mode, the return value has no meaning, and if no hit is found, the callback is called once with 0 ids.

Returns

integer numShapes – numShapes if async is false.

raycastClosest

Raycast closest object.

Arguments

float x – x position in world space.
float y – y position in world space.
float z – z position in world space.
float nx – x component of direction vector in world space.
float ny – y component of direction vector in world space.
float nz – z component of direction vector in world space.
string raycastFunctionCallback – See raycastCallback documentation.
float maxDistance – Max distance of the raycast.
object targetObject – [optional] Target object of the callback function.
integer collisionMask – [optional] The collision mask of the raycast.
boolean generateNormal – [optional, default=false] If a normal should be generated for each hit.
boolean async – [optional, default=false] If true, callback will be called in the next frame and calculations will be done in a background thread. In Async mode, the return value has no meaning, and if no hit is found, the callback is called once with 0 ids.

Returns

integer numShapes – numShapes if async is false.

raycastCallback

A valid raycastCallback function requires the parameters of the following header. The function itself can be renamed as the developer desires:

callbackFunctionName(integer actorEntityId, float x, float y, float z, float distance, float nx, float ny, float nz, integer subShapeIndex, integer shapeId, boolean isLast)

overlapBox

Checks for possible overlaps in the defined box.

Arguments

float x – x position in world space.
float y – y position in world space.
float z – z position in world space.
float rx – x rotation (radians) in world space.
float ry – y rotation (radians) in world space.
float rz – z rotation (radians) in world space.
float ex – x half dimension (meters) in world space.
float ey – y half dimension (meters) in world space.
float ez – z half dimension (meters) in world space.
string overlapFunctionCallback – See overlapFunctionCallback documentation.
object targetObject – [optional] Target object of the callback function.
integer collisionMask – [optional, default=ALL_BITS]

boolean includeDynamics – [optional, default=true] If dynamic objects should be included.

boolean includeStatics – [optional, default=true] If static objects should be included.

boolean exactTest – [optional, default=false] If an exact test should be done instead of a simple AABB collision check.

boolean async – [optional, default=false] If true, callback will be called in the next frame and calculations will be done in a background thread.

Returns

integer numShapes

overlapSphere

Overlap sphere objects.

Arguments

float x – x position in world space.
float y – y position in world space.
float z – z position in world space.
float radius – Sphere radius in meters.
string overlapFunctionCallback – See overlapFunctionCallback documentation.
object targetObject – [optional] Target object of the callback function.
integer collisionMask – [optional, default=ALL_BITS]
boolean includeDynamics – [optional, default=true] If dynamic objects should be included.
boolean includeStatics – [optional, default=true] If static objects should be included.

boolean exactTest – [optional, default=false] If an exact test should be done instead of a simple AABB collision check.

boolean async – [optional, default=false] If true, callback will be called in the next frame and calculations will be done in a background thread.

Returns

integer numShapes

overlapCallback

A valid overlapCallback function requires the parameters of the following header. The function itself can be renamed as the developer desires:

    callbackFunctionName(integer entityId, integer subShapeIndex, boolean isLastAsync (only set if async was true))

Network

streamReadBool

Reads a bool value from the network stream.

Arguments

integer streamId – ID of the network stream entity.

Returns

boolean value – A bool value.

streamReadFloat32

Reads a 32-bit float from the network stream.

Arguments

integer streamId – ID of the network stream entity.

Returns

float value – 32-bit float value.

streamReadInt16

Reads a 16-bit signed integer from the network stream.

Arguments

integer streamId – ID of the network stream entity.

Returns

integer value – 16-bit signed integer value.

streamReadInt32

Reads a 32-bit signed integer from the network stream.

Arguments

integer streamId – ID of the network stream entity.

Returns

integer value – 32-bit signed integer value.

streamReadInt8

Reads an 8-bit signed integer from the network stream.

Arguments

integer streamId – ID of the network stream entity.

Returns

integer value – 8-bit signed integer value.

streamReadIntN

Reads an N-bit signed integer from the network stream.

Arguments

integer streamId – ID of the network stream entity.
integer numberofBits – Number of bits used to send the value.

Returns

integer value – N-bit signed integer value.

streamReadString

Reads a string from the network stream.

Arguments

integer streamId – ID of the network stream entity.

Returns

string value – A piece of text.

streamReadUInt16

Reads a 16-bit unsigned integer from the network stream.

Arguments

integer streamId – ID of the network stream entity.

Returns

integer value – 16-bit unsigned integer value.

streamReadUInt8

Reads an 8-bit unsigned integer from the network stream.

Arguments

integer streamId – ID of the network stream entity.

Returns

integer value – 8-bit unsigned integer value.

streamReadUIntN

Reads an N-bit unsigned integer from the network stream.

Arguments

integer streamId – ID of the network stream entity.
integer numberOfBits – Number of bits used to send the value.

Returns

integer value – N-bit unsigned integer value.

streamWriteBool

Writes a bool value to the network stream.

Arguments

integer streamId – ID of the network stream entity.
boolean value – A bool value.

Returns

boolean value – The sent bool value.

streamWriteFloat32

Writes a 32-bit float to the network stream.

Arguments

integer streamId – ID of the network stream entity.
float value – 32-bit float value.

streamWriteInt16

Writes a 16-bit signed integer to the network stream.

Arguments

integer streamId – ID of the network stream entity.
integer value – 16-bit signed integer value.

streamWriteInt32

Writes a 32-bit signed integer to the network stream.

Arguments

integer streamId – ID of the network stream entity.
integer value – 32-bit signed integer value.

streamWriteInt8

Writes an 8-bit signed integer to the network stream.

Arguments

integer streamId – ID of the network stream entity.
integer value – 8-bit signed integer value.

streamWriteIntN

Writes an N-bit signed integer to the network stream.

Arguments

integer streamId – ID of the network stream entity.
integer value – N-bit signed integer value.
integer numberOfBits – Number of bits used to send the value.

streamWriteString

Writes a string to the network stream.

Arguments

integer streamId – ID of the network stream entity.
string value – A piece of text.

streamWriteUInt16

Writes a 16-bit unsigned integer to the network stream.

Arguments

integer streamId – ID of the network stream entity.
integer value – 16-bit unsigned integer value.

streamWriteUInt8

Writes an 8-bit unsigned integer to the network stream.

Arguments

integer streamId – ID of the network stream entity.
integer value – 8-bit unsigned integer value.

streamWriteUIntN

Writes an N-bit unsigned integer to the network stream.

Arguments

integer streamId – ID of the network stream entity.

integer value – N-bit unsigned integer value.

integer numberofBits – Number of bits used to send the value.

Index

A

actionEventChangeRotorSpeed()
function, 170
activateSpeedTrapFlash() function,
194, 203
addActionEvent() function, 170
addExecuteSet function, 150
addSpecialization() method, 211
agentAttachment element, 138
AI *area markers*, 138
API documentation, 287
Arrays, 47, 48, 54
assert() function, 72

B

Billboard, 188
Boolean logic, 47, 60
Booleans, 47, 50, 51
Bools, 47
Breakpoints, 98, 99

C

Camera
getCamera, 303
setCamera, 304

checkEquality() function, 77
clearArea() function, 153
Collision mask, 199, 310, 311
collisionTrigger, 138
Conditional expressions, 59, 61, 64
Conditional statements, 59–64
cooldownDuration value, 202
currentDetectionSample fields,
199, 202

D

Data types
arrays, 47
Booleans, 47, 50, 51
dictionaries, 47, 48, 57–59
floating-point errors, 47
number variables, 49, 50
setting and manipulating
variables, 48
strings, 47, 51–53
tables, 47, 48, 54–56
Debugging, 4, 85, 87–89, 94, 96, 97,
110, 287
DEFAULT_GAMEPAD, 132
Density map, 148, 151, 152
Dictionaries, 47, 57–59

dirtyFlag field, 213, 215
doCheckSpeedLimit() function, 165
Double-precision floating-point
    number, 47
drivenDistance field, 213–216
drivenDistanceNetworkThreshold
    field, 213
drivenDistanceNetworkThreshold
    value, 215
drivenDistanceSent field, 213

E

effectNode field, 140
elseif keyword, 62
Entities
    ClassIds enum, 300
    clones, 297
    createTransformGroup, 297
    getHasClassId, 300
    getName, 298
    getUserAttribute, 299
    getVisibility, 299
    setName, 298
    setUserAttribute, 299
    setVisibility, 298
Entity relations
    getChild, 302
    getChildAt, 302
    getNumOfChildren, 303
    getParent, 302
    getRootNode, 303
    link, 301
    unlink, 301

F

FarmCon, 3, 12–14
Farming Simulator, 1, 6, 9, 14,
    15, 94
First-person mode, 22, 35
flashFactor parameter, 186
flashTimeRemaining field,
    202, 203
Floating-point errors, 47
For loops, 76
    generic, 66
    numeric, 65
Framed Rotate mode, 22
FSDensityMapUtilExtension.
    lua, 130
FULL axis, 131
Functions, programming
    languages
    argument, 71
    "_" character, 73
    header, 70
    parameter, 72
    procedures/subroutines, 70
    recursion
        base case, 74
        checkEquality() function, 77
        factorial function, 74, 75
        for loops, 76
        references, 75, 76
        stack, 74
    recursive functions, 77
    throw(), 72
    variadic functions, 72

G

Generic for loops, 66
getDefaultSpeedLimit()
    function, 171
getDrivenDistance() function,
    212, 218
getLastSpeed() function, 204
getRawSpeedLimit() function, 165
getRotation, 292
getScale, 296
getTranslation, 289
getValue() script function, 122
getWorldRotation, 292
getWorldTranslation, 288
getWorldTranslation()
    function, 167
GIANTS Developer Network (GDN)
    community forum
        Documentation category, 7
        Documentation section, 5
        Engine category, 6
        Exporter category, 7
        Feature Requests category, 7
        mod creators, 5
        Modding category, 7
        Off Topic category, 7
    Content Creation section, 4
    documentation, 4, 5
    Downloads section
        Editor category, 8
        Exporter category, 8
        LUADOC, 9
        miscellaneous category, 9

        modding category, 8
        Other Tools category, 8
        Studio category, 8
    Farming Simulator, 1
    Feedback category, 7
    Fundamental Reading section, 4
    modding resources, 3
    preview, 2
    Scripting section, 4
    video tutorials, 3
    YouTube, 10
GIANTS Editor, 4, 8, 81, 104,
    128, 176
    application menus
        create, 29, 30
        edit, 27, 28
        file, 26, 27
        help, 31, 32
        scripts, 31
        view, 30, 31
        window, 31
    Attributes Panel, 32–34
    Console, script, 43
    Downloads section, 18
    Scenegraph Panel
        entities, 24
        multiple objects,
            scene, 23, 24
        parent-child
            hierarchy, 24, 25
    Script Editor, 42, 43
    technical requirements, 17, 18
    Toolbar, 34
    viewport, 19

GIANTS Studio, 4, 81, 172, 204
   application menus
      debug, 89
      edit, 87
      file, 86
      help, 90
      view, 88, 89
      window, 89
   create mod scripts
      LUA files, 117–123
      XML files, 109–116
   debugging scripts
      breakpoints, 98
      factorial function, 97
      locals and callstack
         tabs, 99, 100
   diner model, 108
   installation, 86
   mod directory, 105
   mod structure, 107
   mod test, 123
   new mod project, 90–97
   refresh project
      browser, 106
   restaurant project,
      104, 105
   start the game, 94, 97
   technical requirements, 85
Grid option, 23
groundReferenceNodes
   field, 135
GuiElement fields, 234
GUIProfiles element, 230
GUI's xml file, 230

H

HALF axis, 131, 228
High-Level Shader Language
   (HLSL), 185, 186, 188

I

I3D
   cancelStreamI3DFile, 306
   LoadI3dFailedReason
      Enum, 305
   loadI3DFile, 304
   loadSharedI3DFile, 304
   releaseSharedI3DFile, 307
   streamI3DFile, 305
   streamSharedI3DFile, 306
i3d mappings, 116
initSpecialization() function,
   158, 212
inputAttacherJoints field, 136
inputBinding field, 228
Integrated development
   environment (IDE), 85
ipairs() iterator function, 67
isEven variable, 63
Iterator function, 66, 67

J

Joint limits, 136

K

KB_MOUSE_DEFAULT, 130,
   132, 228

L

localDirectionToLocal, 294, 295

localDirectionToWorld, 295

localRotationToWorld, 293

localToLocal, 291

localToWorld, 290

Logical operators, 60, 61

Loops

for, 64–66

iterator function, 66, 67

repeat, 69

while, 68, 69

lowerRotLimitScale field scale, 136

lowerTransLimitScale field
scale, 136

LUA, 9

LUADOC, 9

LUA files creation, Mileage
Counter HUD

InjectSpecialization.lua

finalizeTypes() function, 210

getTypes() method, 211

purpose, 210

MileageCounter.lua

core script, 211

getDrivenDistance()
function, 216

onLoad() function, 213

onReadStream()
function, 214

onReadUpdateStream()
function, 214

onUpdate() function, 215

onWriteStream()
function, 214

onWriteUpdateStream()
function, 214

prerequisitesPresent()
function, 212

registerEventListeners()
function, 212

saveToXML() function, 213

MileageDisplay.lua

background text, 219

createBackground(), 221

createBackground()
function, 217

draw() method, 218

drivenDistance value, 218

getBackgroundPosition()
function, 220

global text rendering, 219

HUDDisplayElement, 217

metric system, 218

MileageDisplay.new()
class, 217

purpose, 216

setScale() method, 219

setTextBold(false), 218

setVehicle() function, 217

MileageHUDExtension.lua

createDisplayComponents()
function, 222

drawControlledEntityHUD()
function, 222

game's interface, 221

LUA files creation, Mileage
Counter HUD (*cont.*)
setControlledVehicle()
function, 222
LUA files creation,
Multibale Spawner
AdditionalGuiProfiles.lua, 251
MultiBaleSpawnerEvent.lua
instructors, 240
readStream() function, 241
register() method, 239
run() function, 242
writeStream() function, 241
MultiBaleSpawnerScreen.lua
component program, 242
createFromExistingGui()
function, 244
GUI elements, 243, 247
INSTANCE field, 243
new() constructor, 244
onClickOk() function, 249
onOpen() function, 245
register() function, 243
show() function, 243
updateBaleSizes()
function, 247
updateBaleTypes()
function, 246
MultiBaleSpawnerUtil.lua
baleTypeIndex, 239
MAX_NUM_BALES field, 238
program purpose, 236
register() method, 239
SEND_NUM_BITS, 238

spawnBales() program, 238
PlayerExtension.lua
*openMultiBale
Spawner()*, 251
registerActionEvents()
function, 250
LUA files creation, Rotating Mower
*actionEventChangeRotor
Speed()* function, 170
FSDensityMapUtilExtension.lua
Deco Foliages, 152
DensityMapFilter object, 150
DensityMapHeightUtil, 153
*DensityMapMulti
Modifier*, 150
DensityMapMultiModifier
object, 150
terrainRootNode, 150
updateRotateMowerArea()
function, 150
getDefaultSpeedLimit()
function, 171
HUD, 170
RotateMower.lua
bool values, 170
control script, 153
currentFillType field, 161
default events, 155
doCheckSpeedLimit()
function, 165
field worker
functionality, 161
getRawSpeedLimit()
function, 165

getRotorSpeedFactor() function, 166

.i3d material holder, 154

initSpecialization() function, 158

math.abs() function, 167

MathUtil.lerp() function, 164

onDelete() function, 162

onLoad() function, 161

onReadStream() function, 162

onTurnedOn() function, 168

onUpdateTick() function, 164

onWriteStream() function, 163

prerequisitesPresent() function, 155

processRotateMowerArea() function, 167

registerEventListeners() function, 155

registerFunctions() function, 156

registerOverwritten Functions() function, 157

savegame.xmlFile field, 161

saveToXMLFile() function, 162

specialization and values, 154

streamReadSpeed Factor(), 154

streamWrite SpeedFactor(), 154

TurnOnVehicle specialization, 156, 169

RotorSpeedFactorEvent.lua purpose, 144

readNodeObject() function, 147

readStream() function, 145

RotorSpeedFactorEvent. emptyNew(), 144

RotorSpeedFactorEvent. new(), 144

run() function, 147

sendEvent() function, 148

vehicle and *speedFactor* arguments, 144

writeNodeObject() function, 145

writeStream() function, 145

sound manager, 171

LUA files creation, Speed Trap Trailer

base Event class, 193

constructors, 194

custom functions, 203

onSpeedTrapRaycastCallback() function, 204

raiseActive(), 203

readStream() function, 194

run() function, 194

SpeedTrap.lua activateSpeedTrapFlash() function, 194

LUA files creation, Speed Trap
    Trailer (*cont.*)
    currentDetectionSample
        field, 202
    flashDuration field, 199
    flashNode field, 199
    flashTimeRemaining
        field, 202
    ignoredVehicles, 199, 202
    initSpecialization()
        function, 197
    onDelete() function, 200
    onLoad() function, 198
    onUpdate() function, 202
    prerequisitesPresent()
        function, 195
    raycast, 199
    raycast node, 202
    registerFunctions()
        function, 195
    specialization, 194
    writeStream() function, 194
LUA programming language
    classes, 78, 79
    conditional statements, 59–64
    data type, 47
    function, 70
    GIANTS Engine, 45
    loops, 64
    programming style and
        efficiency
        GIANTS Studio, 81
        naming convention, 81
        optimization, 82
    readability, 80, 81
    tables, 54–56
    technical requirements, 46
    variables, 46

M

Mathematical operators, 63
Mileage Counter HUD Mod
    creating LUA files, 210
    creating XML files, 208
    extraSourceFiles field, 209
    technical requirements, 208
    testing, 222
    UI elements, 207
Mod contest, 14, 15
Mod creator, 15
ModHub
    account creation
        awards section, 276
        help section, 276
        login button, 274, 275
        messenger tab, 276
        mods page, 275, 276
        register new account here
            button, 275
        rewards tab, 276
    awards, 283, 284
    best-performing and
        highest-quality mods, 10
    categories, 10, 11, 273
    complex systems, 285
    definition, 273
    feedback, 282, 283

financial opportunities, mod
creation, 11, 12
guidelines, 276–278
mods, 274
reference link, 274
rewards, 283
technical requirements, 273
TestRunner, 279
uploading, 280, 282
Money cheat mod
activatable objects, 270
ATM, 270
LUA files
activatable objects, 266
addChange and *forceShow*
flags, 268
addMoney() function, 268
ATMActivatable, 269
ATMEvent, 268
ATMEvent.lua, 262
custom functions, 267
farmId, 263
getDistance() function, 270
in-game notifications, 268
onATMTriggerCallback()
function, 266, 267
onDelete() function, 267
onLoad() function, 266
PlaceableATM.lua, 264
placeable object/trigger
node, 269
prerequisitesPresent()
function, 264
readStream() function, 263

registerEventListeners()
function, 265
registerFunctions()
function, 265
registerXMLPaths()
function, 264
requestMoney() function,
263, 268
run() function, 270
triggers, 266
scripts, 256
technical requirements, 256
testing, 270
XML files
ai filed, 260
atm element, 261
ATM placement, 260
atm.xml, 258, 259
clearAreas, 260
extraSourceFiles, 258
l10n_de.xml, 262
l10n element, 258
l10n_en.xml, 261
modDesc.xml, 256
PlaceableATM, 258
placeableTypes, 258
rotating sign, 259
storeData, 259
translation files, 261
trigger element, 261
MultiBaleSpawner, 235
Multibale Spawner Mod
creating LUA files, 236
creating XML files, 226

Multibale Spawner Mod (*cont.*)
  GUI elements, 225
  technical requirements, 226
  testing, 252
multiTextOption elements, 234

N

Naming convention, 81
Network
  streamReadBool, 314
  streamReadFloat32, 314
  streamReadInt8, 316
  streamReadInt16, 315
  streamReadInt32, 315
  streamReadIntN, 316
  streamReadString, 316
  streamReadUInt8, 317
  streamReadUInt16, 317
  streamReadUIntN, 317
  streamWriteBool, 318
  streamWriteFloat32, 318
  streamWriteInt8, 319
  streamWriteInt16, 318
  streamWriteInt32, 319
  streamWriteIntN, 319
  streamWriteString, 320
  streamWriteUInt8, 320
  streamWriteUInt16, 320
  streamWriteUIntN, 320
Number data type, 47
Number variables, 49, 50
NUM_BITS value, 154

numDetectionSamples + 1
  raycasts, 199
Numeric for loop, 64, 65

O

Object masks, 199
Object-oriented languages, 79
Object-oriented programming
  (OOP), 79
onClickBaleType() function, 249
onClickFileType() function, 249
onClickOk() function, 249
onDelete() function, 162
onLoad() function, 120
onReadStream() function, 162
onRegisterActionEvents() function,
  156, 170
onSpeedTrapRaycastCallback()
  function, 195, 203
onTurnedOff() function, 169
onUpdate() function, 123
onUpdateTick() function, 156
OPEN_MULTI_BALE_SPAWNER,
  228, 235

P, Q

pairs() iterator function, 66
Parent-child hierarchy, 24, 25
Physics shape entity
  getCenterOfMass, 309
  getMass, 309

getRigidBodyType, 308
overlapBox, 312, 313
overlapCallback, 314
overlapSphere, 313, 314
raycastAll, 310
raycastCallback, 312
raycastClosest, 311
RigidBodyType enum, 308
setCenterOfMass, 309
setMass, 310
setRigidBodyType, 308
PlaceableObjectRotate.lua, 122
prerequisitesPresent function, 118
print() function, 48, 65
processRotateMowerArea()
    function, 167
Programming, 9

R

Raycast, 184
raycastCollisionMask fields, 199
raycastNode, 202
Readability, 80, 81
Recursion, 74
registerEventListeners() function,
    118, 195
registerFunctions() function, 156
registerOverwrittenFunctions()
    function, 157
registerXMLPaths function,
    119, 122
Relational operators, 60, 63
Repeat loops, 69

Revolutions per minute (RPM), 141
RotateMower.actionEvent
    ChangeRotorSpeed
    function, 170
Rotate tool, 38
Rotating Mower Mod
    LUA files, 144
    technical requirements, 128
    testing, 172
    XML files, 128
RotorSpeedFactorEvent.lua, 130

S

saveToXMLFile() function, 162
Scope, 66
Script Editor, 42, 43, 81, 85, 92
self:raiseActive() function, 123
SEND_NUM_BITS field, 241
setCallback() function, 244
setDirection, 296
setRotation, 291
setRotorSpeedFactor() function,
    166, 171
setScale, 296
setShaderParameter() function, 202
setTranslation, 289
setVehicle() function, 222
setWorldRotation, 293
setWorldTranslation, 289
spawnBales() function, 242
specs field, 133
speedTrap element, 184
speedTrap specialization, 178

Speed Trap Trailer Mod
  LUA files, 193
  technical requirements,
     176, 204
  XML files, 176
Stacks, 74
STEP_SIZE value, 154
streamReadSpeedFactor()
    function, 154
streamWriteSpeedFactor()
    function, 154
string.format() function, 122
Strings, 47, 51–53

T

table.getn() function, 56
table.insert() function, 55
table.remove() function, 56
Tables, 47
Ternary expression, 63
TestRunner
  definition, 279
  downloading, 279
  erros, 280
  execution, 279
  HTML file, 280
  information/
    troubleshooting, 280
  mod folder, 280
  testing, 279
3D modelers, 5
3D modeling, 4
tonumber() function, 53, 65

Toolbar
  actions and tools, 34
  File, 35
  Mode section
    local/world mode, 36
    rotation mode, 37
    scaling mode, 38
    snapping, 36
    translation mode, 37
  Play, 35, 36
  terrain, 39–41
tostring() function, 65
Translate tool, 37
TypeManager class, 210

U

updateBaleSizes() function,
    247, 249
updateParallelogram
    WorldCoords()
    function, 153
updateRotateMowerArea()
    function, 167

V

Variable, 46
Variadic functions, 72
Video tutorials, 3
Viewport
  Camera, 21
  create menu, 19
  first-person mode, 22

framed rotate mode, 22
grid option, 23
movement and camera
        manipulation, 20, 21
polycount option, 23
selectable option, 23
show option, 22
wireframe and shaded
        modes, 22

W

while loops, 68
workAreas field, 135
worldDirectionToLocal, 294
worldRotationToLocal, 293
worldToLocal, 290
writeStream() function, 147

X

XML files creation,
        Multibale Spawner
guiProfiles.xml
    anchorMiddleLeft/
        anchorTopCenter, 230
    inheritance and traits, 230
    predefined profiles, 230
    profile elements, 230
    purpose, 228
l10n_de.xml, 236
l10n_en.xml, 235
modDesc.xml
    actions field, 228

multiBaleSpawnerScreen.xml
    background elements, 234
    boxLayout element, 234
    content, 231
    GuiElement fields, 234
    GUI layout, 234
    multiTextOption
        elements, 234
XML files creation, Rotating Mower
    l10n_de.xml, 143
    l10n_en.xml, 142
    l10n_fr.xml, 143
    modDesc.xml
        extraSourceFiles, 130
        groundReference
            specialization, 131
        materialHolders, 129
        particles.i3d file, 130
        turnOnVehicle
            specialization, 131
        Vehicle.lua, 131
        vehicleTypes field, 131
    rotateMower.xml
        actions field, 131
        ai field, 138
        animationNode fields, 140
        attachable field, 136
        base field, 135
        defaultLights field, 137
        distanceToGround
            element, 136
        foliageBending field, 138
        i3dMappings field, 142
        inputBinding field, 132

XML files creation, Rotating
Mower (*cont.*)
jointType, 136
l10n field, 132
LIZARD, 134
particleType field, 140
powerConsumer field, 135
powerTakeOffs field, 137
real particle system, 140
rotateMower
configuration, 131
rotSpeed, 140
sounds element, 141
specs field, 133
topReferenceNode, 136
turnOnVehicle field, 138
wearable field, 138
XML files creation, Speed
Trap Trailer
flashShader.xml
billboard, 188
code injection, 192
CodeInjections field, 186
HLSL, 185
setRotation() function, 189
shader *parameters*, 186
vertex shader, 188, 190
l10n_de.xml, 192
l10n_en.xml, 192

modDesc.xml
extraSourceFiles field, 178
storeItems field, 178
vehicleTypes field, 178
speedTrapTrailer.xml
animations field, 182
attachable field, 182
base field, 180
cooldownDuration
field, 184
detectionRadius, 185
foliageBending field, 183
i3dMappings element, 185
mapHotspot field, 180
maxSpeedKmh field, 184
raycast, 184
speedTrap element, 184
storeData field, 179
washDuration field, 183
wearable and *washable*
fields, 183
wheels field, 182
workMultiplier and
fieldMultiplier fields, 183
XML schema, 112

Y, Z
YouTube, 10

Printed in the United States
by Baker & Taylor Publisher Services